Human Goods,
Economic Evils

Culture of Enterprise series
_____

Previously published:

Third Ways:
How Bulgarian Greens, Swedish Housewives, and Beer-Swilling Englishmen
Created Family-Centered Economies—And Why They Disappeared
Allan C. Carlson

Human Goods, Economic Evils

A Moral Approach to the Dismal Science

Edward Hadas

ISI BOOKS

Wilmington, Delaware

Copyright © 2007 ISI Books

The Culture of Enterprise series is supported by a grant from the John Templeton Foundation. The Intercollegiate Studies institute gratefully acknowledges this support.

All rights reserved. No part of this publication may be reproduced or transmitted in any form or by any means, electronic or mechanical, including photocopy, or any information storage and retrieval system now known or to be invented, without permission in writing from the publisher, except by a reviewer who wishes to quote brief passages in connection with a review written for inclusion in a magazine, newspaper, or broadcast.

Hadas, Edward.

    Human goods, economic evils : a moral approach to the dismal science / Edward Hadas.—1st ed.—Wilmington, DE : ISI Books, c2007.

    p. ; cm.
    (Culture of enterprise)

    ISBN-13: 978-1-933859-26-2
    ISBN-13: 978-1-933859-27-9 (pbk.)
    ISBN-10: 1-933859-26-1
    ISBN-10: 1-933859-27-X (pbk.)
    Includes bibliographical references and index.

    1. Economics—Philosophy. 2. Economics—Moral and ethical aspects. 3. Economics—Sociological aspects. 4. Economics—Religious aspects—Christianity. 5. Philosophical theology. I. Title.

HB72 .H33 2007   2007923891
330.01—dc22   0708

ISI Books
Intercollegiate Studies Institute
P.O. Box 4431
Wilmington, Delaware 19807-0431
www.isibooks.org

Book Design by Jennifer M. Connolly

Manufactured in the United States of America

Contents

FOREWORD: THE JOYFUL SCIENCE, *by Stratford Caldecott*		ix
PREFACE		xv
1	What Are We Talking About? (I)	1
2	The Problem with Conventional Economics	19
3	Can This Model Be Saved?	35
4	Starting Again	49
5	Human Nature for Economists	65
6	A Short Discourse on Economic Method	77
7	What Are We Talking About? (II)	87
8	A Few Imperfect Ideas about the Economic Good	113
9	Economic Goods for the World	125
10	Economic Goods for the Economy	147
11	Evil in Economics	157
12	Economic Evils in the World	165

13 Economic Evils in the Economy	181
14 The World of Work	193
15 A Typology of Labor	215
16 Consumption in the World	239
17 A Typology of Consumption	257
18 What Should We Talk about Now?	273
BIBLIOGRAPHY	283
NOTES	299
INDEX	323

When want, sent but to tame, doth war

And work despair a breach to enter in,

When plenty, God's image, and seal

Makes us Idolatrous,

And love it, not Him, whom it should reveal,

When we are mov'd to seem religious

Only to vent wit, Lord deliver us.

—John Donne

Foreword:
The Joyful Science

Around the turn of the century, England lost its only Catholic college dedicated to the exploration of social thought, economics, and politics (Plater College in Oxford). It seems remarkable not only that it was allowed to close, but that it had been the only institution of its kind. In the U.S., fortunately, there are several organizations and colleges, centers, and societies dedicated to this task. The history of intelligent Catholic and Christian reflection on the social implications of the Gospel, and of brave attempts to do economic activity differently in the light of that Gospel, should be much better known than it is. This is a rich tradition. Even if we confine ourselves to the modern period, defined by the rise of various kinds of socialism and the response of Christian leaders and movements from 1891 to 1991, the work of Christian thinkers on economics has been exciting, varied, and often massively sane compared to the mainstream "establishment" economic tradition.

Edward Hadas is a major new voice in this important tradition. He is independent of all schools and parties; he is not the representative of a movement or the follower of an economic guru. Admirers both of G. K. Chesterton and of Michael Novak, though critical of each other, will find the book of interest to them. Hadas is not a "one-idea man." He has the gift, not of simplifying, but of going back to the foundations of the discipline and *rethinking* it—intelligently—from the ground up. What he has tried to do in this book is nothing less than reinvent economics through a careful study of the nature of labor and of consumption. When you come across a section in a serious academic book that begins, "Economies produce stuff," you know you are in the hands of an author who is not afraid of getting back to basics. (I would draw attention especially to his original typology of labor in chapter 15, which he feels offers a number of improvements over the standard models: "The priority given to labors of being and care; the respectful treatment given to women's labor; the integration of reproduction into labor economics; the praise of indirect productive labor, especially of regulation; and the concept of instrumentally neutral labor.")

One of the points he makes is that conventional economists have turned "Capital" into an impersonal force beyond our control. Hadas wants to humanize it.

> Socialists think the entire force of the state is necessary to ensure that the monster Capital does not enslave the people. Capitalists count on "private ownership" (an odd description of the control mechanism for gigantic impersonal corporations), but consider the income from capital, profit, to be fundamentally different from the personal income of wages. Both socialists and capitalists make the same basic error. Capital is not a thing or a force or an impersonal and uncontrollable social construct; it is human—men knowing, sharing, trusting, and working together, and the tools built and operated by men. Any organization of capital—in a family business, a corporation, a government agency, a partnership—is an arbitrary human construction subject to the same moral and practical judgements—is it good? is it useful?—as any other human thing. (10)

In this way Hadas stands in the tradition of the "humane economy" and those personalist thinkers who sought to give priority to the human—such as E. F. Schumacher, with his "economics as though people mattered," and, of course, Pope John Paul II. This is not just a moralistic point, but an ontological one: the human being is actually the ground and purpose of the economy. Any economic theory that does not accept this is merely *unrealistic*.

Hadas believes that conventional economists start out from the "wrong ontological place":

> Like many contemporary philosophers, they do not like to talk at all about the Good—the transcendental, mysterious, divine ultimate that should be at the center of economics. When econo-

mists talk about goods—consumption, production, final and intermediate goods—they have nothing moral in mind, just terms for different varieties of what I have been calling stuff. But such language games are not enough to free them from the moral orientation of human nature. (113)

He shows that "true goods," and even the "transcendental" good, cannot be so easily eliminated from economics, simply by treating money as a meas-ure or substitute for whatever it is that people want. He argues coherently against utilitarianism and other conventional theories stemming from the Enlightenment that reduce the good of economics to mere utility, prosperity, or the satisfaction of worldly desires. He argues for a hierarchy of goods, and in that sense for a moral cosmos a bit like that of the classical and medieval thinkers.

His aim, and he admits it is ambitious, daring, almost unprecedented, is "to combine economics with philosophy and theology," bringing the latter down to earth and the former up to meet them. His aim is a truly "human economy," taking into account the full scope and destiny of the human being. Like E. F. Schumacher (whose other, less famous book, *A Guide for the Perplexed*, was a defense of this principle), Hadas believes in levels of reality and a hierarchy of value reflected in the interior acts and judgments of the human person.

But at the same time, Hadas parts company with the "small is beautiful" brigade at many points. Nor can he be described as "antimodern," as though modernity or the Enlightenment was for him merely a problem to overcome. He gives a ringing endorsement to many aspects of modern life and the globalized economy when he writes, for example:

The industrial economy does not need tremendous improvements. Unlike the academic discipline of conventional economics, which is something of a disaster area, the actual economy works quite well. Of course, adjustment to circumstances is constantly needed. Reforms are always needed for something—central banking, environmental protection, pension funding, and so forth. However, the necessary reforms in such matters do not require anything like a major economic reconfiguration. Indeed, the economic good is so well served that my first advice to would-be economic reformers is to turn to one of the many more deeply troubled aspects of modern society. (280)

Of course, he admits that there are problems, even if our industrial economy is not at the root of them.

> Without a doubt, the modern economy is alienating. No one seems to care much about these soul-deadening patterns and trends. Worse, when attention is paid, for example in motivational campaigns by employers, the supposed cure often seems only to aggravate the disease. Still, economic alienation is among the least significant aspects of modern alienation. (279)

He locates the problem not in the economy, but in the conventional worldview, its antispiritual, indeed materialistic and reductionistic, attitude. To uproot that worldview and to turn things around will take the intellectual (and spiritual) equivalent of "deep ploughing." What we end up with is an approach to economics that does more justice to reality—in all its heights and depths—than conventional economic theories dare to dream.

> The world is too complicated for economism or any of its simplistic peers to be right. If an all-encompassing explanation is to be successful, it must work at a much higher level—the "divine comedy" of creation and redemption comes to mind. The economy is a mundane aspect of life, just one among many. It is neither autonomous nor able to encompass the others. One of the economist's principle tasks is to put the economy in its proper place. (16)

Part of the necessary complexity of economics derives precisely from the fact that it is not an abstract, deductive science (or even, in any straightforward way, an "empirical" science). It is concerned with human beings and the way they act, the things the want, and the stuff they do. And here the Christian tradition gives us a very useful concept: original sin. As G. K. Chesterton says, this is "the only part of Christian theology which can really be proved." An area of enormous concern, then, in this book is the whole question of *consumerism* and how to handle it. Hadas is a critic of the idea that economic growth is the real purpose of the economy, though he admits that it is difficult to subtract consumerism from contemporary industrial economies. (Personally, I wonder if this thought could eventually lead him to take a more jaundiced view of industrialization than the one he adopts here.) By wrestling with this issue, he takes us into areas where other promodern economic theorists hardly ever set foot.

I would not say I agree with everything he says, and you may feel the same, but the point about this book is that you don't read it in order to have your ideas confirmed; you read it to have them challenged. The very clarity of Hadas's thinking makes it easy to find points of disagreement: he does not bury his meaning in a cloud of obscure syntax or technical jargon. In the end, he can offer no simple, ideological solution to the world's ills, but he has done something much more important than that: he has shown why such a solution would inevitably be a false one. He argues that our economy is fundamentally sound (this is where, if I knew enough, I might want to argue with him), but that this should not make us complacent: it can be improved in all sorts of ways that would make it better for us as human beings.

In the end, he comes down in favour of *charity and service*. That is a simple concept, I suppose, but not in the way an ideology is simple. Charity and service are simple words for a vast set of ideas about human nature and how it may attain happiness. "Those virtues," he says, "offer solutions for most human problems, perhaps for all of them. With charity and service, men can accomplish great things, turn darkness into light, sorrow into joy. They are certainly applicable to economics, which should, after all, be something of a joyful science."

STRATFORD CALDECOTT
EDITOR, *SECOND SPRING*
OXFORD

Preface

I am not a trained economist. On the contrary, during my studies I completely snubbed the field. Even in business school, the mandatory course in economics passed over me almost unnoticed. My curiosity was only awakened after starting work as a financial analyst. But when I looked at economics, especially at the mainstream neoclassical model of microeconomics, it all seemed profoundly untrue—both to human nature and to my experience of actual companies, jobs, and families.

After some years of frustration, I set out to write about a better economic model. The work was supposed to take no more than a year. After all, I was well prepared, or so I thought. I had academic training in philosophy and some knowledge of theology, providing insight into the deeper meaning of economic questions. Catholic social teaching gave me an excellent moral lodestar. My years on the job—by then in two continents, with numerous employers and spread over many tasks—had left a thick residue of knowledge of the actual workings of the industrial economy. Finally, I had by then made a reasonable study of both conventional and unconventional economics.

That was somewhat more than a decade ago. But it turned out that economics was much more complicated than I had first believed. There were so many forces and factors at play that it took time to identify and then to understand (as much as I have understood) the most important ones. Also, there was a shortage of time. It is difficult to undertake a venture of this scale within the margins of a full-time job.

The main reason for the delay, however, was a slow but profound shift in my basic perspective. That transition required a major intellectual rebalancing. I grew up in a tradition of left-wing secular Jewish intellectuals. I had converted to Catholicism, and was drawn to theologians who praised the world's goodness, without ignoring the distortions caused by sin, and who called on men to take up their worldly responsibilities with serious goodwill. My job—my labor, as I had come to call it—was frustrating. There were many intellectual challenges, but little virtue. Initially, this background and professional environment led to an easy radicalism. The quick book was to be little more than a straightforward condemnation of the modern economic world and the ideas that have been presented to justify it. That position was clear and allowed me to be faithful to both the anticapitalist thinking of the Jewish left and the antimodernist strand of Catholic social teaching.

But somewhere in the middle of revising the first draft, I realized that a simple "no" was a totally inadequate response to industrial prosperity. That insight should have come much earlier, in fact when I was thirteen years old. Shortly after an uneventful appendectomy, I fell into an argument with another ninth-grader about the good of modern medicine. Under the influence of the 1960s counterculture, I argued that it harmed almost as much as it cured. My friend pointed out that without modern medicine my appendicitis would likely have killed me.

That dialogue came back to me when thinking about what Catholics call the "culture of life," the belief that human life is a good that should be cultivated. That belief has an economic implication—an economic organization that protects and promotes life must have something fundamentally good about it, no matter how many other bad things it protects or promotes. The industrial economy is "pro-life" in many ways. Safer surgery is just one example. By the broadest standard, industry has allowed the world to support many more people and allowed those additional people to live lives that are longer, healthier, and more imbued with knowledge. A life-lover cannot simply dismiss these accomplishments as meaningless.

I was not the first to recognize that something was fundamentally right about the industrial economy. Unfortunately, most of the thinkers who had made the same basic judgment seemed to be in the thrall of conventional economics, accepting much of its flawed understanding of human nature and of the rules of actual economy.

They offered bad explanations for good things. They also seemed almost oblivious to the many ways in which the modern industrial economy really is not good and to the many and complicated ties the economy has to the rest of what I call the modern worldview.

It took me years to find a balanced judgment. As chapter 18 makes clear, that judgment is complicated and nuanced, about as far as possible from my initial simple radicalism. Readers may disagree with some aspects of my evaluation, or even with the overall balance, but I do think that some sort of mixed judgment is inevitable. In this imperfect world, all aspects of society are always made up of interlacing light and shadows.

This book is both hugely ambitious and sharply limited. The ambition is to combine economics with philosophy and theology. Economic activity is part of the life of men, those creatures who are described in the Bible as being made of both the "dust from the ground" and a "breath or spirit from God" (Genesis 2:7). Everything human, including economic activity, is made up of both dust and spirit. In order to understand economics, philosophy and theology need to be brought down from heaven, while economics needs to be brought up from the earth.

The study of economics as a branch of applied philosophy has required some fundamental challenges to the accepted approach. To start with, there has been a redefinition of the field of study. Economics in this book has almost nothing to do with money, markets, or measurements. Rather, it is a study centered on two aspects of the human condition: labor and consumption. Both of those have to be understood in themselves, in their relations with each other, and in how they are practiced in society. That redefinition takes up the first seven chapters of the book.

A thorough moral reworking follows. Economic activity, like anything men do, aims at the good, but the nature of the economic good is far from obvious. This good is the subject of chapters 8 through 13. The ethical perspective makes it possible to create the value-laden typologies of labor and consumption that take up the following four chapters. My hope is that the morally charged analysis will allow a better judgment of individual jobs, the social arrangements of labor and consumption, and the nature of luxury. I am particularly anxious to counter two modern trends—the devaluation of labors of love and overvaluation of what I call "instrumentally neutral" labor, the many jobs that are socially esteemed but serve no great good.

The limits to this book are practical and show up in chapter 18. There I provide both a tentative evaluation of the whole modern economy and a few suggestions for personal and organizational reform. My effort is indeed sharply limited, since many volumes would be required to answer all questions in sufficient detail. My hope is that the ambitious philosophical framework offered in this book proves useful for later and less limited study, by myself and others.

In this book, I talk of human economics. The adjective is in part explanatory. It emphasizes that economics should be studied as part of human nature. But the use of "human" is also polemical. Most economists actually work as if economics were not primarily a human study. They typically take for granted such a simplistic view of economic motivations that the human aspect becomes almost peripheral. Theoretical economists think too little about virtue and meaning, too much and often incorrectly about money, and about abstract and hardly human things such as markets and interest rates. They create largely meaningless equations in a vain effort to make this human study into something more like a physical science. More practical economists are less foolish, but they suffer from the weakness of their theory.

Still, I do not want to frighten off either theoretical or practical economists with threats of abstract philosophy and, worse yet, Christian theology. Although I have no formal academic training in economics, I am now employed in the field (as a commentator) and have come to respect the profession's strengths. I hope to persuade some of my peers that this human approach to economics can be useful in analyzing such concrete problems as unemployment, productivity, and economic growth. So while this book is certainly meant to contribute to a great Catholic intellectual project—the reconstruction of the social sciences in accordance with what can be called "Christian anthropology"—almost all of the arguments are supposed to be understandable by, and possibly acceptable to, economists of all ideological and religious persuasions. Despite the urgings of some Christian friends, I have kept the theology as far in the background as I could.

Conversely, for the noneconomist man on the street, the use of a more realistic picture of human nature is supposed to make human economics more comprehensible and more appealing than the conventional approach. The descriptions and arguments provided here do not rely on any complex economic notions, and the premises—the descriptions of human nature and of economic activity—are spelled out in what I hope are straightforward terms. In some ultimate sense, men will always be a mystery to themselves, but in the economic realm much can be understood without esoteric language or extravagant expertise.

Many people and institutions have been extremely helpful to me over the past decade. My greatest debt is probably to the entire Western tradition. It may seem stupid to thank Plato, Thomas Aquinas, Heidegger, and their many intellectual companions, but it is impossible to imagine writing a philosophical book about economics—or indeed to imagine the development of the industrial economy—without the support of all those rational thinkers and their various attempts to grasp the orders, disorders, and transcendental supports of reality.

It is also impossible to imagine thinking about economics without the genuine insights of professional economists, both in and out of the mainstream. The most helpful books are cited in the notes, but Hannah Arendt and Peter Drucker deserve special mention. I disagree with both of them on most topics, but they were the thinkers who first showed me that it was possible to discuss economics in the context of philosophy, cultural history, and politics. In the flesh, conversations with some very intelligent economists—particularly Martin Wolf, Thomas Mayer, Jim O'Neill, Joachim Fels, Eric Chaney, Thomas Stolper, and Michael Atkin—have all been helpful.

Institutionally, I thank the International Theological Institute in Gaming, Austria, the now defunct Plater College (and its then-principal Michael Blades), and the Association of Catholic Social Scientists, which all gave me opportunities to present some of the ideas in this book. My various employers over the last decade—Swiss Bank Corporation, NatWest Markets, Putnam Investments, and Breakingviews.com—have taught me many lessons and provided time and resources to write, even if much of that generosity has been inadvertent. Readers should be especially grateful to Hugo Dixon and the other editors at Breakingviews.com, who have tried to teach me how to write clearly and concisely.

I am also grateful for the suggestions and encouragement offered by Jennifer Roback Morse, Simona Beretta, and Michel Camdessus. More personally, Matthew Muggeridge deserves special thanks for listening and frequently not understanding. Andrew Abela and Stratford Caldecott have both provided moral support, invaluable intellectual insight, and the opportunity to present various arguments at informal conferences. Peter Kwasniewski, Miko Giedroyc, Tim Kelly, Russell Sparkes, Rod Macdonald, and Timothy Egan were very encouraging.

Yet more personally, from earliest childhood my late father instilled in me a great respect for the life of the mind. He was a warm and penetrating supporter of this project over the years and would have lived to see its completion if I had been more sensible. My wife, Grace Andreacchi Hadas, asked the questions that started the intellectual process that eventually led to this book. Finally, my children have lived with the book for too many years. To all, profound thanks.

1

What Are We Talking About? (I)

What Is Economics?

For most of this book, I will try to answer the question "What is economics?" from the perspective of individuals, workers (or laborers, as I will call them), and consumers who engage in economic activity. This first chapter, however, is a description of the economy as a whole, that is, as an aspect of society. The economy, or economic organization, is indeed only one aspect, which has to fit in with many others—including politics, warfare, artistic endeavor, religion, education, and families. Speaking roughly, the distinctly economic aspect of society includes everything that has to do with jobs and shopping, with the things that are worked at and the things that are bought. The economy takes in most of what happens on farms, in mines, factories, warehouses, stores, financial markets, telephone networks, and so forth. The economy also takes in a smaller portion of what happens in homes, schools, and health-care systems.

This chapter attempts to identify the most important features common to all economic organizations. A casual study of the newspapers, or of the economic commentators they cite, might suggest that there is not much common ground. When the experts talk about economic systems, they mostly discuss differences—between the U.S. free market and the European social economy; between the open developing economies that follow the Washington consensus and those that adhere to a more protectionist model; or perhaps between Communist-style central planning, treated either as a fading dream or a looming threat, and something distinctly Scandinavian. Further, all rich countries are different from all middle-income countries, and both are quite different from the poor.

While these differences are certainly important, they are not great enough to preclude a basic unity of all economic organizations. At the most basic level, there is the unity behind the word itself. Just as the differences among religions are significant, but the ability to describe them all as "religion" shows the existence of some common concern, leading to a philosophy of religion, the fact that an economy is present in every society leads to the possibility of a philosophy of economics, the topic of this book.

My primary practical interest is contemporary economies, especially since I and most of my potential readers live in one of them. Their unity is far more than linguistic. On the contrary, the reported distinctions among the various available models are quite superficial; scratch the surface and a profound cultural unity emerges. Thanks to a remarkable globalization of ideas and practices, the same economic approaches, expectations, technologies, and techniques are now found everywhere. To be sure, these forces of industrialization are less thoroughly and successfully deployed in poor countries than in rich, but failure does not change the accepted economic standard, which is industrial. As for the differences among the various economic models of rich countries, they are microscopic in comparison with the similarities.

A lazy or time-bound philosopher might wish to study only this universal modern economy, forgetting or dismissing its newness; it started sometime between two hundred and fifty years ago (the exact time depends on what features are identified as essential). That, however, would be as philosophically inadequate as a philosophy of religion that took only monotheistic or "world" religions into account. The thorough philosopher should be concerned with what is constant in human nature, not what is found only in the modern world, no matter how widely the modern notions have spread or how obviously true and good they currently seem to be. The deeper, philosophical unity of economics must take in not only all contemporary economies but all economies in the past (and in the future, to the extent that they can be imagined)—hunter-gatherer, agricultural, industrial, and postindustrial. This philosophical challenge has a big practical effect, because the differences between industrial and nonindustrial economies are significant. Indeed, the contemporary economies of Afghanistan and Austria probably have more in common than the Austrian economies of the twenty-first and sixteenth centuries.[1]

What follows is a description of the economic aspect of society, of all societies. It has five parts: stuff, capital, service, authority, and social importance. Each part includes comments on how the industrial and preindustrial economies differ, as well as on the key confusions of conventional economists.

Stuff

Economies produce stuff. More exactly, they transform raw materials—the earth itself, currently living creatures and the residues of past life, the powers and dominions of natural forces (such as light and electricity)—into goods that men can use. Some of those goods, most notably food and fuel, are used up by their very nature, so the economy has to keep producing them at a fairly steady rate. Others, such as clothing and shelter, would ideally last forever, but in fact eventually wear out, so the economy also has to produce them at a steady rate. Some stuff, such as food and fuel, are necessary to stay alive. Other stuff, such as sacred books and tools for worship, are considered necessary for spiritual life. Yet other items, for example pillows and the latest model of an electronic gadget, are enjoyed but in no way required. Some stuff, for example food, is assigned primarily to individuals; some, for example houses, to families; and some, for example roads, to whole communities. The diverse collection of economic stuff hardly changed from the beginning of history to sometime around 1500 (or perhaps 1700 or even 1800). Foodstuffs were the preeminent good, at least in terms of the amount of labor dedicated to their production and their importance in social relations. Fuel, for cooking and warmth, was just as vital but its production usually required less effort. Clothing and shelter were the other basic economic goods; their production absorbed much of the effort left over after food and fuel had been assured for the community. In many preindustrial economies, little was left over, so clothing and shelter were minimal. Then there was the stuff made by craftsmen, most notably furniture, containers, jewelry, and the tools of war. An economy was considered rich when these were available to a significant minority of the population. However, most economies were poor.

By preindustrial standards, all industrial economies are fantastically rich. They produce enormous amounts of stuff. Items that were available but scarce in preindustrial societies are almost all abundantly available. There is an ample supply of not only food, fuel, shelter, and clothing but also of candles, chairs, cleaning products, combs, decorations, dishes, nails, pottery, soap, and weapons. In addition, there is always a surplus of totally new and innovative products, from paved roads to this or that electronic gadget. Virtually every category of worldly human desires has been addressed with remarkable effectiveness.

The rich young man to whom Jesus speaks in Mark 10:17–31, provides a good example of this transformation. His wealth is not described, but it is safe to say that his fine clothes, large house, and numerous servants would have made him rich anywhere in the world at any time up to about 1750. By today's standards, however, he was very poor. His furniture and diet were crude and meager. His house may have been fine, but it was cold and dirty and his health was likely to be poor. His travels were ridiculously slow and uncomfortable—a camel or a carriage versus an air-conditioned car or jet. His access to knowledge (technical, not spiritual) was pathetic. He had no text messages, recorded music, or overseas holidays.

The tremendous increase in stuff production teaches a lesson about the human condition. From time immemorial, it was universally assumed that the natural, physical world was so hostile to men that they could never get it to produce enough stuff for everybody. This assumption of the necessity of scarcity was justified by experience, an experience almost as harsh in temperate as in extreme climates, in rich as in barren soils, and in peaceful as in troubled times. Always and everywhere, famines, plagues, and disease were frequent; life expectancies were short; daily life was uncomfortable; nutrition was generally poor; books were rare. The losing battle with the world could fairly be described as "the economic problem."[2]

The battle is no longer lost. The economic problem has been more than solved among the rich sixth of the world's population. They live in plenty. A much larger fraction, half or more, enjoy a good portion of the contemporary cornucopia of stuff. True, this plenty could be ended by an environmental catastrophe or a modern-style war, since the modern world also holds a cornucopia of destruction. For now, however, the economic problem has been resolved. Famine is unthinkable and infectious diseases are often cured and always kept under control. Potable water, effective sewage, and access to sterile medical equipment are universal. Almost no healthy mothers and infants die from the difficulties of childbirth or infancy.

More than that, there are fresh vegetables from around the world, microwave ovens, mobile telephones with voicemail, running hot water (you choose the exact temperature), easy and fast air travel, open-heart surgery, downloaded films, a list that could continue almost until the computer keyboard—a clever thing, made of a miracle material that adjusts precisely to the touch—wears out. The quality as well as the quantity of available stuff steadily increases. Indeed, the least elaborate machine-made good is now almost always better—more durable and effective, although often not more beautiful—than the finest work of a preindustrial craftsman or housewife. All this stuff is available to many more people. Indeed, so many people can be supported by the industrial economy that it is now man's choices, not the harshness of nature, which limits the population.

This tremendous transformation of the stuff economy is rarely acknowledged by conventional economists.[3] On the contrary, they continue to speak of economics as a study of rationing and scarcity. Further, their almost universal interest in the promotion of "economic growth" is based on the assumption that more stuff is always and everywhere desirable. Modern industrial satiety is rarely considered a relevant consideration. This is an obtuse omission, as a few economists have finally recognized.[4] While crude economic growth may still be good in poor countries, where some beneficial modern stuff is not yet universally available, its value is at least questionable in rich economies. Indeed, more stuff would only always be better than less stuff if stuff were always and everywhere good. That is an unlikely claim about human nature (more on that in chapter 5). In addition, the stuff of economy cannot be considered in isolation. The production and use of stuff demand man's time and effort, which might be better deployed in other ways.

Of course, riches do not stop men from wanting, or thinking that they want, more stuff. Many of the ways in which industrial economies are oriented and organized encourage and satisfy such desires. But stated desires should be evaluated critically. They may not reflect the soul's profoundest desires, but only superficial and morally misguided cravings. Many philosophers and psychologists would say that the desire for stuff is often best understood as not actually a longing for the stuff itself, but as a craving for something deeper and better, a something that the stuff is supposed to bring. Is that hope realistic? A fuller answer will emerge from the remaining chapters of this book, but here is a starting hint. Economists should take seriously a piece of philosophical wisdom that has stood up well through the transition of the stuff economy from scarcity to satiety—that the good of stuff is limited. That is the insight that Jesus offered the rich young man, who was no more willing to accept it than are most conventional economists.

Capital

The goal of the stuff economy is use, but the economist must also be concerned with the tools and techniques of stuff production and distribution. Men use various sorts of power to turn what is given into what is useful. They have knowledge about all sorts of raw materials; they have learned skills of refining, construction, and manipulation; they live in or create communities that work together; they build tools and combine them in machines and factories; and they develop systems of trade and transport to move the stuff in socially integrated ways from the place of production to the place of consumption. This whole collection of ideas, attitudes, knowledge, practices, and equipment is known as "capital."

The massive increase in the amount of stuff in the modern industrial economy is only possible because of a parallel increase in the amount of all sorts of capital. For hard capital, the physical tools of production, the expansion is clearly visible. A world traveler of two centuries ago would have had to search carefully to find a production site that employed more than a few dozen people or utilized more than a few horsepowers of energy. Now he must only go down the highway a few kilometers (a much quicker journey, thanks to the stuff economy's satiety). The landscape is dotted with huge units of production—chains of factories, each filled with complex and powerful machines, each with hundreds or even thousands of workers.

For soft capital (the social supports for production), the changes are less visible but perhaps even more impressive. By a generous count, predominantly agricultural economies might have had a few hundred "job descriptions." Almost all production was coordinated for the needs of nothing larger than a family farm or, at most, a village. Men were rarely obliged to cooperate with strangers, because production was local and trade was rare. Economic knowledge was limited and largely local, often passed down only from father to son or mother to daughter. Now, however, there are thousands of types of productive labor, and the skills required are much more sophisticated. The scale of production is often global, entailing trust of and cooperation with hordes of totally unknown people. Trade and commerce are almost everywhere. An extensive and self-perpetuating economic culture provides a gigantic and readily available reservoir of economic know-how.

The increase in the quantity in the capital economy has been accompanied by a change of scale—from the human to the superhuman. In the pre-industrial economy, the skills and muscles of man, or of a handful of men, were the standard. Tools or simple machines enhanced men's strength, but they were made to human measure. If the spinning wheel, the harness, the horseshoe, the water wheel, or the grindstone broke, another could be made relatively quickly in a fairly small workshop. Animals, which are much stronger than men, could be put to work, but they needed direct human guidance.

Industrial capital is quite different. Consider mining. It was once the domain of men with picks and shovels and of machines that were not much larger than the men who used them. In contrast, a modern open-cast mine has many huge machines and almost no miners. It is much the same in any big factory. Huge, virtually unmanned machines do tasks that once required the strength and dexterity of many men. There are only occasional compromises with humanity—noise insulation or ladders for repairmen. Lighter industry is almost equally, if more subtly, superhuman. For example, electronic products are not really assembled by men; the sterilized line-workers only guide and supervise machines working at tasks invisible to the unaided human eye. Even the scale of organizations of production has become somehow superhuman. A gregarious man may know a few hundred people, but large companies or economic systems—the pharmaceutical community or the air-traffic control network—bind together hundreds of thousands or even millions of men in overlapping economic networks.

The superhuman economy works amazingly well. Take the production of food, the most basic type of stuff. Industrial capital has multiplied the typical preindustrial farming family's production twenty or thirty times.[5] Further, the industrial farmer works fewer and shorter days with far less physical demands than those of his preindustrial predecessor.[6] The increases have been even more significant in industries that depend less than farming on the gifts of nature. For example, the hours of labor needed to make a ton of steel have shrunk by something like 99.9 percent since 1600, and by 90 percent over the last century, while the quality of the steel has improved tremendously.[7] Traditional women's domestic productive labor has also been changed almost beyond recognition. Most of the stuff that used to be made at home is now produced in factories, and machines have whittled away the once onerous labors of cleaning and heating to almost nothing.

The increase in the productivity of capital has eliminated a scarcity of labor in just the same way that it has allowed the elimination of the scarcity of stuff. In most preindustrial economies and in the early days of industry, it was common for men to die because their labor was not productive enough to earn the stuff necessary for survival, and hard physical labor was the lot of all but a few aristocrats.[8] That is ancient history. Now only about one-fifth of men work in the stuff economy, while women almost never think of housework as a full-time job. The idleness that efficient capital has spawned has been spread around society through a series of social and economic innovations—shorter work weeks, weekends and vacations off work, extra years of schooling and retirement, pointless employment (discussed in chapter 15).[9] The leisure time freed up by industrial capital has been so great that about as many people are now employed, directly and indirectly, in occupying that time through "leisure industries"—travel, entertainment, sports—as are employed producing stuff.[10]

This successful superhuman scale of production is connected—as both cause and effect—to a change in the view of nature and man's place in it. Preindustrial men wrestled nature into a human world, but they generally saw the humanized world as a small, temporary, and fragile break in the nonhuman uniformity of nature. (This broad cultural generalization is subject to the usual caveats.) In contrast, the human world in modern industrial societies extends throughout nature. Men and their equipment are found almost everywhere in the land, sea, and air. Men believe that they should be able to know and master the inner workings of everything in the world, from the microscopic to the cosmic.

In the capital economy, this modern view of nature translates into a titanic confidence in the human ability and responsibility to overcome whatever physical obstacles are thrown in man's path.[11] Is a river flooding? Dam it, change its course, build up its banks. Are people hungry? Produce more food, ship in the excess from somewhere else. Is a disease ravaging? Find a cure. This is excellent, as far as it goes, and it goes further than anyone would have imagined before the advent of the industrial economy. Still, the philosopher knows, or should know, that this confidence is fundamentally illusory, and not merely because of a temporary technological incapacity in the face of a problem. The illusion is more profound—no machine will conquer death, no consumption stuff can be produced that will give happiness or meaning to life.

Although industrial capital is in some ways superhuman in its scale and operation, it is very much a human creation. The physical stuff comes from God or nature, but men must transform it into something useful. Industrial capital is constructed out of the trust, knowledge, and efforts of men, of course while still relying on (God-given) human intelligence, men's social nature, and the close correspondence of men's thinking with the way the world actually works.

Conventional economists simply miss this humanization of capital. On the contrary, while correctly considering capital to be central to the industrial economy, they reify Capital into an impersonal force that is not only more powerful than men, but almost beyond man's control. (Capital is usually described more in physical and financial than in human terms, reflecting the narrowness of the conventional approach.) Socialists think the entire force of the state is necessary to ensure that the monster Capital does not enslave the people. Capitalists count on "private ownership" (an odd description of the control mechanism for gigantic impersonal corporations), but consider the income from capital, profit, to be fundamentally different from the personal income of wages. Both socialists and capitalists make the same basic error. Capital is not a thing or a force or an impersonal and uncontrollable social construct; it is human—men knowing, sharing, trusting, and working together, and the tools built and operated by men. Any organization of capital—in a family business, a corporation, a government agency, a partnership—is an arbitrary human construction subject to the same moral and practical judgments—is it good? is it useful?—as any other human thing.

Caring

Economies do not only produce stuff for men to use. They also involve the labor of men, and especially women, being useful to each other. As humans, we almost always need or desire some sort of human help. In childhood, we wish for adult love and guidance. In ignorance, we wish for knowledge. In sickness, we wish for care and cures. In physical or mental weakness, we look for protection and help. In traveling, we wish for hospitality. Our bodies can always benefit from physical attention—athletic training, beautification, and, at the end, the appropriate respect for corpses. Our souls are just as incomplete without others helping us with religion, education, entertainment, and therapy. The provision of all of these services constitutes what can be called a service or caring economy.

This caring economy has been much less changed by the coming of industry than has the stuff economy. Apparently, the amount of stuff available has relatively little effect on man's social needs and desires. Industry has led, however, to two shifts in caring. First, much more time is dedicated to the caring economy, thanks to the amazing effectiveness of capital. That additional time has allowed all human needs that can be met to be met and many new desires to be found and satisfied. Second, the modern, caring economy is much more professional than the premodern. There is more knowledge, training, and specialization. How much good the increase in time and professionalism has provided is a subject for debate, but that debate has more to do with human nature and competence than with economics.

Indeed, economics can provide only a relatively narrow perspective on the care that the caring economy provides, because that economy is so deeply integrated with the rest of society and human experience. Of course, the stuff economy is also not totally isolated from the rest of society. The construction and operation of hard capital require scientific and technical knowledge, which relies on universities and other largely scientific organizations.[12] Soft capital is even more social. The relations of trade rely on trust and a common language of commerce. Those cannot flourish without powerful and reasonably protective political authorities.

Still, the caring economy is much less economic than the stuff economy. True, there are economies of the family, of education, of health care—the organized networks of provision, the arrangements and compensation of those who provide these services, the supporting networks that train, supervise, and discipline the providers. However, the boundaries between these economies and other domains (social, political, cultural) are unclear. The analysis of the most economic aspects of the caring economy—for example, of the working hours of nurses or the pay demands of teachers—generally needs to be supplemented with expertise from other fields. Indeed, the economic aspects of many sorts of care are considered among the least valuable, both by those involved and by outsiders. For nurses, teachers, or mothers to worry too much about wages or to complain too much about their hard toil is somehow unseemly.

Conventional economists do talk about the service economy, but without giving much thought to either its definition or its differentiation from the rest of society. Instead, they usually assume that economists should only be concerned with service or caring tasks when those who provide them are paid for their pains. This implicit definition fails the basic philosophical test of historical universality. Many types of care, for example nursing and psychological counseling, were typically done outside of the cash economy in preindustrial societies but are typically paid jobs in industrial economies. The move to pay and increased professionalism is certainly meaningful sociologically, but the economist should be concerned primarily with the common nature of tasks and those who work at them. This conventional economic confusion, or at least the endorsement of it on a social scale, leads to one of the more bizarre economic judgments in modern societies—that it is an obvious improvement when mothers stop working "at home," that is, with their children without pay, and start "working," that is, at paid jobs with other adults or with machines.

More significantly, the conventional economists' emphasis on money misses what is perhaps the most outstanding feature of the caring economy: its focus on the good of others. The conventional analysis does not merely miss this focus, it actively denies it. The conventional idea that money defines the caring economy misleadingly suggests that there is a hidden selfishness, the desire for more money, at its center. I will offer a description of caring labor that is certainly more generous and I hope more satisfactory, but only after placing economics on a more solid moral and anthropological foundation.

Authority

Both the stuff and the caring economies require authority. That statement cannot be justified formally without some postulates about human nature (coming up in chapter 5), but it is certainly plausible. After all, communities in all other aspects of society—politics, armies, families, organized religion, and academic departments, for example—have clear hierarchical structures, even if the authority is often limited or precarious. Humans do not seem to be able to undertake any venture together without having some sort of rules and various sorts of leaders to set, change, and enforce them. There is no obvious reason to expect the economic aspect to be unusually anarchic. This argument from analogy can be supplemented by observation—economies, both preindustrial and industrial, in fact do have all sorts of rules, rule-setters, and leaders, and the economy is in fact closely tied with political and other types of authority.

There seems to be a rough correlation between the scale and complexity of the economic organization and the scope of the economic authority. In preindustrial economies, most production was done on largely self-sufficient family farms located in almost entirely self-sufficient villages. The economic authority was almost indistinguishable from the general rules of family and community. Only small groups of traders, craftsmen, and moneylenders had their own structures of economic authority, which generally included subservient but mildly hostile relations to the political authorities. Cities were rare, and big industrial complexes did not exist.

As the products and networks of production became more complex, economic authorities have also become more complex, centralized, and far-reaching. Consider cities, which have come to dominate population structures. Cities make excellent economic sense for both the stuff and professional service economies—distances are short, skilled laborers are numerous, and communities of like-minded industrialists and researchers can flourish. Cities, however, are complex and will be chaotic without strong central authorities to provide infrastructures such as roads, water, electricity, schools, and police. In effect, the same economic forces that promote cities also promote strong economic and political authorities.

More generally, the need for authority, in particular for government authority, increases when industrial capital becomes more productive through economies of scale (using "economy" in a sense that is otherwise almost obsolete), that is, by making the most use of the available tools and technologies and of the various networks of distribution and information. The logic is simple. The larger the scale of production, the less personal relations can be relied on to establish the standards and rules required for uniformity and efficiency. Authoritative administrations are needed to set, change, and police these standards. Then, the larger the economy, the more centralized and powerful the administrations must be. In addition, the more powerful the administrations, the more they should be oriented directly to the public good. Finally, the more these administrations are thought to serve the public good, the more they will drift into the sphere of politics and government rather than remain in an autonomous economic arrangement. Thus, it is hardly surprising that the history of the industrial economy is largely a history of increased productivity accompanied by more economic authority, housed both in largely economic entities such as corporations and in largely governmental entities such as regulatory agencies and central banks.

The trend toward centrally monitored structures and centrally set rules should be kept in mind whenever terms such as "rugged individualism" or "entrepreneurial spirit" come up in economic discussions. Isolated economic action has long contributed little to modern industrial economies. It was not brave individuals, romantic trappers, and lone pioneer farmers who made America's wilderness wealthy. The wealth came from centralized thinking—the standardized gauges and carefully maintained support networks of canals and railroads, the telegraph network, and a unified financial system.[13] By now, almost all of the economic action is made by teams, corporations, and networks that are guided by well-understood rules, rules that mesh easily with the gigantic administrations that make up modern government.[14]

The increasing economic role of government irritates most conventional economists. They are quite reasonably frustrated by the way in which central authorities stifle organizational and individual flexibility and creativity. Those losses, however, must be taken in the context of the gains provided by the complexity of modern industry and by economies of scale. Less reasonably, many economists are enthralled by an unrealistic "market" model of economic organization in which the interactions of atomistic individuals are imagined generally to be self-regulating. The many conceptual weaknesses of this model will be discussed in the next chapter, but a leading practical one is this combination of a bland acceptance of big business with a blind resistance to big government. It is certainly possible to have neither, as in pre-industrial economies, or both, as in industrial economies, but big business without a big regulatory government is hard to imagine. (Historically, this correlation of increasing economic complexity and the size of government has extended to the government regulation of income distribution, but the economic rationale for those government programs is different.)

Social Importance

At the beginning of this chapter, the economic aspect of society was described as no more than one of many. As a study, economics must try to deal with the relations of its particular part, the distinctly economic organization, to each of the others and to the whole. Unfortunately, this intellectual effort is likely to be unsatisfactory. As a specialist, the economist can only see the whole from a narrow perspective. His limited range of expertise threatens to make him sound like the tailor whose sole response to a papal audience was a guess at the Holy Father's suit size. Alternatively, if he merely throws in his personal opinions about noneconomic topics, he begins to sound like a show-business celebrity expounding ignorantly on political questions, as if excellence in one domain automatically extended to others. In the next four chapters, I will try to avoid the second danger while discussing economics as a typically modern way of looking at the world. For now, I will try to avoid the first risk by making a few broad, but still basic, observations.

To start with, the economy is deeply and inextricably entwined with everything else in society. Relations with science and politics have already been mentioned. I have hinted at the generally subservient role of economic considerations in matters of knowledge and love. In general, any attempt to analyze a particular situation or problem solely in economic terms will always prove inadequate. Even when it comes to something as basically economic as getting food on the table, there is much more involved—religion, if the fertility of the soil is thought to be a divine gift; scientific knowledge, if it is thought to be a matter of human ingenuity; social status, in the decision of who should get what food; cultural symbols, in how the food is prepared and presented; and psychology, because the giving and sharing of food is a prime way of expressing love.

Many conventional economists deny that the economy needs to be integrated with everything else. At best, they try to treat economics as an autonomous study. They argue, or more often simply assume, that the economy has its distinct motivations and rules—self-interest, the preference for the present over the future, a peculiar sort of "rationality." Neither the applicability of economic rules to other domains nor the economic applicability of noneconomic motivations and rules is considered to be the economist's affair. That assumption is foolish, since economic organization is obviously intimately connected with so many other aspects of society, and because men do not seem to think about economic things in a distinct way.

All too often, however, economists add arrogance to their foolishness by trying to integrate everything else into the economy. In other words, they believe that all social questions—political, religious, sociological—can and should be reduced to economic ones. For example, they think that the lower fertility rates seen in rich countries for the past two generations must be caused by something economic—too much wealth, too little wealth, or not enough group childcare facilities. In this economic reductionism, they follow, perhaps at a distance, Marx's idea that "material relations" are the key to all social understanding.[15]

Economists are not the only modern intellectuals tempted to reductionism. Other single categories—for example, national character, evolutionary laws, and sexual drives—have their fans. Each monomaniacal explanation has its own claimed motivations and rules.[16] The number of these one-cause-explains-all theories is suggestive of their inadequacy. The world is too complicated for economism or any of its simplistic peers to be right. If an all-encompassing explanation is to be successful, it must work at a much higher level—the "divine comedy" of creation and redemption comes to mind. The economy is a mundane aspect of life, just one among many. It is neither autonomous nor able to encompass the others. One of the economist's principal tasks is to put the economy in its proper place.

The question of the proper place for economic concerns in society turns out to be extremely difficult. Indeed, most of the rest of this book aims at providing the start to an answer, by identifying and evaluating the economic good—or, as it turns out, the various economic goods. Those goods must then be placed appropriately within a broader hierarchy of goods, both social and more personal. As a start, I have already rejected one extreme evaluation: that the economic good is the only, or the highest, good. Other things matter as much or more. In the next chapters, I will also reject the other extreme: that the economic good is valueless. That rejection, however, relies on a statement about human nature—that the good of men is expressed, at least in part, in their everyday life in the world. Rejecting the extremes, however, still leaves a vast middle ground.

While the philosophical judgment is elusive, the modern practical judgment is clear. The economy and its perceived goods have become more highly valued. No preindustrial society cared enough about economic matters to create large factories, global distribution systems, or extensive economic regulations (see chapter 4). The development of the industrial economy required a higher valuation of the economic good. One sign of this revaluation is the willingness routinely to sacrifice evenings at home, Sabbath rest, and family unity to the industrial organization's "need" for production. Similarly, the optimization of industrial production is now the most important consideration in the organization of transport and housing. Social status is not entirely determined by economic status, but the correlation is much closer than it was in most preindustrial societies; and the direction of causality is much more likely to run from wealth to social prestige than the other way around. Even political structures are increasingly seen as primarily serving prosperity, rather than prosperity being seen as useful for its support of national military prowess or aesthetic glory.

The Question about Economics

If it were not for conventional economics, this chapter would largely have made some pretty obvious comments: the resolution of the economic problem of scarcity should change the way people think about economic needs and desires; the techniques of production are a mix of the divine (or given) and the human, particularly the human willingness to work together; work done at home or for other people is as valuable as work done in factories or with stuff; complicated economies need more extensive governance than simple ones; and economic activity is far from the be-all and end-all of society. In conventional economics, however, each of these claims is either rejected outright or accepted only with difficulty.

The discipline appears to be fundamentally confused. That appearance is right—conventional economics is based on false premises about human nature, comes to many false conclusions, and ignores many important economic facts.

Still, conventional economics should not simply be ignored, for two reasons. First, despite their severe intellectual handicaps, economists have learned some fairly important things about the way economies work. Their insights into such topics as prices, monetary systems, trade policy, industry structures, and financial markets should not be discarded. Economists disagree about everything, but it would be foolish not to try to learn from their debates. This book hardly touches on any of the questions that conventional economics can help answer, but that silence should not be taken as disrespect.

The second reason is quite relevant to this book. Conventional economics has been successful in the simple sense of being able to gain adherents. As the conventional wisdom, it is believed or half-believed by almost everyone who gives economics a thought. It has to be the starting point for any attempt to construct a more plausible model of economics. So before starting again, I need to explain the deep sources of error in the conventional theory. The roots of the conventional view spring from the core of the modern worldview, so the intellectual equivalent of deep ploughing will be necessary to pull them all up. That deconstruction or extirpation is the subject of the next chapter.

2

The Problem with Conventional Economics

There can be no doubt that the modern industrial economy works well, at least by some standards. I will provide a more refined judgment in the last chapter of this book, but any system that has been able to resolve the economic problem cannot be all bad. The titanic claims for industrial capital may ultimately be illusory, but advances in technology have truly allowed a large number of human problems to be solved. That success suggests that the shapers of the industrial economy—in business, politics, research, and general cultural formation—know, and have always known, what they are doing in some basic sense, whether or not they understand the deepest principles underlying their techniques.

Unfortunately, conventional economists, the professionals who are supposed to understand exactly those deepest principles, do not know what is really going on. True, their basic ideas come out of the same modern worldview (which I will talk about in more detail in chapter 4) that has inspired both scientists and technologists in their successful development of capital and so many others in their successful dedication to industrial prosperity. However, practical success in some domains—in this case science, technology, and prosperity—does not imply the truth of all modern ideas. Indeed, for conventional economics, most of the founding notions of the discipline are wrong and most of the supposed laws and rules are some combination of wrong, misguided, and meaningless.

The economists' most basic problem is anthropological, in the philosophical sense of that word—the "logos" (reasoned principle or nature) of "anthropos" (man).[1] The first section of this chapter lists nine basic and erroneous claims about human nature, all of which are accepted with more or less enthusiasm by almost all professional economists. (Some modified views are discussed in the next chapter.) These bad ideas both limit and distort the economists' vision. The second section deals with the especially peculiar utilitarian characteristics of the neoclassical economic model, which has dominated the field for the last century. Finally, there is a discussion of why economics is often called the "dismal science," and whether it really needs to be one.

Nine Bad Ideas about Human Nature

The first day of the first introductory course in economics sets the tone for everything else, all the way into postgraduate work and beyond. The professor defines the field—generally in terms of scarcity, choice, or money—and gives a few hints about the analytic techniques that will be used—mathematical, monetary, or "rational." If the teacher is sophisticated and direct, he might introduce economic man (*homo economicus*). That odd creature embodies human nature as economists see it, at least for the purposes of their study.[2] Even if economic man is not cited by name, students will rapidly become familiar with his characteristics. Indeed, by the time they hear about the "golden rule" of neoclassical economics—markets balance when marginal cost equals marginal revenue—they will be taking for granted that when it comes to economics, this is how men are. The principles that guide this economic man are listed here. They are not entirely consistent with each other, but their contradictions are rarely severe enough to cause any sort of theoretical crisis. They do share one common attribute—they are all wrong.

1) The transcendental is not relevant to economics. Sure, a man might go to church, meditate at home, or sometimes ponder about the meaning of a life that ends in the mystery of death (a meaning, if there is one, that is presumably concerned with things more durable than economic stuff). For the conventional economist, however, such matters are irrelevant. Speculations about deeper things are simply not his business. This economic inattention to the transcendental is supposed to be neutral to claims about supernatural goods, but in practice inattention easily slips into hostility. So, for example, economists generally treat arguments that hard work can be sanctifying or that poverty can prepare men for heaven as absurd. This is all wrong. Men have an inerasably transcendental orientation that guides them in everything, even in worldly economic activities. Indeed, worldly prosperity is only valuable to the extent that it aids men in their transcendental search for meaning. Religion, in particular the world-loving transcendentalism of Christianity, can play an important role in economic analysis.

2) Economics has nothing to do with morality. Conventional economists want to be ethically as well as transcendentally neutral. If the good is a meaningful concept at all—a claim that makes many economists deeply uncomfortable—then it is one that should stay in the domain of philosophers and other airy-fairy types. Economists think they are limiting themselves to hard facts—what men's actions show about their economic desires. The main hard fact, or so the economists claim, is that people want more, in particular more consumption goods. In practice, this "more" serves as a basic economic good. This is all wrong. Men rarely if ever act without some sort of ethical intent—they always search for the good, a good that has at least some hint of the transcendental about it. If they do look for more stuff, it is because they believe that this stuff is in fact good. Of course, ethics is complex. The good cannot easily be identified or followed in any domain, including economics, but it certainly cannot be reduced to mere quantity.

3) All economic ties are contractual. According to conventional economic anthropology, each man is an economic island, interested only in his own good. These islands, however, are not fixed, but bump into each other. The collisions are regulated by freely negotiated contracts. In turn, these are guided entirely by each individual's search for his own advantage; they are unconstrained by any previous obligations. The result is not so much a society as a contractual quasi-society, a place without tradition or fixed rules and with the open-ended possibility of any number of new contracts. This is all wrong. Men are by nature social, and they naturally live in societies that have many structures—of family, religion, and government, to name a few, as well as the economic structures of labor and consumption. Contracts can be useful, but they are only manifestations of deeper structures of law, trust, and community.

4) *Men's economic behavior follows physical laws.* Economists suffer from physics envy. They want to base their field on simple, elegant, and pervasive mathematical formulas. Newton's laws of mechanics were the first inspiration, but the laws of thermodynamics, most notably the conservation of energy, have had more direct influence, especially in the neoclassical model.[3] Economic transactions are thought to conserve latent utility (or pleasure or happiness). In any transaction, the total utility, like the total of money, is the same at the end as at the beginning. All of this can be expressed in terms of mathematical functions. This is all wrong. Men—their motivations, joys, hopes, and fears— can rarely be reduced to numbers in any meaningful way. Economists' equations might explain something, but whatever they explain is not what should be central about economic activity—how well it serves the human good.

5) *The economic life is a constant struggle.* This idea comes out of social Darwinism, the vision of human society as guided by an unending, inevitable, and universal struggle for survival.[4] This theory, generated by biology envy, does not mesh easily with the last, generated by physics envy, but the struggle-view lies behind the widespread praise of competition as a force that drives the economy forward. This is all wrong. Amoral social Darwinism offers a most unrealistic interpretation of all human interactions, but it is particularly inapplicable to industrial economies, which rely extensively on trust and cooperation and which demand the support of entire communities. Competition can be helpful, but it needs to be controlled and channeled with great care. Otherwise, like any struggle among men, it is more likely to prove mutually destructive than uplifting.

6) *Perfection is within reach.* Economists love to talk about perfect markets and the optimization of "welfare." They assume that well-directed economic effort will be rewarded by coming closer to these perfect states. The belief in an unceasing ability to do more economic good helps justify a dismissive attitude towards any tradition—political, cultural, or religious—that gets in the way. This is all wrong. Men can and should strive to improve their lot, including their economic lot, but they should never expect too much.

Life in the world, no matter how economically enriched, will always be marred by moral weakness. Traditions can provide valuable anchors. Economic perfection is a dangerous goal, as the Communist experiment demonstrated.

7) *Economic freedom is a good found in free choice.* Many conventional economists consider freedom, along with "more," to be an economic good. Their definition of freedom is the one endorsed by philosophical liberals—freedom is choice. So an economy is freer—better—if people have more choice in their consumption, more choice in their jobs, and more choice in who they contract with. This is all wrong. The liberal understanding of freedom is inadequate.[5] True freedom is found in the ability to live up to the true and the good, the transcendental true and good. Unrestrained choice can restrict rather than enhance this freedom, for example when the choice is for addiction or some other evil. The value of free economic choice is particularly hard to determine without some sense of the social context in which the "free" economy is set.

8) *The good economy is controlled by the beneficent state.* Some conventional economists prefer order and efficiency to freedom of choice. For them, the road to economic optimization is blocked by the steady inability of men to act in their best interest and by their tendency to waste time and energy in petty squabbling. The assumption that the perfect is possible leads to the conclusion that this inability and waste can and should be overcome by extensive government controls. At the extreme, this line of thought leads to praise of the total central planning of jobs and production. This is wrong, just as wrong as the simple praise of freedom. Governments are fallible in much the same way as the individuals they govern. Wise governments certainly play a part in the search for the economic good, but they are never good enough to create perfection.

9) *Economics rules.* The tendency towards economism was mentioned in chapter 1. The idea is that behind all of men's actions lurk economic motivations, motivations that only economists can fully understand, because only they are trained to apply the correct mundane, mathematical, amoral, individualistic, competitive, and optimizing logic to situations that noneconomists might try to think about in more noble terms. This is all wrong. Economic motivations are hardly relevant beyond the domain of economic activity. The

conventional tools of economic analysis hardly provide any insight into economic motivations, let alone noneconomic issues. Residents of industrial societies may well be more oriented to the satisfaction of economic desires than their preindustrial predecessors were, but other concerns—spiritual, social, romantic, aesthetic, political—still predominate.

The Utilitarian Mistakes

The central topic in any introductory economics class is the neoclassical model of economic equilibrium. Much of the rest of an economist's career is spent modifying or backing away from this model, but no conventional economist really feels comfortable too distant from the world of markets, supply and demand, marginal factors, and differential equations. It would take too long to analyze each of these ideas, and much too long to analyze the many modifications that are made to save economic appearances. However, I can briefly go through some of the underlying notions—including the key idea of a market—in the hope of suggesting how deeply flawed the whole approach is.

The emphasis on money is especially misguided. Money sits at the core of the neoclassical model—economic man's ability to match supply and demand through finding a mutually acceptable money-price for each piece of stuff. This price can only be optimal for both sides if it fairly represents all of the good in the thing. It is true that the theory refers to the "utility" that the money creates rather than the money itself. However, since money is treated as the only source of utility, it comes to the same thing conceptually. (In theory, economists may admit the existence of "psychic income," a pleasure that comes without any direct monetary value, but in practice, cash on the table, or in the bank account, is what matters.) In addition, more money is assumed to be better than less money.

This monetary emphasis is true to the utilitarian roots of the neoclassical theory.[6] Jeremy Bentham, the founder of modern utilitarianism, wished to reduce the metaphysical notion of the good to the strictly physical, individualistic, and completely quantifiable ideas of pleasure (plus) and pain (minus). The physical aspect, which was to be measured by skin or brain chemistry, was dropped by later theoreticians, who turned utility into an almost empty concept: that which people want. This substitution of a concept for a measurable physical quantity causes a major philosophical problem for a supposedly precise and mathematical approach to human nature, since it is hard to measure what people want. Money comes as a godsend, since its good is vague enough to include nonphysical pleasures and it is as numerical as any measure of skin excitement. No wonder economists are the only utilitarians who try to use quantitative utilitarianism as a practical guide to decisions. They seem to have a quantitative measure of pleasure right at hand.

Not really, though.

Money clearly plays an important role in the organization and operations of industrial economies. It is a useful tool for allocating stuff and services and for indicating social status and relations. Money, however, is simply a poor measure of the economic good. To start with, the utilitarian assumption that more is always better is not true for most of the things that are valued in monetary terms—for example, food, comforts, or time spent on the job (in which the conventional assumption is that less is better). On the contrary, the best is most often found in the mean, while more generally leads to undesirable excess.[7]

More generally, while prices may indicate costs or preferences, as economists point out, the whole idea that money can be used to quantify and compare goods is faulty. It is not simply that there are some goods that money cannot buy; it is that the value of goods, including the most economic ones, cannot be measured numerically in any meaningful way. No collection of prices can really express the absolute or relative value of having enough to eat, of a comfortable life, of a luxury vacation, of the ability to talk to distant friends and relations, of a job that makes one happy, of being able to stay at home to take care of one's children. Of course, money cannot even start to compare any of these goods, which at least can sometimes be bought with money, with those that money truly cannot buy—eternal life, wisdom, happiness, a good marriage, honor.

More technically, money is a problematic measure of value within the monetary world. The same amount of money buys different goods at different times and places. Goods that cost the same amount of money—say a certain amount of food and a certain amount of entertainment—would seem to have quite different, and not obviously comparable, values to the purchasers. Even the same money buying the same food has quite different human values when the food fends off starvation and when the food is excess to requirements. Money is an instantaneous measure—there is a price paid now—but many economic goods (for example, houses) have a value that stretches out over years. Economic activity helps to create or damage such goods as clean air, safe streets, and "free" entertainment or health care, but these goods come either without any obvious price or with a value that seems quite different from the obvious price.

Economists have developed a series of tricks to try to get over these disadvantages. The different values of money over time and place are dealt with by the construction of artificial equivalent-monies that have a constant value—seen for example in so-called "real" Gross Domestic Product (GDP) calculations. To deal with the different values of same-priced goods and the different times that money is used there are arbitrary mathematical schemes that change money into value. The problem of nonmonetary goods is tackled with a series of calculations of "imputed" monetary values. Unfortunately, the solid, quantitative, and objective nature of money is lost in all these adjustments.

Besides the utilitarian theory's reliance on money, its assumption of universal selfishness is also a problem. This selfishness—or self-interest, as it is more politely named—is required for the functioning of the archetypical neoclassical interaction, the balance of supply and demand through price. The suppliers and the demanders of economic stuff must have no interest in the other side's utility in the transaction. Without that assumption, the key balance of supply and demand cannot be derived mathematically.

In Bentham's physical utilitarianism there is hardly any issue. Since I am only interested in my physical pains and pleasures, which cannot be shared, there is no question of a broader vision (unless I somehow get pleasure from other people's pleasure). In reality, however, men often look beyond themselves in their search for the good. A quick observation of the labor of mothers, fathers, coworkers, soldiers, or lovers shows that men frequently search for the good of others, often so resolutely that they willingly make huge personal sacrifices. A more Christian analysis suggests that men should search for the greatest good, which involves a profound denial of all selfishness and self-interest. Men do not live up to this high standard of total generosity, but that failure does not invalidate either the orientation or the effort.

Economics is not even a particularly promising domain for postulating a merely selfish good. The most typical economic unit is the family—the father and mother (or stepparents or lovers) who take care of each other, of children, and perhaps of other dependents. Even conventional economists sometimes concede there is a common spirit within a family that cannot be expressed as the enlightened selfishness of the individual family members. Industrial economies include all sorts of broader communities—neighborhoods, cities, countries, companies, unions, industries—that elicit the unfeigned and unselfish dedication of their members.

The consequentialism of utilitarian thinking is basically silly. The idea is that the only way to make a decision is to weigh the utility value of alternative choices. Whichever has the highest value is then chosen. Enthusiasts for this felicific or hedonic calculus are not deterred by the observation that men generally appear to base decisions on rightness rather than on likely consequences. They merely posit the existence of an unconscious practice—that the calculations are done by some decision-making mental faculty, which then translates the numbers into conscious ideas of morality.

Among social scientists, only economists have tried to put this strictly numerical, hedonic calculus into practice. They are undeterred by the unknowability of the future. That is dealt with by the use of probabilities, as if the likelihood of future events could be calculated. They are also undeterred by the inability to compare the value of utilities far into the future, indeed into the indefinite or infinite future. That is dealt with by the assumption of an exponential rate of decay of the value of good, an idea that piles implausibility upon implausibility. All these assumptions do not come cheap in terms of lost simplicity. The equations of rational choice involve many, many terms.

Indeed, the whole mathematical rigor of the system is a big problem. It is not seen as such by economists. One of the main complaints about efforts, such as this one, to make the study of economics more human is that the new conclusions often cannot be expressed in equations. Such a descriptive approach demotes economics from the rank of hard science, where the economists wish to place it, to the vague territory of social science or, worse yet, to a branch of philosophy, that font of fuzzy ideas. The real economist yearns for elegant or simple equations, but he is not afraid of adding complexity as necessary. There are many such necessities—functions that account for uncertain outcomes, that convert cash into a measure of the good, that convert future pleasures into current ones, and that deal with the relationship between capital and stuff. The end result is a wonder of mathematics. Unfortunately, the more equations are added to economic analysis, the further it travels from the human reality that should be its subject matter. At best, the complex mathematical models describe a stylized version of reality, but the equations themselves only detract from the observations and intuitions that generate them.

All these bad ideas and their accompanying equations lead away from human reality towards another place, one inhabited only by economists. The ultimate destination is the land of the perfect market, where price balances unlimited supply and unlimited demand. The word "market" is borrowed from commerce, but the analogy is misleading, since actual markets rely on social structures that balance trust and temptation. The utilitarian market relies only on pure self-interest.

In the perfect market, there are no effectively unified communities—men who consume what they produce, men who share the travails and triumphs of the economic life, who make sacrifices for each other and for their possible heirs. Indeed, all the complexity of capital and production, not to mention the unilateral labor of care, is simply ignored. Only transactions matter. The economy is not embedded within a society with laws, customs, and a complex set of social goals. No, in the perfect market there is only an agglomeration of utility-seeking individuals. They come together in economic effort only when, and as long as, the interaction adds to each party's quantity of individual utility. The interaction is always a contractual exchange—a precise this for a precise that. The utility is instantaneous, felt now, and selfish, felt only by me.

The economists' perfect market is so unrealistic that it can give little insight. The professionals do recognize the unreality. In a move filled with philosophical irony—for economics is supposed to be an empirical science based on observation, not on hypothetical intellectual constructs—they admit that in practice markets are always imperfect. An honest economist will even allow that industrial economies have steadily become less like the ideal, as capital has become more complex and governments have become more closely integrated into the economy. But only a few rebels see that the norm, the perfect market that is supposed to stand behind the actual "free market" economy, is no more than a figment of the utilitarian imagination.

There is much more to economics than can be found in the conventional economist's philosophy.

Beyond the Dismal Science

For the most part, the modern worldview has been tremendously optimistic. Some date its birth to the Renaissance, which planned to bring back the lost glories of the Ancients. Others go for the Reformation, which expected to bring back the lost glories of the early Christian church. For economists, a more likely starting date is the eighteenth century, when the Enlightenment (that was the optimistic name its exponents gave it) brought forth the first analysis recognizably economic in a modern sense. The Enlightenment's goals were nothing less than knowledge, freedom, and perpetual peace. More recently, the psychology of self-help has held out the promise of emotional equilibrium for all. Not for nothing is the United States, with its "can-do" philosophy and constitutional cheerfulness, considered the archetypal modern society.

Yet economics, which is as modern a study as can be imagined, has long been known as the dismal science. The phrase was coined in 1849 by Thomas Carlyle and stuck immediately. Why has this grim description seemed so appropriate? One explanation is descriptive. Many leading economists, particularly in the nineteenth century, were gloomy, even desperate. The early economists mostly interpreted the first signs of a new economic order as harbingers of cultural disaster. They saw a landscape blighted by hideous factories located in cities beset by growing squalor. What would later be identified as "unemployment"[8] seemed to be both inevitable and socially incendiary. Economic change seemed to be beyond any sort of political control. The intellectuals were frightened by the increase in population and did not notice the corresponding spread of consumer goods. They deduced an increase in misery and a cheapening of life.

This supposed gruesome reality inspired recommendations of either a strong stomach or revolutionary change. The hard pragmatists, most notably Thomas Malthus and David Ricardo, considered widespread misery to be an inevitable part of the modern economy. The revolutionaries, generally identified as socialists, believed there was a better way. They agreed that the current economic system could produce only wretchedness, at least for the masses, but they thought that a new and better economic arrangement was possible and desirable, even though its creation would likely require the overthrow of the whole social order.[9]

The early-modern tradition of economic despair has not died out completely. The neoclassical model still assumes that economic choices are the resolutions of bitter conflicts among needy economic actors, leading some economists to describe their study as the rationing of unhappiness. There is also a small but influential group of deeply gloomy modern economists who predict the eventual coming of something awful—a shortage of natural resources, the exhaustion of human ingenuity, or the failure of all economic systems. Finally, there is an even smaller and scarcely noticed school of antimodern economists who adhere to the nineteenth-century belief that industry is synonymous with disaster.

Ultimately, however, that descriptive explanation is inadequate. For at least the last half-century, economists have largely been optimists. The cheeriness is not entirely new; Malthus wrote his essay on the inevitability of war and famine in response to Condorçet's prediction, in the true Enlightenment spirit, that modern ingenuity would eventually resolve the economic problem. More recently, the dismal battle of economic agents in the neoclassical model has been subsumed into a model based on faith in the goodness and perpetuity of economic growth.[10] Earlier predictions of inevitable imbalance—whether monetary, demographic, physical, or cultural—have been largely discredited. Rather, most economists believe that the industrial economy can find ways to correct its weaknesses (perhaps with the help of the government). At worst, conventional economists argue for the necessity of some level of unemployment, an unemployment that should be temporary for any affected individuals and that always comes with reasonable compensating welfare benefits. Even the socialists of dire revolution have given way to the socialists of the perfect welfare state.

While economists have mostly been cheerful for several generations, their reputation remains dismal. I do not mean by that that they are criticized for inaccurate predictions or poor policy recommendations. As far as everyday usefulness goes, economists are not alone. They are in a close race to the bottom with psychologists and political scientists. No, economists are thought to be dismal because they take such a small, low, and inhuman view of men's motivations and of the underlying reality of all situations.[11] Ask an economist why mothers do or do not have more children, why beer becomes more or less flavorful, why religion waxes or wanes. The answer is always the same—it's the money. Ask an economist how to figure out whether to build a new road, teach more literature, or allow more immigration. The response is always the same—estimate, calculate, and ignore anything noble or good.

That dismal reputation cannot be shed by more optimistic expectations about potential economic growth rates, or even by a less hostile initial response to government programs that noneconomists praise on the grounds of justice or some other virtue that economists can barely recognize. The dismal nature of economics can only be shed completely by starting afresh with a new anthropology, followed by new definitions of economic activity and the economic good.

Such a renewal is exactly the purpose of this book. Human economics, as I call the result, aims to make economics more realistic, beyond the unwarranted economic pessimism of the early moderns, the base economic optimism of most contemporary practitioners, and the somewhat carping pessimism of antimodern moderns.

Perhaps an example might make the human approach a bit clearer. Consider a trip to a well-stocked modern supermarket. Years of effort have allowed the creation of thousands of emporiums of an awesome opulence, offering an abundance of stuff almost unimaginable to a premodern consumer. These goods come from all over the world, they are kept fresh for weeks if not years, and even residents who are considered poor are able to afford an ample supply, with ample choice.

The response to this vision by either a premodern noneconomist or an early modern economic pessimist would most likely be stunned silence. I would hope that the premodern's interest would be ignited by the sight and that he would be inspired by the good of so tremendous a supply of food. I would also hope that Malthus would return from the supermarket visit with the happy admission that his pessimism had been completely unjustified. (Of course, it is quite possible that any visitor with fixed ideas would find a way to ignore this unsupportive evidence.)

The conventional optimistic economist responds to the consumer cornucopia with simple pleasure—the fully stocked supermarket shows that the economic system works. His response is fair, as far as it goes. The supermarket's abundance can legitimately be considered the culmination of economic history, or at least a shining example of the full resolution of the traditional economic problem. I might argue with the conventional economist about just what the "system" is that is working, but I would not quarrel with his basic judgment.

Still, the economist should recognize that for all this goodness, there is also something wrong, not with the supermarket itself, but with the cultural expectations that it carries and perhaps with the amount of effort that has been dedicated to it. That "something" is hard to identify, but perhaps its clearest sign is the consumers' overall response to this good. The conventional economist, who thinks that consumer happiness is the goal of economic activity, should be disappointed. Consumers rarely show Malthus's hypothetical stunned but happy silence. More common responses are a dazed indifference, complaints about prices and service or resentment over aggressive displays, which seem designed to encourage unwanted purchases. The problem does not seem to be inadequate industrial development. On the contrary, the supermarket's scale is already almost superhuman. It seems improbable that even more variety, convenience, and comfort would create more consumer happiness.

The antimodern modern responds to supermarkets with horror—at the crassness of the whole thing, at the preference for abundance over quality, at the emphasis on marketing rather than on the simple distribution of goods. Such a single-minded horror is too narrow a response—these unattractive shadows are cast by a truly good light of plenty. Still, the antimodern modern is in a good position to identify what is wrong with this accomplishment. The supermarket's problem is that the abundance is so resolutely worldly.

Supermarkets, no matter how well-stocked, cannot be great goods in themselves. Such mundane excellence has too little of the transcendental to offer men much meaning. On the contrary, the effort that goes into creating supermarkets and the consumers' great effort in using them suggest an exaggerated respect for the goods of everyday consumption. It may even be said that the supermarket's overemphasis on the comforts and pleasures of consumption causes moral rot in much the same way that the failure of its refrigeration units would cause the beautifully displayed fresh vegetables to decay. The customers' lack of enthusiasm reflects the emptiness of the delight implicitly promised by the heaping up of so many goods of so little human value.

Human economics attempts to draw what is best out of all three of these modern responses. From the pleasantly surprised pessimists, it is important to learn that men are capable of remarkable economic accomplishments, including correcting previous mistakes. The conventional economist teaches that there is a system in industrial economies that works remarkably well, so well that it seems almost automatic. Finally, the antimodern modern reminds us that modern economic accomplishments look substantially less impressive when they are viewed within the broader context of the modern experiment.

3

Can This Model Be Saved?

When Thomas Carlyle coined the phrase "dismal science," both the industrial economy and the laissez-faire ideology of the free market were still quite new. He was far from alone in his scathing reaction to the belief that impersonal market forces should have free reign, whatever the consequences. Social reformers disagreed with conservative critics such as Carlyle about what was to be done, but they shared his dislike of both the new economy and the new economics. Such critics were not placated—far from it—by the development of the neoclassical model at the end of the century. Rather, the inhumanity and futility of conventional economic research and analysis have remained frequent themes, both for noneconomists and for some disgruntled members of the profession.[1]

Some of the critics moved beyond complaining to attempting to construct their own models of economic activity. These alternative economists generally had mixed feelings about the model they were trying to change or overthrow. They disliked some or all of its premises and conclusions, but they could not really imagine living without it. After all, the conventional economists were the only professionals who had thought coherently about some pretty knotty problems—why there were gluts and depressions, how a monetary system should be organized, the right level of profits, the value of landlords, the advantages of tariffs, and so forth. The conventional economists, classical and neoclassical, may never have reached a consensus, but they framed the terms of the debate. The critics, who were mostly trained in the discipline, were reluctant or unable to move too far away from these terms.

The result is that unconventional economists, past and present, generally abandon only some of the conventional theory. They offer variations rather than true alternatives. To my knowledge, there has never been an attempt to rebuild a coherent intellectual edifice for economics on a sound anthropological foundation. This book aims to lay that necessary new foundation. The full edifice will have to wait, but I am confident that those old knotty problems—and the new ones that have come up in the last century—can all be addressed more successfully by using the categories developed here than by any manipulation of the conventional model.

My belief in the wrongness of the old and in the need for, and value of, something quite new is subject to challenge; perhaps the conventional model can indeed be saved by some alterations or innovations. That would certainly be an appealing alternative for economists. Just as a homeowner is glad to hear that his house can be spared demolition by extensive repairs, a well-trained professional would much prefer being spared a complete re-education. Of course, noneconomists might be less impressed by any such piecemeal solution. The potential buyer would generally rather see a new construction than a shored-up old one.

I might have written this book even if I thought the old model could in fact be saved—I am more like the new buyer than the old seller of the economic model. Still, it is certainly worth looking at the leading heterodox variations in order to see if an alternative approach could spare me the trouble.

What follows is no more than a sketch, ignoring nuances and internal disputes. I have somewhat arbitrarily divided the alternatives into four families: theoretically radical, practically radical, antimodern, and Catholic. I apologize for all oversimplifications, confusions, and omissions, but I do not believe that more detailed study would change my basic judgment: that none of these variations really does the job.

Theoretically Radical Economics

The most common reforms offered by conventionally trained economists involve the addition of nonutilitarian ideas or the subtraction of some of the more grating utilitarian constraints. The efforts are worthwhile almost by definition, because the conventional utilitarian anthropology is so simplistic and erroneous that most changes are improvements. Unfortunately, the new ideas that have been offered are generally flawed, sometimes by their authors' almost inevitable attachment to some or all of the "canonical assumptions" of selfishness and individualism, sometimes by the discipline's fascination with abstract mathematical formulations, and sometimes by the use of anthropological assumptions that are unattractive despite being non-utilitarian. Institutional economics is the best accepted variation.[2] What is subtracted is the neoclassical model. Nothing much is added, other than the peculiar observations and unsystematic insights of the various writers. Few of these have been quite as clever or as quirky as Thorstein Veblen, generally taken as the founder of the school. He gets credit for rejecting the then-new neoclassical approach, but loses much of that for offering in its place only a jumble of sociological observations. (I discuss Veblen's best idea, conspicuous consumption, in chapter 16.) His followers, who still rumble on in a few universities, have never managed to provide anything like a coherent economic model. There is also the new institutionalism epitomized by Douglass North, which does not even attempt to eliminate neoclassical ideas. Its approach to institutions is generally naïve and marred by a fundamentally individualistic anthropology.

Humanistic economics has received little attention since its formulation in 1988, but it was a worthy effort to build economics on a non-utilitarian anthropological foundation.[3] However, the choice of Abraham Maslow's humanistic psychology as a base was unfortunate.[4] Maslow's assumption that needs are met in upward sequence—from the physiological up to "self-actualization"—deprives humanistic economics of any transcendental anchor and tends to reduce too much economic activity to the animalistic.

The bounded rationality of Herbert Simon is less ambitious but more attractive.[5] Simon, who largely studied noncorporate organizations, was particularly unhappy with the emphasis on maximization.

He developed a more modest notion of economic purpose—to "satisfy," to find suboptimal but satisfactory resolutions. This approach to purpose is certainly more accurate than the assumption of incessant maximization, but it accepts without question the nonmoral and individualist core of utilitarianism. Indeed, Simon's "bounded rationality" is little more than a modified utilitarianism.

Altruism is a more attractive purpose than utility, self-interest, or even bounded rationality. Unfortunately, the economics of altruism offers only a limited form of that virtue—the pleasure that I get from the pleasure that you feel. This is quite distant from any sort of generous interest in the greater good.[6] In other words, this altruism only adds a motivation of enlightened selfishness to the simple selfishness of utilitarians. Economists have not rushed to endorse this quasi-utilitarian "altruism." It has fallen into the same unfortunate middle ground as bounded rationality. Both are too suggestive of the complexity of men's motivations to please simplicity-seeking utilitarians, so they have largely been ignored by the profession. On the other hand, they are too narrowly mundane to be very attractive to non-utilitarians.

When it comes to distinctly feminine labor—which tends to be unpaid, unselfish, and unproductive, at least in monetary value—the conventional model is almost completely mute. Unfortunately, self-declared feminist economists fail to seize the opportunity to develop an alternative view, largely because they are trapped within feminism's internal debate on the meaning of sexual differentiation.[7] In addition, they have generally been poisoned by their professional training, finding it hard to throw off the conventional assumptions—that economic actors are selfish, at least when they are acting economically, and that real economic analysis is based on monetary values.

There have been various efforts to analyze economics in terms of anthropology, sociology, and psychology.[8] These range from the useless (for example, attempts at Darwinian analysis) to the genuinely insightful (for example, the anthropological exploration of the symbolic social meaning of money). Similarly, anyone interested in the economic aspects of social stratification would certainly be better off talking to an economic anthropologist than to a conventional economist, whether capitalist or Marxist. Still, these cross-disciplinary efforts are at best piecemeal and generally marred on the economic side by the acceptance of too much of the conventional model. The model is diluted rather than discredited or abandoned.

Finally, post-autistic economics is not so much a school of thought as a cry of despair.[9] The thinkers are united only in their dislike of the neoclassical model, which they describe, quite correctly, as sitting in autistic isolation from the real world. Unfortunately, they have no positive agenda other than to call for greater diversity in economics instruction. That is certainly worthy; economics should be treated as a sort of philosophy, in which the elusive truth must be approached from many directions. Still, the lack of coherent alternatives limits the potential of the post-autistic movement. It appeals most strongly to students, who will presumably either succumb to the conventional worldview or leave the profession for something less frustrating. The post-autistic writing is worth noting because it is a particularly striking example of the intellectual impotence that marks all heterodox economics. The aspirations are high, but the necessary intellectual tools are lacking.

Practically Radical Economics

The economists I have just discussed may not be happy about everything in industrial economies, but their discontent is centered on the economics, not the economy. Another sort of discontent starts with the economy. Its malfunction is seen as either the source or the sign of bad economic theory. These practical radicals tend to be revolutionaries who wish to overthrow the current system and replace it with one based on better economics. For them, economics is basically the intellectual side of a radical, practical agenda.

The ancestors of this type of thinking were the early ninteenth-century utopian socialists.[10] They were considered members of the developing discipline of economics (not yet generally called by that name), but they stood out for their belief that the industrial economy's reliance on hostility, cruelty, and exploitation was unnecessary. Rather, they thought that economies based on men's natural beneficence would be hugely productive and completely peaceful. The expectation of moral perfection doomed all of the communities established to put this theory into practice.

For example, New Harmony (in Indiana) lasted only four years. Practical failure, however, has not eliminated the utopian temptation. Many radical critics of conventional economics suffer from utopian delusions. Rather than dealing with the economy in place and human nature as it is, they offer a fairly detailed blueprint of the perfect economy that is around the corner.

Karl Marx was the first person to refer, quite disparagingly, to "utopian socialism," but neither his sneering rejection nor his claims for a purely scientific approach should be taken at face value.[11] Marxism is a fairly broad church, but few of its sects escape completely from the utopian vices. All of Marx's elaborate and often insightful analyses of the "bourgeois" economy were presented to support a determinist explanation of history, a story that will surely culminate with a violent revolution, followed by a Communist utopia in which all men are rich and all labor is meaningful. On the other hand, Marxist economic anthropology is depressingly conventional. Indeed, Marx is the father of the belief that men are so much economic creatures that history is driven solely by "material" motivations.

Marx was confident that what he called "capitalism" would inevitably lead to the ever greater enrichment of "capitalists" and the ever greater impoverishment of workers, whose desperation would inevitably, although perhaps only eventually, spark a revolution. Marxists responded to the abject failure of that prediction in two ways.[12] Leninist communism ignored reality and kept Marx's revolutionary emphasis. It promoted the use of coercion and central planning, all in the service of the ultimate society of peace, trust, and freedom. Social democracy kept Marx's economic dream but promoted democratic institutions, labor unions, and the welfare state as peaceful stepping stones on the road to true socialism. Social democracy is no longer utopian, now that all rich countries have more or less endorsed it and the Communist endpoint has largely been forgotten. Indeed, social democracy is now so far from utopian that it suffers from the spiritual bankruptcy of the resolutely mundane.

Marx's revolutionary utopianism has inspired a remarkable amount of wickedness, not to mention some inefficient industrial economies. That dark success, along with the somewhat lighter success of near-Marxist social democracy, can easily give a misleading impression of Marx's own economic thinking. While Marx the young

Hegelian had wide-ranging and interesting ideas about society, Marx the economist thought he could explain absolutely everything in terms of a single unlikely variable—"material relations." In other words, Marx the economist was the sort of cranky thinker whose works are normally found in ill-printed pamphlets or unreadable privately printed tomes. He just happened to be a crank whose key, simple idea fit in perfectly with the dominant contemporary worldview.

There are still many economic cranks with various radical agendas, but they mostly fall far from the cultural mainstream.[13] There are the self-proclaimed Marxists in poor countries (some of whom still appeal to particularly ill-informed masses) who blame "capitalism" for all sorts of evils. There are also self-proclaimed anti-Marxist extremists, who often share the Marxist belief in economic motivations as the center of society but who reject Marx's communism for an alternative, "libertarian" utopianism. Libertarians, like Marxists and many other single-idea men, are sometimes insightful, but it is wrongheaded to believe that men can construct a complex industrial economy without simultaneously constructing complex regulatory structures, including structures designed and monitored by governments.

Then there are conspiratorial thinkers who are persuaded that some evil cabal—Jewish, capitalist, governmental—has taken control of the global economy in order to impose its wicked hidden agenda. They are joined by the critics of central banking, reserve banking, and paper money and by the believers in the need for total economic self-sufficiency of families or tiny communities. In every case, the extreme complaints pick up on some half-truth and turn it into two imaginary worlds, the current one that should be destroyed and the future one that should be created. Most of these thinkers are fundamentalist believers in the conventional economic anthropology. They simply think that someone or some evil force is getting in the way of the natural individualism of the perfect capitalist economy.

Antimodern Economics

One group of economic extremists comes closer to rejecting the conventional anthropology completely. They are the antimodern moderns, the thinkers who want to give up on industry altogether. In many ways, these are the direct intellectual heirs of Carlyle, although they tend to be more enthusiastic than he was about some modern notions, for example, the abolition of a hereditary aristocracy. These critics generally claim to be unmoved by the economic accomplishments of industry, even if they now use the Internet to distribute their screeds on the dangerous pointlessness of technology. To them, such economic goods provide only an illusion of improvement. The advances of technology are merely the attractive baubles that cannot cover up, to the discerning eye, the underlying modern reality of moral and cultural decay.

Some of these thinkers are more poets than economists.[14] Like all good poets (and all interesting one-idea men), these antimoderns often provide insightful critiques, in this case of the spiritual effects of many modern economic arrangements. The basic argument, that the coming of industry has something sacrilegious and monstrous about it, has a certain truth. As poets, they rarely feel obliged to discuss "what is to be done" (as Lenin once put it), but only a can-do modern would use this impracticality as evidence against the cultural claims. For my purposes, the more pertinent weaknesses are the disregard for the good effects of the industrial economy and the generally unquestioning acceptance of the conventional economists' assumption that the industrial economy is necessarily cruel and impersonal. Of course, the poetic case is only strengthened by this reliance on the dismal theories of their enemies.

Some antimodern moderns are more practical.[15] The best known are probably the agrarian distributists inspired by G. K. Chesterton (although his economic thinking was vague enough to inspire some quite different interpretations). These thinkers are practical only by low poetic standards. Like the poets, the agrarians largely leave the purely economic interpretations of the modern economy to the modern economists. Their concern is to restore some of the virtues of the fulfilled, close-to-nature farm life of yore, a life now drowned by the monetizing tide of industry. The case is only strengthened by the monetizing explanations of conventional economists. Some agrarians also see farming as pro-Christian and the industrial economy as anti-, again taking the generally antireligious conventional economists' word for the latter judgment.

Antimodern ecologists are closely related to the agrarians.[16] Ecologists do not need to be antimodern; the industrial economy can use its own resources to face environmental challenges. Many ecologists, however, prefer to see a direct conflict between industrial production and the good of nature. Some "deep" ecologists even argue that men stopped respecting nature when earth-scarring agriculture replaced hunting and gathering; industry just compounds the damage. The radical ecologists' approach to conventional economics should be familiar by now. While their own economic goals are bold, including massive depopulation in the service of reduced production, in their economic analysis they meekly accept the utilitarian understanding of "industrial capitalism." It is easy enough for them to believe that a capitalist economy described by its proponents as nonhuman is also anti-nature.

One group is missing from this list of antimodern modern economic ideas—a conservative school of economics. That gap is puzzling, since many of these thinkers are identified with modern political conservatism—the effort to conserve what is good about the current order, including whatever is good about relatively new modern traditions. Economic conservatives could, for example, be skeptical about economic growth and critical of economic penalties for marriage while being enthusiastic about industrial agriculture and inoculations. However, economists who call themselves conservative are generally anything but. Rather, they are zealots who call for a totally revolutionary economic arrangement, the combination of a complex economy with simple structures of governance.[17]

Catholic Economics

The most plausible claimant for an economic analysis that is both truly alternative and sound is Catholic social teaching (CST, also known as Catholic social doctrine), developed by the Catholic Church over a little more than a century.[18] Indeed, if I had to recommend one economic text to a noneconomist it would be John Paul II's 1981 encyclical *Laborem exercens*.[19]

It is not surprising that Catholicism should come fairly close to offering an antidote to the utilitarian anthropology of economists; the opposition of utilitarianism to Catholic beliefs could hardly be more complete. Utilitarians, however, merely stand toward the extreme end of modern anti-Catholic thinking. There are few topics of greater modern unanimity than the rejection of much of the Catholic worldview.

This intellectual antipathy is seen in the general indifference of non-Catholics to all Catholic thought, including CST (with the partial exception of the development of the pan-European welfare state after the Second World War).[20] The converse, however, is far from true. Catholic intellectuals have persistently tried to learn from, adapt to, and influence the developing modern worldview. CST is a fine example of that response. It attempts to answer distinctly modern questions using the insights of both the premodern Catholic tradition and modern social and economic thinking. If economists bothered to look, they would learn a great deal.

To start with, they would learn that the human good should be the goal of everything economic. Of course, that is a heretical idea to conventional economists, who try to avoid talking about any sort of good and who think not in human but in impersonal terms. Theirs is not the world of men, but of the production factor known as labor and the consumption factor known as households. The popes do not see the economic world in this way. True, John Paul II accepted the conventional notion that "capital" is in opposition to, and often in conflict with, "labor." Still, he stated that the good of "labor," which he identifies as the good of man, should be preeminent.

Conventional economists would be humbled to find that the human good is not purely economic. CST fully rejects Marxist reductionism, so economic concerns should not dominate social arrangements. On the other hand, CST also fully rejects the contrary argument, that economic concerns are not worthy of the attention of truly religious men. Rather, the theology of the Incarnation (God's assumption of manhood in all its aspects, including the economic) leads to an appreciation of the potentially redeeming (sin-countering and meaning-providing) nature of economic activity. From this perspective, it is recognized that the industrial economy has supported many human goods.

CST is also helpful in its rejection of the radical individualism of conventional economic anthropology. In the Catholic worldview, men are inevitably social and bound primarily by ties of love.

(Again, this is based on a theological claim, that "God is love.") Any particular human society is limited to its own members, but CST endorses what might be called a "God's-eye view" of mankind. From that perspective, there is only one society. All men—past, present, and future—are neighbors. So when it comes to economic justice (a theme not discussed in detail in this book) all of the economic goods that we produce should be ordered to the good of all men. This doctrine of the "universal destination of goods" does not invalidate all claims for "private property," but it does transform property from a defensive and distancing barrier to a responsibility-bearing gift. According to CST, economists cannot avoid the practical implications of this vision—most notably, the persistence of the global wealth gap as prima facie evidence that the rich, who have so much property, are not living up to their responsibility.

The interest in the social leads CST to a helpful analysis of one aspect of the industrial economy—its impersonality. The great global community of the industrial economy is certainly a remarkable achievement, but it relies on an almost anonymous sort of economic trust. For example, the mutual confidence of thousands of total strangers is required for driving on a public road. That is impressive, but it does not create a sense of community among the physically close but psychologically isolated drivers. More generally, the development of industry has been accompanied by the disintegration of many traditional types of economic communities.

Finally, CST is admirably moderate. For example, it has dismayed two sets of Catholic intellectuals by avoiding both blind anti-"capitalist" fury and equally blind pro-"capitalist" enthusiasm.[21] John Paul II did not credit the fall of communism to the wisdom of "capitalism," but to the anthropological weakness of Marxism—its reductive ideas about human nature, ideas shared by many "capitalists" that have also harmed noncommunist industrial economies.[22] Similarly, CST approaches government realistically, neither as a panacea nor as a necessary evil, but as an important, although always flawed, human organization.

For all its virtues, CST does not provide a complete model for sound economics. Like the other alternatives discussed in this chapter, it relies excessively on the categories and approach of conventional economics. That is easy to understand, since knowledge of economic theory is not included in the papal job description, but it is unfortunate, since too many bad ideas are accepted either uncritically or in a confused way. John Paul II, who spent most of his prepontifical adult life in a country dominated by Marxist thinking, saw that the prevailing economic vision was inadequate, but often seemed to accept the Marxist assumption that economics is a free-standing and almost self-sufficient discipline. This led him to endorse the conventional view of a war of factors of production.[23] More generally, there have been only sporadic and largely unsuccessful efforts to refine or redefine the conventional ideas about such economic concepts as property, profits, interest rates (usury is a long-standing interest of the church), unions, free trade, corporations, and the government's economic role.[24]

This dependence on bad ideas has certainly not crippled CST completely. Most notably, the analysis of socialism first published in 1891 was prescient, even prophetic.[25] It can be paraphrased as a complaint that the cruelty of capitalists and the negligence of governments have allowed the flourishing of an even worse force, atheistic socialism. And so it proved. When governments and employers started to act responsibly, radical socialism's appeal started to melt away. On the other side, the atheist socialist government of the Soviet Union really was worse than anything that could have been imagined in the ninteenth century. I believe the more recent analysis of the problems of the "modern business economy," what I call the "industrial economy," will prove equally prescient.[26]

So can this model—the standard utilitarian and neoclassical model taken for granted by virtually all working professional economists—be saved? The daily toil of many economists is technical enough that for them the question is not urgent. As for the model itself, the answer is an unqualified "no, it cannot be saved." The various additions, modifications, and efforts to create a parallel approach fall short. They cannot overcome or ignore the wrongheaded nature of the conventional model. In simple terms, its assumptions about human motivations are wrong, its view of men in society is wrong, and its search for equations is wrong. It is time to start over again.

The conventional model should be jettisoned with the same thoroughness that scientists abandoned the "humor" model of medical psychology at the end of the nineteenth century. That model was never true, but it dominated Western thinking on the topic for more than two millennia. All that is left of that theory now are linguistic traces—a phlegmatic disposition here, a sanguine expectation there. The conventional economic model is almost as misleading as the humor model, and it is poorer in poetic metaphors (too dismal). Still, some phrases may be worth saving. I look forward to the day when only specialists can remember the pseudoscientific origins of such phrases as "opportunity cost," "declining marginal utility," and "perfect markets."

4

Starting Again

The history of economics is hardly something about which to boast. After starting during some of the darker byways of the Enlightenment, the field was quickly taken over by utilitarians, who thought men and their dreams could and should be reduced to numbers.[1] Their bad ideas have flourished for two centuries. Later, many intelligent professionals were taken in by Marxist economics, which is only a little better than a crackpot theory. As for current practitioners, almost all of them take for granted the primacy of economic motivations that are both unrealistic and unattractive. Most assume the basic truth of the neoclassical model, despite an almost total lack of supporting evidence.

These are massive intellectual errors, so large that the only possible explanation for their wide and sustained popularity among so many intelligent men is a misunderstanding at the most basic level. Such unfortunate intellectual growths must have deep roots in a confused view of the world. My desire is to replant this field, this discipline of economics, with healthier seed. However, my new plants need new soil—a complete reconceptualization, which is the purpose of this chapter. It starts by explaining why economics must be a distinctly modern discipline, and why that need is difficult to satisfy solely with distinctly modern ideas.

Something Modern

Economic activity, as compared to economics, is not new or modern in any sense. Indeed, it is as old as mankind. Nor is tremendous economic effort particularly modern. Indeed, although the social importance of economics issues has increased, the efficiencies brought by industrial capital have actually allowed men to reduce the portion of their lives, expressed in either time or energy, dedicated to economic activity. Nor is the debate about the right way to go about the economic life really new. Wealth has been vaunted by misers and conquerors and despised by saints and philosophers for millennia. When Jesus condemned the excessive desire for wealth, he was joining an already well-established tradition.

Economics, however, is new and modern. Not until two or at most three centuries ago was economic activity thought to merit its own academic discipline. Before then, cultural and metaphysical observers of all varieties—historians, chroniclers, philosophers, political theorists, spiritual teachers—showed a degree of inattention to all things economic that now seems little less than amazing. To say that the study of economics as we know it simply did not exist is hardly an exaggeration. There was not even a word for it; "economy" and its derivatives only took on their current meaning during the nineteenth century. Historians of economic thinking may speak of the economics of Plato, Augustine, or Thomas Aquinas, but they are only teasing out theories from a few scattered references. In the texts themselves, other topics—politics, social status, law, warfare, and almost anything other than what we would recognize as economics—take precedence.[2]

Historians of economic activity must also be content with careless references. The silence of the historical record suggests that there was relatively little interest in directly economic matters. When slaves rebelled against their masters, their paramount concerns were usually social, not economic.[3] When capital leapt in sophistication—for example, with the development of sophisticated crop rotation or the establishment of trade routes between Europe and Asia—contemporaries hardly noticed. The development of steam power in the late eighteenth century was the first technological change that seemed historically important at the time, and it was almost another century before many practitioners of production saw themselves as the principle engines of progress.

What Changed?

In retrospect, the noneconomic vision seems almost blind. How could the many intelligent and imaginative observers of the world not have paid more attention to something as important, changing, and amenable to improvement as the economic life? And why did it take so long, more than a century after the beginning of what is now identified as the Industrial Revolution, before economic progress became a theme for cultural commentary? Other changes in the way people lived—the Renaissance, the Enlightenment, the Revolution in France, the blossoming of Romantic sentimentality, the awakening of national self-consciousness—were proclaimed and celebrated as they occurred. Why so little attention to the economic shift? To modern eyes, the economic change seems if anything more important than the others, since it affected everyone all the time.

Economic history provides some insight into the indifference to economic issues present in preindustrial economies. To start with, there was little about economic activity that attracted attention. Economies always seemed to work as they always had. Changes came slowly enough that the patterns of labor, production, consumption, and trade could be seen as matters of well-worn tradition. Only with the benefit of modern hindsight does it seem easy and obvious to divide preindustrial history into economic epochs, from the Stone Age to the early capitalist.

Similarly, there was no practical need to ponder the goal of this activity. Economic success (ignoring philosophical and spiritual objections) was immediately understood in an economy of scarcity. For the poor, it was more food, clothing, and other basic stuff, as well as the ability to support more children. For the rich it was more visible signs of abundance, expressed in the tokens that were then available—gold, servants, feasts, clothing, houses, and the leisure to pursue cultural and intellectual pursuits. For a society, it was a growing population, which offered the labor required for grand projects such as conquest and monuments. These varieties of success were certainly elusive and when gained were easily lost, but recognizing them was easy enough.

Economic ignorance also played a role. Premodern thinkers did not know that paying closer attention to economic matters would allow vast increases in population and tremendous improvements in health, knowledge, leisure time, communications, transportation, and comforts of all sorts.[4] Perhaps if some premodern thinkers and leaders had anticipated the glories of the industrial economy, they would have been more interested.

Such economic explanations of familiarity and ignorance are helpful but incomplete. Historically, this intellectual indifference continued for a long time after the economy started to change substantially. A satisfactory explanation requires ideas.

Which ideas, then? There are many of them, but they can be grouped together in a simple phrase—the modern worldview. The industrial economy could only develop after the spread of a new way of looking at the world. And what is this modern worldview? Intellectual and cultural historians argue about the idea. When did it start? Sometime between 1350 and 1789. What are its most salient characteristics? Choose from the following list and you will get the general idea: the separation of religion from society, trust in human ability, a belief in progress, the dismissal of tradition, the construction of mathematical sciences, the search for freedom. Why has the modern worldview continued to develop from its inception to the present day, expanding to become ever more modern as it took in, for example, the praise of romantic love (in the early nineteenth century), women's suffrage (a century later), and gay rights (yet another century later)? That is a trickier question.

For all of these debates, the historians do have more or less the same understanding of the division between premodern and modern, between old and new.

The premodern worldview was predominantly nonworldly. Almost always and everywhere it was taken for granted that the higher gifts of human reason should be used primarily, perhaps even exclusively, to serve the spiritual good—to explore the undying, the divine, the underlying nature of reality, and to promote the true, the good, the beautiful. The best men in any society, those who were gifted with a good mind and provided with a good education, were expected to turn away from everything particular, changing, and everyday and towards the universal, eternal, and transcendent. Intellectuals in ancient Babylon, Athens, Rome, or Pataliputra would not even have considered using their talents to improve the tools of production. The worth, the dignity of the intellectual life called them to higher planes.

This nonworldly orientation was not limited to professional intellectuals. The political, sociological, and religious elites considered the current way of the everyday world to be good enough, unworthy of additional attention. Glory, piety, and conquest were usually the preeminent goals of the community. Economic innovation was a waste of time and effort, perhaps even a threat to a divinely approved social order. Each man may have searched for a better economic life, but that goal was easily sacrificed to other, higher ones—social, intellectual, and religious. Of course, economic changes did occur, but often in times of social collapse, perhaps after conquest or a natural disaster.

The modern worldview, in contrast, is profoundly worldly. Indeed, it is so thoroughly worldly that it is separated from the premodern, nonworldly worldview in almost every aspect of intellectual and practical life. Modern judgments differ on nearly everything—how the world works, what should and should not be changed, what tools of analysis are legitimate. The premoderns searched for the immutable; moderns expect and look for change. Premoderns saw numbers as signs of relation and perfection; we moderns use them to count and quantify. Premoderns strove for moral ideals; moderns hardly believe in truth or goodness. Premoderns saw daily life as a dull distraction from what was important; we often identify "the good life" with a happy unrol-ling of the most common experiences. Premoderns tended to believe that everything makes sense when and only when seen from a divine perspective; moderns ignore the divine and vacillate between a simple confidence in human ability and a gnawing fear of human inability.[5]

Intellectual and cultural history is, of course, more subtle and more complex than this sort of polarized summary would suggest, but economics is so firmly on the modern side of the intellectual divide that analysis of the border regions is hardly relevant. Economics is dedicated to the everyday and the common. Economic activity involves striving in the most typical and dull ways for the most mundane of delights. No wonder, then, that economics appeared fairly late in the unrolling of the modern worldview. It took time for societies—both the leaders and the led—to abandon enough of everything previously considered glorious about the human condition that they were willing to turn to something that had been previously considered base.[6]

New and Old

Clearly, economics must be a modern discipline. It might be possible for a modern to study only premodern philosophy or literature, but the idea that economic activity should be studied is itself so modern that no configuration of premodern intellectual tools and techniques could hope to deal with it.[7] Even if premodern ideas could be stretched to deal with the premodern economy, a doubtful proposition, they certainly could not extend sufficiently to take in many everyday modern economic phenomena—for example, employment as the primary type of economic relationship, an economy based on fiat money and credit, ubiquitous economic bureaucracy and female caring professionals.

Yet, the last three chapters have shown that modern attempts to find an intellectual vocabulary suitable for economic analysis have failed pretty miserably. The first set of bad ideas—the preeminent importance of property, the reliance on self-interest, the inevitability of massive poverty, the wretchedness of labor, the inhumanity of capital—was succeeded by an even worse one—the marginal utility analysis of neoclassical economics. All efforts at improvement have fallen short, largely because they use only modern ideas.

The answer to the dead end of conventional economics must start with a new set of first principles. Considering the inadequacy of purely new approaches, it might be advisable to dust off some old ideas and put them to economic use. These old ideas must be modernized to fit into the necessarily modern study of economics. They also need to be supplemented with some purely modern notions. Some combination, I believe, provides the best intellectual soil for the would-be human economist.

The selection of modern ideas is challenging. On one side, the ideas must be truly modern. The analysis of something as big and mundane as the economy requires intellectual tools well suited for use in explaining everyday life. On the other hand, as attentive readers will have noticed, I have grave problems with much modern thinking. Indeed, while I have rejected some ideas found in conventional economics on almost technical grounds—they are inaccurate descriptions of the economy—I have rejected others because they are inadequate—not just wrong for the economy but wrong in themselves. For example, I consider utilitarianism to be indefensible, at least in any form that would be recognizable to Bentham or Mill. That dismissal rules out using much of the work in modern social science, not merely in economics. I am at least as hostile to the struggle images of social Darwinism, not to mention Hobbes's materialism, Locke's radical individualism, and Hume's denial of the existence of human nature. Also, and perhaps most significantly, I reject the modern rejection of religion. In my view, any economic analysis that ignores or devalues the religious perspective on economic activity is fatally wounded. Thus, I am merely a "cafeteria modern," taking what I want and leaving what I do not from the rich array of modern notions.

This collection of old and new can be considered my own personal worldview—useful for my purposes and appealing to my judgment. Such an idiosyncratic synthesis is all too typically modern. Like some modern painting—in this case a picture of men, society, and the transcendental—my presentation may perfectly express my ideas to myself, and can perhaps speak with almost equal lucidity to the few readers who share most of my principles, but it will seem more or less strange to the rest.

I cannot see how to avoid this intellectual atomism completely, but I find it extremely frustrating. The whole goal of this book is to present a model of economic activity that can reasonably claim to be universal, which includes being (in theory) universally acceptable. Without a shared tradition of presuppositions, this effort will fall far short.

Fortunately, there is one tradition that I can turn to—the Catholic. To be sure, there is no single Catholic philosophy, but at least I can rely on some steady principles about God, man, and the world. My worldview, and all of human economics, is consciously designed to be in complete accord with those principles.

The Catholic ground helps me feel more universal, but it is likely only to frustrate, irritate, or infuriate those who share the antipathy of the modern worldview to almost all things Catholic. For these skeptics, I have a request. Even if you are unhappy with some of the assumptions or their implications, please do not simply dismiss the basic intellectual approach. The technique—first to describe the background of economics, ontological (in this chapter), anthropological (in chapter 5), and methodological (in chapter 6), and then to describe economic activity in that context (in chapter 7)—has its own merit. It provides a clear basis for discussion of differences of opinion.

Of course, a more purely modern worldview would lead to somewhat different descriptions of the background, which in turn would produce a different description of the economy, culminating in different judgments about the economic good. Such differences, however, do not invalidate this quasi-axiomatic approach to the social sciences. Indeed, I believe it to be more fruitful to argue about principles and their implications than, as is typical in conventional economics, almost entirely about conclusions.[8] It is probably not necessary to go as far as I have away from the modern worldview to generate a more realistic approach to economics, but I must leave efforts at more modest improvements to others. This book aims at an almost completely new beginning.

Some Old Ideas, Somewhat Updated

Start with the idea of order. *Men live in an ordered world.* Their experiences are no mere hubbub, their ideas no mere jumble. Rather, there are categories and relations. There may or may not be an overarching "theory of everything" (I would argue for a religious framework of that sort, but it is not strictly necessary for economics), but words and concepts (for example, "job," "stuff," "consume," "justice") always have fairly consistent meanings, and these words and concepts can always be put together in fairly consistent ways (better, bigger, older, before, because, attached, tends toward). The order of any particular thing may well be disputed. (Can this economy be best expressed in terms of money, or does money only sometimes express what is going on? Does money mean only cash, or does it include loans, or perhaps loans plus lines of credit?) In the rest of this book, I will suggest many possibly disputable orders—in human nature, in the activities and social arrangements that are primarily economic, in the hierarchy of economic goods and in the types of labor and consumption and their relative value.

Causes are a particular type of order or relation. The idea that one thing brings another about is not hard to grasp—we rely on it constantly. There are human causes ("I pushed the chair over") and physical causes ("Gravity made the chair fall"). Causes, however, have proven philosophically difficult, so much so that some modern philosophers consider them to be illusory. In economics, questions of causality are central. Is it men or something nonhuman that causes most economic changes?—I answer "men." Can we speak about "society" as a cause?—I am reluctant, but sometimes have to. Can we speak about "unconscious desires"?—I am less reluctant. Just why do we go to work in the morning? Why does work make us happy or unhappy? What causes the connection between labor and consumption?—Read on for my full answers, but I can say already that many of the causal structures I offer are substantially different from those given by conventional economists.

Everything has a nature. By its nature, fire releases energy in particular ways. By their nature, molecules store energy. Of course, the actual nature of any particular thing, including economic arrangements, is often debatable, both because it is hard to determine what is essential about the thing (is the nature of a factory to produce a particular type of stuff or to provide profits for its financial investors?) and because there can be disordered appearances that hide true natures (a shortage of raw materials stops both the factory's production and its profits, but does not change its nature). In chapter 1, I provided my view of the nature of the industrial economy. That description ignored or downplayed many characteristics that conventional economists would have considered essential—for example money, credit, and trade. In chapter 6, I will offer my description of the nature of economic activity. It, too, will be different from the description that conventional economists would provide. Crudely, I will say that only labor and consumption are essential, while they would focus on exchange, equilibrium, choice, and production.[9]

The nature of men, *human nature*, is a particularly controversial and difficult topic, because it is very difficult for men to take the ancient advice to know themselves. The next chapter presents my views, but I can say already that men's economic activity should fit into the whole of their human nature. I can also repeat the complaint of chapter 2—conventional economists start with a distorted and debased picture of human nature. Their "economic man" must be rejected completely.

Things should be good. In other words, the nature of all things, the way they would be if nothing got in the way, is good. What is "the good"? Like causality, it is an idea that we use all the time in everyday life but which philosophers find elusive. "Good" certainly expresses a rightness or excellence of some sort, but of what sort is hard to say. The word is sometimes used to mean exemplifying or being in complete accord with the definition of a thing—as in a good meal or a good carpenter. Alternatively, it can be used to describe something ideal and almost beyond normal human experience—a good man, the goodness of God, the form of the Good. In line with the Platonic-Aristotelian-Thomistic philosophical tradition, I accept the underlying identity of those two senses. A meal is good because it in some way participates in, gets close to, reminds us of the truly and ideally good meal, the meal that fully fulfils the nature of the meal, even though such a perfect meal cannot actually ever be eaten. (At least it cannot be eaten in this life. Christians will recognize that the perfectly good meal is the heavenly banquet.)

Much of this book is dedicated to identifying the *economic good*, or, as it turns out, the various economic goods. From the perspective of most modern philosophers and the conventional economists who follow them, such a search is fundamentally misguided. They find the good-by-nature claim deeply objectionable. It brings in vague and probably imaginary transcendental notions; it assumes an objective good; it implies that that this good can be identified (since otherwise the claim would be useless, even if true); and it glosses over the nearly universal presence of evil (most things are far from the good that they supposedly tend toward).

This venue is not for fundamental philosophical debate, but I do not see how economics can be discussed without some quasi-transcendental idea about some sort of goods, if only the desire to maximize "utility." I would go further. Ultimately, there is something about the economic good, about all aspects of the good and indeed about all things, that remains a mystery to men. In everything that we think about, do, or experience, there is at least a shadow or a hint of something that transcends or goes beyond our everyday experiences and normal categories of thinking. It is this mystery, or some variety of it, which so attracted premodern men to the superworldly. The mystery may have many parts, or all of its various names may be partial descriptions of a single great mystery. Theologians talk of God. Philosophers speak of the mystery of being, of the wonder of existence, of the "thrown-ness" of experience (I find myself as if thrown into the world). Scientists feel awe at the beauty of it all, the simplicity and elegance of the laws of nature. The relation between order and mystery is itself part of the great mystery.

Premodern philosophers were not much interested in the mysteries of the changing and everyday world. They cast their eyes to the heavens (which they thought were unchanging) and beyond, to the transcendentals of the Good, the True, the Beautiful, the One. Some modern philosophers, those who reject at least some aspects of modern antitranscendentalism, are not ashamed of turning towards the mysteries found in this mortal life. Economists should follow them.[10] Until we can see the *economic wonder*—in the beautiful harmony of the economic community that emerges out of our love and striving, in the generous cornucopia of stuff that the world hides behinds the veils of human ignorance and laziness—we have not fully appreciated the nature of economic activity.

For believers, God is the ultimate mystery. Most of the details of religious belief are not directly relevant to economics, but one biblical claim about the nature of God is, because it is also a claim about the nature of men. The statement that men were created in the "image and likeness" of God (Genesis 1:26–27) implies that when men act in fully human ways they are in some way acting as God acts—because their humanity is the image, the likeness of the divinity. If this biblical claim is accepted, then there is something of the divine about all of human nature. Since economic activity is fully part of human nature, it, too, must have something of the divine about it. That divine something may well be modest—economics is concerned with earthly rather than the infinitely more valuable heavenly treasures—but economists should give it the attention it deserves.

The Christian teaching on love helps create a bridge between the ultimate mystery of God and the everyday mysteries of economics.

In particular, that teaching emphasizes that *love is fully expressed in the form of gift*. The highest gifts are of our selves (in some sort of devotion to a higher cause, in marriage, in personal friendship), but our labor and consumption are also ways to express our love for each other, to accept God's gifts in creation and to pass them on. This economic ontology of love and gift is the direct opposite of the conventional economist's ontology of self-protection, self-interest, and pleasure. The decision of which view of reality is right is central to the analysis of economic activity. It is also a fundamental choice about "the meaning of life."

Disorder makes the choice difficult. Things should be good, and perhaps they are good by nature, but in the everyday world things are often not good at all. Men should love, but do not. The world's gifts prove meager. Life is full of sadness and ends in death. Perhaps disorder, or evil, is stronger than order, which is part of the good. Perhaps those much-vaunted mysteries are no more than illusions, childish comforts that knowledgeable adults should cast away. Then the only love that matters would be self-love. Then the good of economic activity would not be the center of economics. Rather, economists would primarily study the abundant signs of economic disorder—toil, want, frustration, imperfection, laziness, deception, greed.

Economists cannot be expected to answer fully the great philosophical question of the meaning of evil, but any plausible theory of economics must take this disorder into account. The conventional answer is a combination of moral reversal (self-interest is the basis of economic relations) and denial (the combination of self-interested individuals produces a good outcome). I do not think that answer is plausible. The Christian answer to that question is a story of sin and the possibility of redemption. That will be reflected, although not explained in theological detail, in the rest of this book.

Some New Ideas

This world matters. I have already described the deep worldliness of the modern worldview and have stated the need for economics to welcome this worldliness. It is fair to ask whether everyone else should be as enthusiastic. The objection of premodern philosophers has been mentioned. Religious believers should be upset by one aspect of this turn to the world—the turn away from the mystery of the divine. Pragmatists should note that the striving for human autonomy (the idea that men, not God, make the laws) and control (the idea that men, not God, should shape the world) has caused much social disruption and personal unhappiness. Still, Christians should find the idea that men's imperfect lives in this world are worthy of study and improvement in perfect accord with their understanding of this life as a road to salvation, a place for love, and a potentially purifying vale of tears. Christian love should not merely be spiritual, but quite worldly. It should encompass all economic activity, both joyous and painful.

Meaning should be found but can be lost. One direction of the modern worldview is towards alienation, the human position of being other. There are many words to describe this loneliness in the cosmos, some of which will come up in the course of this book. The pair of "meaning" and "meaningless" is a good starting point. Economic activity, like anything else about men, should have meaning. It should make sense, seem valuable, be in accord with human nature. Ideally the meaning should be both subjective, felt by the economic actor himself, and objective, a genuine contribution to the economic good. The modern experiment (the development and implementation of the modern worldview) has demonstrated the fragility of meaning when men feel cut off from the mystery of being. Economic activity has not been exempt. Labor is always hard, but it can become something much worse: pointless. The satisfactions of consumption can become empty. The psychological result of meaninglessness is despair. One of the key questions for the human economist is whether, and if so to what extent, the industrial economy promotes alienation, meaninglessness, and despair.

Society shapes men and men shape society. The individualism of conventional economics is only one strand of the modern worldview. Outside of economics, it is usually paired with another, social determinism. "Society" is seen as a single agent, an "it" that shapes its parts (the individual men and their organizations) for its own purposes. Such reifications are not entirely justified—organizations cannot literally think or want—but they are not entirely unjustified either. In some ways the economy can be treated as an "it" set in the broader "it" that can usefully be called society. The causality works in two directions. The decisions of men are in some way shaped by the society they live in, including the economy they work and consume in. Society and the economy, however, are also shaped by the decisions of men, both the inspirational decisions of leading men and the shared decisions of led men.

Some motivations are unconscious. More precisely, the explanations that men give for their actions are frequently less persuasive than those which are based on postulated but unrecognized "drives" or desires. Conventional economists believe that economic actors are only modestly more aware of the "invisible hand" of "market forces" which they enact. Marxists have an even more elaborate set of unconscious motivations, based on the not-understood economic motivations of class. The reliance on such unconscious motivations carries many dangers. Philosophically, their existence and nature can be neither demonstrated nor disproved. Morally, they can be used to deny men's freedom and responsibility. These risks must be taken seriously, but it is almost impossible to analyze the complex social patterns involved in an industrial economy without coming to the conclusion that many actions and facts are best understood symbolically or in terms of some social "function" of which the actual economic actors are, at best, only partially aware.

Finally, truth is elusive but never out of sight. In the turn from the eternal and divine to the changing and worldly, a great certainty has been lost. Modern thinkers try not to regret the loss, arguing that the certainty was always illusory and that the replacement—doubt and searching—is more in accord with human nature. Whatever the merits of that claim, the moderns have won the epistemological war, at least when it comes to the study of men themselves in their worldly whirl of activity. Men cannot see themselves clearly enough to come to final answers. The limits of knowledge are particularly acute in social studies. It is all too easy to assume that the current way of arranging things is either entirely natural or particularly depraved. In the midst of such obscurity, no economic theory can be more than a draft, a step along the way toward an unreachable truth. Some modern thinkers deny that the way actually goes in any direction—to them truth is a discredited premodern illusion. I reject such intellectual nihilism. Men can always make their understanding a bit less imperfect. They learn more, both from the world itself and from those who have studied before them. As they learn, they approach the truth—about economics as about more elevated matter—more closely.

So that is the way things are—orderly and good, yet plagued with disorder; mysterious and meaningful, yet subject to alienation; men who are worldly and yet touched by the divine; societies that guide and yet are guided; and truth that exists and yet remains out of reach. Such a heap of ambiguities and near-contradictions is not a suitable foundation on which to build a hard science, but then economics is not, nor should it be, anything like a hard science. No, economics is a human study, and men cannot meaningfully be reduced to the ciphers of scientific variables. Such dehumanization cannot really make economics into a science, but merely into a dismal simulacrum of one. Economics deals only with certain actions of men, but it must take men in their entirety—in their grandeur and their greed, their generosity and their neediness, their restless ingenuity and their foolish stolidity. It is to men, to the economic aspects of human nature, that I now turn.

5

Human Nature for Economists

Since economics is a study of men, economists need to know about human nature—what is essential to men. That knowledge of course, must be deepest where it concerns men in their economic activity, but the economic aspects of human nature cannot be isolated from the rest; human nature is (I can say already) completely integrated, so that the economic, like all other aspects, both contributes to and depends on the whole. Economists should not try to escape this deep interconnection by drawing a misleading boundary between economic and noneconomic man.

Someone who knows nothing of literature or philosophy might think that human nature could be uncovered in an uncontroversial way, through some sort of disciplined labor of introspection and observation. Are we not men who can know ourselves? Of course, anyone who studies philosophical anthropology, the study of human nature, quickly learns that what one self-observer finds obviously true about human nature another finds almost as obviously false. Philosophical training may increase the sophistication of the descriptions, but it does not seem to narrow the differences of judgment. Depending on who is asked, men are purposeless machines, ciphers in a cosmic process, imprisoned free spirits, or children of God; all essentially identical or differing fundamentally because of sex or caste; blank slates shaped entirely by experience or largely formed before birth; and so forth. There are almost as many variations as there are philosophers. If the philosophers cannot agree, it is foolish to think that an economist, even a philosophically minded one, could present a completely persuasive picture of men as they are.

The Catholic tradition simplifies the task. The following list of attributes has the support of revelation, tradition, and authority. Of course, many non-Catholics will likely consider those supports empty. I can only ask them to suspend their disbelief, remembering that Catholic anthropology has attributes that might deserve some respect. It is well-tested. It has been developed and articulated over two millennia in a wide variety of societies—Christian and non-Christian, stable and unstable, prosperous and poor, preindustrial and industrial. It is also plausible and realistic. It calls on only a few unconscious motivations to explain how men live. Rather, it largely corresponds with what men say they want from life and to what their actions suggest they want. Finally, and of particular appeal to the universalist strand of the modern worldview, it is not elitist, but rather respects both everyday experience and the aspirations of the common man. In the Catholic view, no man—whether peasant, priest, or king—is fundamentally worth more than any other.

1) Men are moral. No human activity (with the exception of the automatic tasks of the living body) can be described solely in mechanical terms. Rather, men's actions always have purposes. They aim at some desired goal. From the actor's own perspective, that desired goal is always considered to be good. This uniform direction of desire is expressed simply in Thomistic terminology—men always will the good. Of course, the will may be misdirected. What I think is good may differ from what is really good. Indeed, I all too often will something which is objectively bad. Alternatively, even if my ultimate target is objectively good, my understanding of how to obtain that good may be faulty.[1]

The limits and failures of the will are significant enough to make the study of all human activity, including economics, complicated and frustrating, but these limits do not reduce the necessity for moral discourse. Economics should not stray too far from its ethical center—man's constant and unavoidable search for the good.

Some philosophers, both modern and premodern, claim that using the same word ("good") to describe both the goodness of economic activity—for example, of a good day's work or of a good meal—and the goodness of virtues—for example, of true love and honest conduct—is misleading. They claim that the two sorts of goodness are substantially different. This is not merely a quibble about words, but rather concerns the mystery of reality.

Economists can make two contributions to this debate. Against the doubters, they can point out that the goodness of economic action is commonly accepted as part of the goodness of men. A good man should "do a good job," "earn a good income," and even "eat good meals," however these different sorts of economic goodness may be defined. In favor of the doubters, economists can point out that these economic goods are commonly considered less valuable than goods such as truth and justice. A man loses less of his goodness by giving up good meals than by giving up his good character. An effective contract murderer provides an extreme example of the limits of a narrow view of economic goodness. As far as his job goes, he is good—he always gets his man. However, his job does not go very far. The minimal goodness of professional competence hardly features in the moral judgment of the murderer.

The two contributions are both valid. Taken together, they provide a basic truth about economics. Economic goods are really good, but their goodness is often secondary, or subservient, to other, more important goods (more on this in chapter 9).

The ubiquity of men's moral orientation can be expressed in terms of freedom: men always have the freedom to act in accord with the good. To be sure, the effectiveness of this freedom, in economic activity as much as in any other human effort, is circumscribed by the limits of men's bodies, knowledge, ability, and will, and by the constraints of existing social structures. Some of the desired economic good will always remain out of reach. Such pragmatic limits, however, do not tarnish the imperishable moral glow of freedom. Further, these pragmatic limits should not be exaggerated, at least in economic matters. The free actions that once developed and now sustain industrial economies have supported a remarkable amount of economic good.

2) Men are morally weak. Men's desire for the good is usually, perhaps always, distorted or disordered. In the traditional language of Christianity, men are sinful. Sin, which I will generally call moral weakness, presents all sorts of philosophical problems, in essence because this "disorder" is a turn away from the good order described in chapter 4 as fundamental to reality. How can men, and indeed the world they live in, be both ordered and good by nature and disordered and bad in practice? The answer to that question, if there is one, transcends the terms of human knowledge. The great mystery of evil must be left to philosophers, theologians, and mystics, but the reality of moral weakness is a readily observable fact that economists should recognize.

The unavoidable presence of this weakness means that men are never so good that their every wish and whim should be respected. An economic organization should not aim to give each member whatever he thinks he wants, because many subjective desires are misguided. Rather, the organization should have a higher aim—to serve the objective and durable economic good, that is, to provide what the members would want if their desires were not disordered. Of course, that raises the crucial question of what the objective economic good really is.

On the other hand, moral weakness can only exist as a distortion of an underlying virtue. Animals cannot really be bad because they cannot really know what it is to be good. Men can be bad because they cannot avoid moral judgments. Somewhere inside even the worst men is some potential to recognize the true good and some thwarted desire to search for it. The universality of the imperfect desire for the good implies that an economic organization that truly aims at the encouragement of economic virtue will be welcomed, although perhaps only unconsciously and grudgingly.

The combination of the first two aspects of human nature draws a helpful moral outline of economic man. Indeed, when it comes to the moral struggle at the center of the human drama, economic man is no different from noneconomic man. We are "good but weak." We crave and search for the good, but often disagree about what is good and often do what is bad. We try to be fair, but are prone to judge ourselves more generously than others. We too easily yield to the selfish desires and to pleasures that corrode our bodies and souls. We exaggerate our own power, importance, and needs. We all too often want to take more than we want to give. And yet, our desire for goodness, and our real goodness, often has the last word.

3) Men are different from things and animals. Men are unique. They are different in many significant ways from other living creatures, from inanimate objects, and from the forces of nature. Men's moral orientation is one important manifestation of their uniqueness, but it can be found in almost every aspect of human experience. Unlike anything else in the visible world, men are religious, philosophical, articulate, curious, analytical, passionate, and humorous. This human difference is sometimes felt to be a privilege, sometimes a responsibility, and sometimes a burden, but it can never be wished away or destroyed.

One aspect of this uniqueness is the constant desire to convert the nonhuman world into a human home. In other words, men never live in a humanly meaningless "nature," but always in a "world" that has been converted from nature into something human, a world that is man-made, man-directed, and man-oriented. This imposition of a distinctly human order onto the world is not primarily economic. Indeed, economic activity is so animalistic that it might be thought not to contribute much to men's distinctness. After all, in the most basic economic activities—the protection of life and the production and consumption of food—men might appear to use nature just as animals do.

Economic activity, however, does reflect men's special position. Animals can do remarkable things in their search for food, but only men can routinely and flexibly overcome their physical limits by the creation of tools, by the mastery of such natural processes as fire and fermentation, and by the sharing of tasks in laboring communities. Unlike animals, men do not labor and consume merely for the sake of survival and reproduction. They want more from, and more than, clothing, shelter, and food. Economic activity plays a significant role in men's effort to create a distinctly human home in the midst of a nonhuman world. It provides some of the meaning of life.

In the most primitive cultures, the hunter/gatherer economies, the physical results of economic activity were unimpressive, no more than simple food or rudimentary shelter. In all other cultures—economies based on plunder, agriculture, or industry—the economic world is elaborate. There is the physical world of carefully constructed and highly productive farms and factories, houses, roads, and cities; the social world of economic cooperation, rivalry, tradition, and innovation; and the supporting structures of trade and money. Men also use their economic activity in order to "express themselves" in noneconomic ways. For example, they can make and consume things that are beautiful, articulate their feelings, and advance and store their knowledge.

4) *Men want more from the world.* Men are not content with their current situation in the world. In the face of physical decay and death, they search for the fullness and abundance of life. They want to develop further everything that distinguishes them from the compulsion, apparent randomness, and nonmorality of the given world of nature. In other words, they want to make their human world ever more human.[2] Their dissatisfaction with what is received is more metaphysical than material. Men do want to have more stuff, but they more profoundly want to have both a greater mastery of the physical world and a greater spiritual independence from it. Like everything human, this desire for a greater fullness is essentially good, but it can easily be distorted into selfishness and pride.

The wish for greater fullness is generally present in economic activity. In this domain, its attributes are often quite material. Men would usually like to consume more and better and to labor more productively. Even in economics, however, the physical is sometimes secondary. The desire for more control—men would like to make the physical world more supportive and less hostile—is certainly material, but the power itself is generally felt to be meaningful. When it comes to the desire for more interesting and more generous labor, the economic fullness is almost entirely psychological or spiritual.

Just as the search for the economic good is often considered less valuable than the search for higher goods, the desire for economic fullness is often judged to be less pressing than other human desires, most notably than the noneconomic aspects of both the need to maintain distinctly human order in the world and the need for the transcendental. These higher concerns made premodern societies economically conservative—they often rejected innovations which would lead to better labor and greater consumption in order to preserve what they perceived to be higher goods of culture and religion. In modern societies, however, the current social order is more often sacrificed for the sake of a greater economic mastery. Indeed, one of the marks of industrial economies is a shift in the balance—to a greater acceptance of the economically efficient and better and to less loyalty to the socially established and virtuous.

5) *Men want more than the world.* The most uniquely human aspect of human nature is the spiritual or religious. Even some materialist anthropologists admit as much.[3] The urge to do more than merely survive, or even than to survive in some sort of style, is common to all human cultures. In other words, men wish to participate in the mystery described in chapter 4. They search for a supernatural, superrational, supersensual, and superpractical meaning somewhere—religion; a heroic life; a noble death; love, whether romantic, maternal, or filial; sexual relations; social relations. The importance that men give to the transcendental search can be gauged by the despair that overcomes them when they feel that this search is vain. Men desperately desire to find the meaning of, or participate in, this "something-beyond," which they might call the transcendental, the spiritual, or the divine.

Economists study labor and consumption, activities that are usually far more concerned with worldly necessities than transcendental truths. This worldly focus makes it difficult for them to look upward to the something-beyond. Still, the search for the transcendental both limits and helps to form men's economic activity. The limits are most visible in the preindustrial disdain for the mundane. The transcendental formation of economic activity may be less clear to modern eyes. The more personal side of that mystery can be seen in the moral goodness attributed to labor, a goodness that is rarely limited to the labor's narrow functionality. It also shines through in the desire to make consumption not only comfortable but also beautiful and distinguished.

6) *Men are social.* Men are tied together by many different formal and informal relations. They are always members of a family, of communities, of a people, of the human race. They are tied to other men by labor, kinship, religion, location, politics, and common interests and experiences. They are tied to those who have come before them by memory, tradition, history, and respect. And they have a tie of responsibility to those who will succeed them. Then there are the inherited communities created by a common language. All of these communities are inevitable, but the equally inevitably human moral

weakness ensures that they are rarely harmonious, either internally or externally. There will always be discontent and rivalry.

Economic activity depends crucially on the unity and divisions of human communities. There is always some sharing of the gifts of labor and the goods of consumption. The more sophisticated the economy, the greater is the sharing and the greater the need for strong, resilient, and complex social structures to organize and allocate both labor and consumption and to control the damage from men's weakness.

Some social organizations are primarily economic—focused on labor, consumption, or the intermediate economic processes of production and allocation. Exclusively economic groupings, however, do not seem to be possible. From the most primitive trading systems to the most sophisticated multinational corporations, economic relations within an organization are always reinforced, and often superseded, by noneconomic rituals, ties, and responsibilities. Presumably, the need for noneconomic structures reflects the general inferiority of purely economic goods.

7) *All men have the same human dignity.* Behind men's many differences lies a single great commonality—that of human dignity (or worth or moral value). This claim is less obviously correct than the preceding six. Indeed, the existence of a single shared value of "being human" is not an obvious deduction from the observation of men's physical, social, intellectual, and psychological variety. In practice, the rich and powerful, for example, are almost always treated as more worthy than the poor and socially humble. Even in theory, the belief in the equality of human dignity is hardly universal. Rather, it is largely limited to Christian thinking and to some strands of the modern worldview (which borrowed and secularized the Christian idea). The Christian explanation of this unifying feature is quite simple—men share the fact of being made in the image of a loving God. Modern non-Christian explanations tend to rely on the claim that human equality is "self-evident."[4]

The economic, social, and political implications of this human commonality are controversial. Radical egalitarians argue that uneven allocations of anything in society—rights, privileges, goods, and difficulties—are always unjust. In practice, their recommended social uniformity is an unrealistic goal. Men seem always to create or to find hierarchies of authority—in families, social structures, and governments. Indeed, one of the hierarchical practices of families, the authority of adults over children, seems to be a physical necessity. These ubiquitous hierarchies and differentiations do not necessarily violate men's common dignity. On the contrary, while it is just to respect men's universal dignity, it is also unjust not to respect their needs, their genuine distinctions, and the varying goodness of their actions.

The two requirements, to respect both men's commonality and their differences, are not directly contradictory, but they are not easily reconcilable in actual social arrangements, even before taking men's moral weakness into account. To favor excessively either the universal or the differentiated is possible. In general, Catholic philosophers used to be too respectful of existing unjust arrangements, while many modern thinkers overestimated men's commonality. Catholics have learned from the egalitarians, for example, to understand extreme poverty as a correctable insult to men's universal dignity. Conversely, the egalitarians could learn to respect some traditional economic distinctions—for example, those based on sexual differences.

In some ways, the commonness of human dignity is most clear in economic activity. Labor provides the same sort of worth to all men's lives. The contents of the labor of a construction worker, a nurse, and a university professor differ profoundly, but they provide much the same sense of excellence and meaning in return for much the same obligations of time, effort, and responsibility. Also, the commonality of labor is stronger than most social divisions. The labor of mothers, whether poor or rich, always involves the same tasks and has the same transcendental dignity. Consumption is also an equalizer. Eating does the same thing for all men, from beggars to kings.

However, economic activity is not always interpreted as demonstrating human equality. It can also be used to reinforce beliefs of unequal human dignity. The traditional Indian caste system, which is based on a claim of radical differences in the value of different human lives (at least in their current incarnations), uses types of labor as markers of caste membership. Similarly and more universally, the sexual division of labor has often been interpreted as a support for the claim of women's natural inferiority to men.

8) Men and women are different. The claim that the differences between men and women are significant would have seemed uncontroversial until a generation ago, but it is now rejected in many legal systems and derided by many intellectuals. The social, psychological, and economic distinctions between the sexes have not disappeared, but they are generally attributed to a widespread social misreading (universal up to a generation ago) of the meaning of physical differences. This is not the place to debate the meaning and value of different forms of "feminism," so I will simply state my own judgment (which is in accord with the Catholic teaching). It is right to assume that men and women have the same dignity, but it is also right to respect the tension between the masculine and the feminine as one of the foundations of society and as an invitation to the transcendental mystery of the unity and mutual need of the two sexes.

In economics, this sexual tension is most evident in labor. Masculine labor and feminine labor were clearly delineated in every preindustrial society and until very recently in industrial societies. These sexual divisions seem to have both respected and exaggerated true sexual differences. The line, however, between appropriate and inappropriate sexual differentiation in labor is not easily drawn, largely because men's moral vision is particularly clouded in sexual matters. That faulty vision is not corrected by trying simply to ignore all sexual differences. In any case, the contemporary effort to be "sex-blind" in economic activity has been only modestly successful. Sexual differences have persisted, most notably in the feminine preference for reproductive and caring labor. I believe that this practice reflects the reality—men and women really are different in economically significant ways.[5]

Compare and contrast. On one side is the conventional "economic man," whom I wish to relegate to the dust-heap of intellectual history. In the words of John Stuart Mill, he is "an arbitrary definition of man, as a being who inevitably does that by which he may obtain the greatest amount of necessaries, conveniences, and luxuries, with the smallest quantity of labor and physical self-denial with which they can be obtained," a being "who desires to possess wealth, and who is capable of judging the comparative efficacy of means for obtaining that end."[6] On the other is the man whose eight characteristics have just been described: good but weak; in the world but not completely of it; who can only be who he is in a community of men; equal in dignity with all others but not necessarily equal in society; and whose gender matters. I have no hesitation in saying that the former description can only generate a stunted economics, while the latter at least has the potential of creating an economics that is a worthy subject of study, and one that is worthy of its subject, men themselves.

The next question is how to turn this picture of human nature into a study of economics. That is the topic of the next chapter.

6

A Short Discourse on Economic Method

René Descartes wrote his *Discourse on Method* in 1637. Like this book, it was an attempt to start over in a discipline—philosophy—that the author judged deeply corrupt. Descartes' method, radical self-examination, was a big part of his message. It has been highly influential in the formation of the modern worldview. Some traces of the Cartesian mix of claimed empiricism and actual leaps of faith can still be found in the conventional economic method—first create a model out of idealized mathematical simplifications of apparently logical first principles and then compare reality to that ideal. For conventional economists, that comparison throws up a long series of deviations, which they must labor at identifying and explaining. The labor takes various forms: sometimes they add wrinkles to the model; sometimes they merely measure "market imperfections." The conventional method then moves on to recommendations, usually to try to make the world look more like a perfect market.

The human economics that I wish to develop cannot follow the conventional method. Not only does it eschew any sort of mathematical simplifications, but it also assumes that economies will remain imperfect, because they reflect the unavoidable tensions of human nature—good but weak; worldly but transcendental; social but individual; male and female. All economies will be seen as attempts to deal with the relevant aspects of these tensions in socially acceptable and morally attractive ways. A full resolution is out of reach.

So how should the human economist proceed? This chapter first offers a five-part method. It then discusses three possible keys for economic analysis.

I want to emphasize that my claims for this method are far more modest than Descartes'. Its elements are nothing like the "clear and distinct ideas" of Descartes, nor are they supposed to provide the last methodological word. These elements should not even be considered steps that must be taken in order. Logically, they move from first to last, but the later stages help shape the earlier. I prefer to think that these elements provide a helpful outline of what should eventually emerge from human economics.

1) Identify the subject matter. What is economics about? I have already let slip my answer to that question—economics is about men in the world, in particular about the two human activities of labor and consumption. That answer will be explained and, to some extent, justified, in the next chapter. It will be expanded further in chapters 13–16, which look at economic activity in more detail in the light of the good. I believe that my description covers everything that conventional economists mean by economics. The conventional description includes too little and is badly focused; mine covers more and covers it more clearly.

2) Identify the goods. What makes economic activity good? The importance of the good for economics came up in both of the preceding chapters. The economic good is worthy of study because it is truly good, but it is by no means the only or highest goodness toward which men strive. One aspect of the discussion of the economic good, found in chapters 8–12, is the effort to put the economic good in its human place. That discussion also covers the noneconomic goods that are supported by economic activity, the marks of a good economic organization (just, equitable, efficient), and the corresponding external and internal economic evils.

This book is mostly concerned with these first two elements of the human economic method—a universal description and the establishment of a universal moral standard. Those are worthy goals, but I am aware that many readers are likely to be more interested in the economy they live in. I share that practical interest. This book came to be written in large part because I wanted to make sense of the industrial economy. Like so much philosophy, the book was thought out backwards, attempting to move from the particular of the industrial economy to the general rules of economics.

The remaining three elements of the method take the argument back to the particular level. There are traces of these elements throughout this book. The concluding chapter provides a more concentrated sketch of my views.

3) Describe the economy under study. The economist who knows what he is studying (the economic aspect of human nature) and what he is looking for (the economic good and its lack) has the basic tools for describing any particular economy in any desired level of detail. That description has two parts. Internally, the economist must identify the predominantly economic structures—how they work, in theory and in reality; what goods they are most centered on; what goods they actually provide; how they affect the physical world; how they affect the economic actors involved. Externally, the economist must identify the ties between the economic and the noneconomic—how social and economic hierarchies are related; how the search for economic goods is integrated into the search for other goods; how political, religious, and other noneconomic structures guide and are guided by economic considerations; how society judges, rewards, and punishes different types of economic behavior. These questions are all extremely difficult to answer. Men are mysteries to themselves, and societies are tangled webs of virtue and vice, of hope and fear, of beauty and ugliness.

The economist is in a particularly poor position to address the relations of the economic with the noneconomic aspects of society. His perspective is too narrow because economic concerns are so often of less value, both in theory and in practice, than noneconomic ones. In my discussions of noneconomic structures and goods, I try to be modest. That reserve should not be taken as indifference. I have many strong noneconomic opinions, but they do not belong in a book on economics, where they can be neither fully explained nor justified.

4) Evaluate the economy under study. Economic weaknesses cannot be isolated and weighed. Rather, they are bound up, apparently inextricably, with the good. Indeed, some sorts of goodness seem to have a painfully close association with some sorts of weakness. When the efficiency of production is favored in a factory, the personal economic concerns of workers are often slighted. The connections between the economic and noneconomic are usually even more convoluted and contrary.

Still, it is possible to make both general and specific economic judgments. The main weaknesses can be identified—this evil is allowed to flourish, that good is thwarted. One economy can be judged to be more desirable than another, although that judgment may need to be tempered by noneconomic comparisons. Within an economy, the treatment of some groups, usually the poor, may be wrong, or the production system may be good in this way and bad in that. Any particular praise or blame may be disputed, but doubt does not excuse timidity. Economists can and should make value judgments.

5) Suggest improvements. Such value judgments are implicitly prescriptive, since any identified weakness can always be addressed by changes in practices, attitudes, or policies. Perfection is out of human reach, but no current social configuration can possibly be the best that men can do. Indeed, each new generation has the responsibility to understand, purify, and improve what it inherits. The economist can participate in this process by suggesting both general and specific changes—an improved hierarchy of economic goods; new practical goals that approximate those goods more closely; new arrangements of economic tokens, such as money and taxes, that are likely to help a society come closer to those practical goals; even detailed rearrangements of economic units such as factories and companies.

Many conventional economists are enthusiastic about giving advice. They are generally much too arrogant, however. The workings of the economy are too complex, too poorly understood, and too subject to human freedom to be modeled with anything like precision. Even a cursory glance at the history of professional advice on industrial, financial, and corporate policies suggests that economists have trouble keeping up with reality. Human economists have the advantage of a more accurate understanding of human nature, but that understanding only teaches them that men are too complicated to be helped by simple all-purpose recipes for improvement. On the other hand, men want the good too much not to try to do better.

Any field of study has its key concepts—the equivalents of grammatical structures that help students parse this or that part of reality. Conventional economists have their own list—utility, supply, demand, GDP, equilibrium, marginal thinking, labor and capital, rent and profit, and so forth. I have rejected most of these and downgraded the rest to the status of sometimes useful tools. Here are three other concepts that come up in my economic discussions with nonprofessionals. I reject one, treat one with caution, and accept one enthusiastically.

Appearances

Appearances should be mistrusted. They do not so much deceive as often mislead. Economists cannot simply rely on what they hear, see, or measure. They must interpret, often calling on unconscious forces.

One basic problem is that economic actors often do not know what they are doing. If the existence of unconscious motivations is accepted, that ignorance comes by definition. Individuals cannot be consciously motivated by something about which they do not know. This incapacity can make surface descriptions both inaccurate and unhelpful. For example, a corporate executive may explain his motivations in terms of his desire for "profit." His explanation may not be accurate, because he is actually guided by forces that he either does not understand or cannot articulate—say, society's desire for his company's product, or his own desire to win the approval of his peers. Even if profit is a good description of his goal, the statement is unhelpful because it skirts over the most important issues—what he means by profit (over what time, using what measure) and the economic and social meaning of this search.

In industrial economies, the gap between perception and underlying patterns is often quite wide. For example, an individual air traveler's accurate description of a ticket price and of flight experiences provides no more than a hint of the complex economic-social structures of the air-transit network. Even a collection of individual testimonies is likely to be highly misleading—the network is so much bigger than the passengers who use it. The only way an economist can hope to understand the whole network is by postulating basic patterns—of technology, leisure and business travel, employment, and so forth. The postulated patterns can then usefully be tested against the testimonies.

Another problem with relying on appearances is that it is not always easy to know which appearances to trust. In particular, social reality can be quite different from economic reality. An economist who studies the automotive industry by looking at the practicalities of consumption (in this case car trips) or production will see only modest distinctions between luxury and economy cars. A sociologist who looks at status and advertising messages will see great distinctions. Sometimes, however, it is the other way around—the economist sees, or should see, a meaningful distinction that the sociologist misses. There is a crucial economic difference between the helpful labor of a doctor and the largely superfluous labor of a marketing executive (see chapter 15). Sociologists miss that objective distinction because the two professionals have much the same social status in industrial societies.

Monetary appearances are particularly deceptive. Money is a useful tool for economic organization. It is also a sociological fetish (to use Marx's word). It is, however, a very poor standard of economic value. It is tautologically true that a salary of 2X is twice as large as a salary of X, but that ratio gives no information about the different economic goods that those salaries can obtain (or their relative sociological status). Those goods cannot be compared in any quantitative terms, monetary or nonmonetary, since there is no meaningful mathematical ratio between, for example, the good of food and that of holidays.

Wealth

The concept of wealth is certainly meaningful. It seems to be present in all societies, sometimes as a fairly smooth gradation from more to less, sometimes as a clear division between the wealthy few and the poor or nonwealthy many. The definition of wealth also varies. In industrial economies, it is usually defined in the monetary terms of assets and income. The standards of wealth in preindustrial economies were more varied. They included money, to be sure, but also the economic control of land, of men, of industry, and the opulence of consumption.

Many economic observers believe that wealth is not only socially meaningful but a helpful guide to the economic good. There have been two types of judgments. One, enthusiastically endorsed by conventional economists, is positive. A wealthier person or economy is not just "better off" than a poorer one. It is intrinsically better, given its greater production of economic "goods." The other judgment is just as straightforward, but negative. Wealth is inevitably deleterious to the real good, which is spiritual. The wealthy man's social and worldly advantages are nothing but a sign and enactment of his spiritual decay, and the wealthy society is almost by definition weak and easily conquered. This negative attitude is now rare, but it was once common.

Both sorts of dependence on wealth as a standard of economic judgment are unhelpful. To start with, wealth is more a social than an economic concept. The standards, tokens, and social responsibilities of wealth vary too much across societies for wealth to pass the test of economic universality. Then there is the satiety of stuff in industrial societies. When everyone else has more than enough, the wealthy are in a different position than when they alone had enough, and when their social-economic superiority allowed them to have master/servant relations. No matter how wealthy an employer in the industrial economy is, his relations to an employee will be structurally less domineering than the relations of the least powerful master to his servant.

More significantly for moral analysis, the goodness of wealth cannot be determined without some additional information. Wealth has a great potential for good. Wealthy individuals can be exemplars of charity and patrons of the arts. The wealth of industrial societies can provide many economic goods—for example, more people living longer and healthier lives, with greater knowledge and more time for prayer. (Of course, many wealthy individuals and societies do not realize these potentials.) The case against wealth is also strong. Wealthy men may well be more easily tempted to greed, sloth, and all sorts of arrogance than poor men. The evil of wealth, however, is no more absolute than its good. Some sorts of wealth can coincide with holiness.

Wealth, however it is defined in a particular society, is itself neither good nor bad. Rather it is best seen as a tool, a "means" in the traditional philosophical vocabulary. The economic good is the end, which this tool serves sometimes but not always.

The Transcendental Aura

The last concept is the transcendental. It has come up already in several places and will continue to be central to the economic argument, as it should be for all of life. I would imagine that conventional economists will find my demand to establish the transcendental as an economic concept hard to take, perhaps the most difficult aspect of human economics to swallow. Even readers who are more sympathetic to this concept may have trouble seeing how it fits in. Here are four examples of the transcendent in economics.

First, economists should look approvingly on most sorts of economic sacrifices. To willingly dedicate something economic—leisure time, labor effort, consumption—to a higher good is good. In Christian terms, such sacrifices make men true to their divine vocation to love. Catholic social teaching suggests that the analysis of economic structures should include a search for sacrificial elements. Following this approach, investment is not only a selfish search for later profits or a morally dubious quest for greater production. It is also and primarily a sacrificial effort for the good of future laborers and consumers. More generally, the orientation to the good of others—the worldly manifestation of the transcendental act of sacrificial love—provides a much better methodological lodestone for ethical analysis than does happiness or wealth.

Next, even the worldliest elements of economic life can bring timeless meaning. In particular, Catholic social teaching emphasizes the value of labor, from the most menial to the most sophisticated. Labor offers an intrinsically good combination of sacrifice and excellence. Indeed, labor can hold the same sort of human significance as contemplation, which too many Christians have traditionally considered greatly superior. More generally, small gestures of generosity in consumption, attention to the goodness of creation, and dedication to the human vocation to humanize the world can all be imbued with something transcendental, a something that should be encouraged to flourish.

Poverty can hold spiritual goods, as Christians have long taught. Desirable poverty can take many forms—moderation, spiritual detachment, willingness to depend on divine generosity, restraint toward the natural world, and sacrifice for the sake of social solidarity. The methodological challenge of integrating the good of poverty into the study of economics is tremendous. Still, the task is not impossible. I make a stab at it in chapter 16.

Finally, while it may not be helpful to invoke the transcendental good in every detailed study of each corner of economic activity, the terms of any economic analysis should always include some sort of transcendental orientation. For example, the best location for a new airport will be determined by the study of such mundane matters as commuting routes and bird migration patterns, but the results of the study depend on the interpretations of such underlying terms as productivity, convenience, and respect for nature. Those interpretations require a transcendental perspective.

7

What Are We Talking About? (II)

It is finally time for a more formal introduction to human economics. The preparation has been long, perhaps too long. My only defense for the mass of introductory material is that it was added in direct response to the confusion and incredulity of early readers. Neither economist nor layman could see the whence (philosophy), whither (morality), or wherefore (description rather than theory) of the argument. I hope that the preceding chapters have provided a sufficient background. I can promise that two important features will persist—no equations and a good amount of philosophy.

Just as in chapter 1, the best place to begin is at the beginning and with the most fundamental question, which can now be answered more rigorously: What is economics?

Economics is primarily the study of two human activities—consumption and labor. The full meaning of these terms should become clear in the course of this chapter, but the starting point is quite simple. Consumption is what consumers do. It starts with the use of the basic economic stuff discussed in the first chapter—food, clothing, shelter, and fuel. Labor is what workers do. It starts with paid jobs, but it also includes many kinds of similar unpaid effort. Economics is secondarily concerned with the implications of consumption and labor—the techniques involved in the production of stuff; the social arrangements of economic activity; the social allocation decisions for economic activities and goods; and the interaction of production with the physical world. These concerns are important, but considerations of space preclude extensive attention in this introductory book.

As might be expected, the definition of the field as the study of consumption and labor sets off human economics sharply from the conventional approach. Economics is typically defined as the study of "man's conduct in the business part of his life," "the mechanics of utility and self-interest," "human behavior as a relationship between ends and scarce means," or the "objective quasi-natural laws and processes governing the production of commodities, their values and money."[1] The first of these definitions, from Alfred Marshall, and the third, from Lionel Robbins, do try to approach economics as a study of human activity, but the "business" and "behavior" in question turn out to be largely trading, not labor or consumption. More prosaically, economics is often defined as the study of money, of scarcity, of wealth, or of production and exchange, all of which have more to do with things than with men and their activities.

My focus on consumption and labor is not, however, entirely novel. It is a modification of the young, philosophical Marx's vision of economic activity as definitive of human nature.[2] It would have seemed acceptable, if not obvious, to most early-ninteenth-century economic thinkers, who were interested primarily in men's well-being. Nor is it completely alien to contemporary conventional economics, which is certainly concerned with both topics. Most importantly, this definition is in accord with an everyday understanding of economic activity as being mostly about jobs (labor) and shopping (consumption). Still, this definition is distinct in its emphasis on men and in its clear focus on the deeper, moral meaning of these activities.

There is not much point in trying to defend the new definition with abstract arguments. They will be much less persuasive than experience. The rest of the book should provide some of that, and I hope that the text will show that this definition is intellectually apt and practically helpful. One preliminary comment might, however, be useful. Neither consumption nor labor is a self-evident concept. Each is a grouping of many quite diverse activities. For example, consumption includes the use of a house, the eating of a meal, and a trip to a foreign country. Labor includes the play-adventures of children, the loving care of parents, and an office worker's paper-shuffling and meeting-attending. The common notions behind each of these two concepts are subtle, but I believe true to human nature.

The next two sections describe consumption and labor, respectively. They are followed by a discussion of why and how consumption and labor should be studied together in a single field, and then by a brief consideration of four secondary economic topics.

Part 1: Consumption

What Is Consumption?

Conventional economists talk a great deal about "the consumer" and the "consumption function," but (as might be expected) they have not given much thought to what consumption really is.[3] The most obvious starting point for a more adequate definition is the word's noneconomic meaning—to use something up completely. A fire consumes its fuel, romance consumes a passionate man, disease consumes the body of a tuberculosis ("consumption") sufferer. In the same way, men consume, or use up, their food and clothing. Translating that notion into economic terms, consumption could be described as the using up or destructive transformation of something.

Such a description of consumption is helpful but too rough; it misses two crucial aspects of consumption in economics.

First, unlike noneconomic consumption, economic consumption should be seen as the end of a process of human choice and action. The consumption by fire or romance and the consumption of flesh are all marked by necessity. The consumers (fire, romance, disease) have no significant choice in the matter; they cannot change their destructive paths. Some aspects of economic consumption—for example, the physiological need to consume food—are similarly tinged with necessity. For the most part, however, consumption involves a purposeful transformation of the world. The purpose makes the transformation meaningfully human.

Even the consumption of food usually involves this "humanization." Some transformation of the given world is usually required in order to make food that men can consume. In order to make it into food that men want to consume, the complex transformations of cooking and serving must be added. The importance of choice and effort in consumption is more evident as the consumption goods get more complex. The need for warmth creates a necessity for clothing, but there is little necessity in the clothing that is actually consumed. There is almost nothing of necessity in the consumption of games, books, or telecommunications equipment.

Second, unlike noneconomic consumption, economic consumption does not always use up the consumption goods. Consider the difference between consuming food and consuming housing. Food is of no use as a consumption good if it stays in the form of food, rather than being ingested in the body. A house is different. The house is the consumption good, but it is not used up in the process. If a house worked like food, it would be consumed by tearing it down, not by living in it. Similarly, while a car is worn down by use, that weakness is an unwelcome byproduct of the consumption. Conventional economists call these goods which are used but not used up "consumer durables." That etymological contradiction (what endures is not what is used up or consumed) points the human economist in the right direction—toward a definition of consumption which does not call for total destruction.

Taken together, these two modifications of the noneconomic meaning of consumption suggest that the human economist should look at consumption broadly, as appropriation rather than destructive transformation. Consumption consists of man's physical and conceptual appropriation of the nonhuman world. When men consume, they put some part of the world to use for their purposes. What they consume, the stuff or consumption goods, is what they take out of the world and make their own. Consumption, therefore, can be defined more precisely as making human use of the world.

This definition takes into account all consumption, from gathering nuts and berries to watching television, from finding a bed of leaves to sleep under to using the latest antiwrinkle cream, from the luxury of eating grapes out of the hands of a slave-girl to the luxury of helicopter skiing. In every case, men have taken something of the world, transformed it to make it their own, and are now making human use of the transformed and humanized consumption good.

The economics of consumption is truly a *worldly* study, in the positive, modern sense that it helps men understand how they make the world part of their unavoidable spiritual reality. Because it is of both the world and of men, consumption always is marked by a mix of the crudely physical and the transcendental.

This definition of consumption in terms of men and the world may take some getting used to. Here are a few implications and refinements.

Consumption ties men to the world, but some sorts of consumption are much more exclusively physical or transcendental. For example, the berry picked and eaten in the woods is little touched by the special reasoning of human effort. Unless the berry-picking is accompanied by human rituals (blessing, arranging, cooking), it verges on the animalistic. Conversely, in a concert men are consumers of music, but the physicality of the instruments and concert hall is far less important than the human effort of music-making. This activity is quite human, but only marginally economic, because the physical world plays so small a part.

The consumption of music shows that consumption need not be the best way to understand a particular human action. Economic analysis can capture only a small and relatively minor portion of the experience. Similarly, a child can be seen as consuming the instruction of a teacher or even the love of his mother, but to look at that activity in such terms almost always hides more than it reveals. Indeed, understanding the child's learning or being loved as consumption indicated a faulty view of human nature. The distinct status of men in the world implies that the relations of persons should have neither user nor used, so a description of human relations in terms of consumption is only relevant when human relations are distorted from their best and truest course. For example, the sexual relations of a man and a prostitute can be described as consumption, while the physically similar relations between husband and wife cannot.

There is no room for anything like money in this definition. Money is only used for appropriation, which is what conventional economists typically identify as consumption. They are interested in shopping, or more generally in exchange, the give-and-take pattern of labor and consumption in a society. That is important—I will discuss it later in this chapter—but it is not consumption. The actual human activity of consumption can come without any shopping, and it almost always comes well after the consumption good has been appropriated (made the consumer's own). The monetary and nonmonetary mechanics of appropriation have an influence on the goodness of the consumption, but only an indirect one. Excessive attention to appropriation, by either economists or consumers, tends to obscure the true nature of the activity. Consumption is not men taking from each other, but men taking from and humanizing the world.

Consumption is ultimately done by one person at a time, but that does not make it essentially selfish or conflictual. The goal of consumption is not merely, as conventional economists have it, to get the most or to get a "good deal." Rather, it must also have a moral component, to serve the good. Since men are essentially social, that good will have something common about it. Families, for example, consume together, and part of the goodness of consumption is found in each consuming only his share. (Of course, moral weakness often gets in the way of that commonality.)

Finally, consumption should be seen as a process that continues through life with few clear borders, not as a long series of distinct transactions. Certainly, consumption goods can be divided into clear units—for example this loaf of bread, that bed. Such divisions are central to the planning of production. For the human economist, however, the focus should be on the activity, not the goods. As a human activity, consumption is continual, almost constant. Food is desired throughout every day and bedding used and appreciated every night. The human desire for consumption goods is so steady that a few hours of deprivation (of food or toilet paper, for example) can be hard to bear. Consumption, correctly understood, is a steady and sustaining element of human life.

Comparing Consumption Goods

Conventional economists love to compare the value of different consumption goods, and they have an easy technique. Are three steaks worth more than five books? Do Italians consume more than the English or the Indians? Just add up the relevant prices. A few adjustments may have to be made, but the basic judgment is simple—whichever collection of consumption goods costs more is worth more.

That approach is highly misleading. This sort of comparison needs to be approached delicately, since only identical consumption goods can be compared directly. Three steaks are more than two (if the steaks are the same size and quality), but more need not be worth more. That can only be determined by considering the value to the consumer, who is a person with many complex needs and desires. That a particular man has more steaks than his neighbor does not necessarily imply that he is better fed, let alone better in some profound sense. Even if three is better than two for Mr. X, it may be worse for Mr. Y.

A common term helps. In respect to calories or protein, a meal of two steaks can be said to be worth more than a meal of two pieces of fruit. In respect to fructose and certain vitamins, the fruit meal is worth more. If the comparison is to be meaningful, the common term must be relevant. For example, two books may weigh less than one concrete block, but books should probably not be judged by their weight. There are likely to be many relevant common terms, including protein, vitamins, and weight, but these terms are themselves not obviously commensurate. There is no clear rule for determining whether the protein in the steaks is worth more than the vitamins in the fruit.

For all of these caveats, some comparisons are possible. It is fair to say that the typical Italian today consumes more than his grandfather or more than the typical Indian today (leaving aside the value of that superiority). This broad statement can be made only because contemporary Italians come out on top of so high a proportion of common-term comparisons. Many grandfathers and grandsons can be paired, as can many Italians and Indians. In each pair, consumption can be compared, both directly and according to many common terms—calories, items of clothing, pieces of furniture, years of education, and so on.

The same comparative process applied to contemporary Italy and Britain would be unlikely to yield so clear a judgment. There are too many difficulties in deciding who is typical and too many disputed calls in comparing consumption goods. While the diet of Luigi from Verona was clearly better than his grandfather's—look how much taller he is and how much more variety he has in his food—the comparison with Nigel from Basingstoke is much less clear. It depends what you value most—fresh foods, convenience, quantity, choice, and so on. The conventional economists' habit of putting precise numerical values on such comparisons—average consumption in the U.K. is 7 percent higher than in Italy today and 46 percent higher than in the U.K. twenty years ago—is nothing less than bizarre.

Of course, conventional economists base these comparisons on a common term—money. Unfortunately, money has no clear or consistent value of any sort. The only information contained in the statement that one basket of consumption goods costs more than another is that more money is necessary to buy the one than the other. Such a statement is tautologically true, but has no nonmonetary content. Conventional economists also err in assuming that more consumption is necessarily better than less. A moral analysis is required to decide whether the greater consumption of the Italian is better than the lesser consumption of the Indian. In turn, that analysis must rely on a hierarchy of specific economic goods and evils (mine will be offered in the following chapters). That analysis will be about as far as possible from a quantitative comparison. It is no more plausible to say that one consumption pattern is 8 percent better than another's than it is to say that one person's behavior is 8 percent better than another's.

Part 2: Labor

What Is Labor?

Labor has its own human meaning that is at least partly independent of consumption. In order to understand that meaning, the human economist should call upon many disciplines—the philosophical study of *homo faber* (man the tool user),[4] the sociological study of meaning in activity,[5] psychological insights into labor and personality,[6] the historical study of farm, craft, factory, and office labor, and theological reflection on labor, creation, and original sin.

Taken together, these collateral studies suggest that labor should be defined as the anthropological correlative of consumption. If consumption is making human use of the given world, then labor is making the given world useful to men. Consumption goods are what men take from the given world; labor is man's contribution to the given world. When we consume, a bit of the world gives up its form and becomes ours—or even, in the case of food, us. When we labor, we are making our mark on the world that surrounds us, giving up a little bit of ourselves in order to make the world somehow different, somehow better, and somehow more our own.

In early industry or simple agriculture, laborers were often referred to as factory or farm "hands," as if the rest of the human body and human nature were irrelevant. That approach is much too narrow. Labor calls on many elements of human nature. It involves not just hands, but much of what gives men their basic dignity. It calls on intelligence, in order to learn how a task is done, to perform it correctly, and to develop new tasks. Some of that intelligence involves logical thinking, while some involves the human ability to tie together brain and body in physical dexterity. Labor can require strength or patience. Labor usually demands sociability, for few tasks can be completed by one person working in solitude. At its best, labor elicits or rewards passion, whether for excellence or for some particular goal. There is also room for wisdom, the ability to see things in their most profound sense. Many types of labor also entail human sympathy, sometimes even love.

Most of the observations of the human meaning of consumption also hold for labor—its fundamental position in human nature, its superphysical core and meaning, its setting in a human community, its fundamentally continuous nature, its immeasurability, and its need for ethical evaluation. In four important ways, however, labor differs from consumption.

First, they differ in their necessity. There is a human requirement for both consumption and labor, but the needs are almost directly opposed. The necessity of consumption is external and animalistic. In order to stay alive, men must use the world through consumption. In this vital obligation, men are no different from animals. The necessity of labor, on the other hand, is internal and humanly meaningful. Labor, in which men touch and transform the world, is part of the fundamental human yearning for meaning, both in the world and beyond it. Men can certainly survive without much labor, but they need labor in order to live out their human nature most fully.

Second, labor and consumption have opposing sorts of freedom. The freedom in question is neither the negative libertarian freedom from any constraint nor the trivial freedom of random choice, but the freedom to search for the good. Men are most free in their consumption when they are most active in their judgment and will, because it is in that willing and judging that they mostly make the world their own. The human freedom of labor, on the other hand, emerges most truly when it is approached in what might be called a spirit of passive receptivity. Labor is freest when it is most in accord with men's nature—as a sort of vocation, something to which a person is called. Men are often called to be active, but they are most free when they try to accept simply, rather than manipulate, the call to action.

Third, labor is more extensive than consumption. While virtually all consumption is preceded by some labor of production, labor involves far more than the production of consumption goods. That difference was missed by the founders of economics, who lived in still predominantly agricultural early-modern economies. Writing as political thinkers before either the emancipation of women or the recognition of the importance of childhood, they were concerned only with the daily toil of males. Most male labor did then go to production, so the omission of nonproductive labor was not a significant mistake. (Many of these economists also had ideological reasons to dismiss the value of much nonproductive labor, such as that of lawyers or priests.) Human economics, however, deals both with all humanity and with highly efficient industrial economies. The wider perspective shows that much labor is nonproductive.

Finally, the human meaning and value of labor is more social than is that of consumption. To be sure, consumption is best understood in its social context. Without that context, a meal is easily reduced to mere food and clothing to mere warmth. Still, ultimately it is my consumption and mine alone that keeps me alive and comfortable. In contrast, the labor of a single individual is almost meaningless. Meaning comes only with social context. In almost every economic organization, the role of the priest is a distinguished one, while picking up rubbish is considered undistinguished. Those evaluations have nothing to do with either the inherent satisfaction or the physical usefulness of the labor. Rather, they emerge from largely noneconomic distinctions between the sacred and the profane, or the pure and the impure. Similarly, the general dismissal of the value of maternal labor in industrial economies can only be understood in the context of socially accepted ideas of the human good. More generally, the meaning of different types of labor can never be separated from the complex hierarchies of social caste or the moral categories of virtue and dignity.[7]

However the dignity of labor is apportioned in a particular society, it cannot be eliminated. By its nature, labor expresses and enhances men's natural goodness. Men labor not only in order to get what they need or want, but because they need and want to labor. They want that labor to be excellent in itself and to express something about themselves. This human focus is lost in most conventional economics. Quite typically, Marx spoke about the "labor power" that the laborer sells.[8] He should have realized that this power is actually the offering—whether well or badly compensated—of men to the world. The center of economic interest in labor should not be the pay or what is produced but the laborer himself. Otherwise, the meaning and dignity of the activity is lost.

Labor must be evaluated along several dimensions: the intrinsic good promoted, the social evaluation of the good promoted, the rewards received by the laborer, the satisfaction actually felt by the laborer, the satisfaction that the laborer would feel if he were not morally weak. "Productivity," a single standard of good labor that is much loved by conventional economists, is much too simple. Some labor that is objectively highly productive—for example, running machines in factories—is subjectively unattractive because of its alienating treatment of laborers as quasi-machines. In some types of labor—for example, labors of affection—productivity is itself a dehumanizing concept. The complex goods and evils of different types of labor will be discussed in chapters 8–12.

Labor and Work

The choice to use the word "labor" rather than "work" may be surprising. There are some good reasons to have gone the other way. "Labor" is part of the traditional vocabulary of economics, but its use is depressingly impersonal, since it is considered as a "factor of production" rather than as a description of human activity. Adam

Smith, for example, spoke of the task-related "division of labor," rather than of any sort of "specialization" of men's activity. In "labor markets," men, or at least their labor-power, are explicitly considered as things to be bought and sold. In addition, Marxists added a misleading revolutionary ring to "labor." Its faint echoes can still be heard in the title of "labor unions" or even (very faintly indeed) in the British "Labour Party." "Work" also has the support of contemporary everyday language. When men speak of their economic activity, they generally refer to "work"—"I'm going to work," not "I'm going to labor." In contrast, "labor" sounds almost undignified. Further, "work" is the preferred term in sociology and theology.[9]

My choice was determined by the broader English connotations of the two words. (This problem does not arise in other languages.) "Labor" always has a distinctly human sound to it. Machines cannot labor, although they can work. In addition, "labor" carries intimations of necessity and pain, for example in the "labor" of women in giving birth. Conversely, the use of "work" in physics provides a distinctly nonhuman intimation, and both "piece-work" and "works of art" suggest that "work" has less to do with the workers than with what these men are doing. All in all, I believe that "labor" better captures the consistent place of this activity in the rhythm of human experience.

Here are a few examples where my distinction fits in better with everyday language. Mothers are often described as "not working," but their labor is—I will argue—more important than most paid jobs. Men are said to stop working when they retire, but their rest from labor should only be temporary. Indeed, whether in retirement or unemployment, without labor men's personalities start to wither away. Similarly, when men are too sick to work, they continue to labor—at regaining health or simply at staying alive.

Hannah Arendt drew a philosophical distinction between labor and work.[10] She used "labor" to describe the repetitive tasks of production, tasks which she considered almost animalistic. In contrast, "work" describes the tasks of constructing something durable. Craftsmen and intellectuals work. In her view, there is a definite hierarchy—work is more valuable than labor (and action, the task of statesmen, is more valuable still). Arendt's philosophical dedication is admirable, but the distinction unfairly denigrates what she calls labor and unfairly elevates what she calls work. She is closer to the social hierarchies of Aristotle than to the universalism of the Catholic tradition. She might not mind that identification, but it is not in line with the vision of human nature that undergirds this book.

Original Sin

Men have mixed feelings about labor. Although they both need to labor in order to remain fully human and want to labor in ways that best reflect, form, and express their personalities, they are always somewhat dissatisfied with their actual labor. Labor always seems somehow hard, and almost any sort of labor soon becomes in some ways boring. This universal and simultaneous presence of desire and dislike may sound, or be, irrational, but it is nonetheless quite human. Men are good but weak, both at the same time. The biblical discussion of this weakness (Genesis 3:17–19), which Christians refer to in their discussion of "original sin," ties human weakness directly to the life of labor.[11] Men will find the production of food toilsome, and women will labor painfully at childbirth. The toil or hard work of labor is an unavoidable punishment for men's sinfulness. (The original temptation [Genesis 3:6] is also in part economic, since it is related to the intemperate consumption of an irresistible fruit.)

The irrational but undeniable pain of labor is paradoxical. Men hate their labor because it is hard, but it is hard largely because they hate it. Labor often involves no more repetition, exertion, or difficulty than sexual relations or eating, but the desire to avoid those activities is usually considered a sign of mental disorder, while avoiding labor is seen as an all-too-human, "natural" desire. Still, the theology of labor does not end with the curse. There is also a hint that bearing this punishment of toil humbly and cheerfully in some way helps men be less morally weak. Conventional economists sometimes argue that less labor, and particularly less toil, is simply better than more. If only it were that simple. Hard work can be good for the character (and for the soul).

Of course, it can be painful to acknowledge that goodness. Indeed, the universal dislike of labor leads most men to see their own labor as unfairly difficult and insufficiently appreciated. We are tempted to shirk at work or to seek greater rewards for our toil.

Those are the wrong responses, of course. If we looked at our truest nature, that is our good nature freed of our moral weakness, we would see that in shirking we are departing from what we truly, deeply want to be. Unfortunately, the knowledge that everyone else feels unjustly treated in labor and that the feeling is almost universally exaggerated is rarely enough to allow us to overcome our moral weakness. In such matters of the heart and the will, the only effective weapon is strong moral standards, often fortified by a powerful religious sensibility.

While most conventional economists simply want to minimize labor and its difficulties, others go to a different extreme. Struck by the energy and enthusiasm that is put into leisure activities, they try to develop schemes to make labor as enjoyable and rewarding as leisure. That effort is doomed by the nature of leisure, for one of the marks of leisure is that it is freed of the dull weight of compulsion (see chapter 14).[12] Because that weight is so fundamental to fallen human nature, leisure can never amount to more than a small portion of labor. More generally, no scheme can make all labor unceasingly interesting or "fun" for anyone. Labor cannot be perfected; it can only be redeemed, that is, helped by the unexpected contribution of an outside force—such as the love that lightens the load of caring for family members, or the sense of duty that calls a soldier to risk his life in his labor.

Part 3: Labor and Consumption

Physical and Metaphysical

Why are labor and consumption placed together in a single field of study? The obvious answer is that each is physically required if men are to have the other. That response is not entirely wrong. Almost all consumption requires preliminary labor. What we consume comes from the world, is formed by human hands, and has been guided by the human mind—it is the result of labor. A life of consumption may require very little labor to support it, as in that led by (possibly imaginary) naked, ground-sleeping fruit-eaters, but some labor is always present. In less friendly climates and more complex economies, the labors are much more substantial. It is not quite true that the need for labor increases with the quantity and quality of goods consumed. Capital makes that relation indirect. Still, there is a rough correlation. Complex modern consumption goods can be produced only through the constant and carefully organized labor of thousands of men.

Labor also requires consumption, but the need is much simpler. The laborer requires energy and health, and thus the consumption goods which keep him strong, in order to labor.

On the other hand, most labor and consumption are not physically tied together. Much labor does not lead to consumption, even indirectly. In particular, caring and instrumentally neutral labor, both described in chapter 14, produce little or nothing that can be consumed. Even more common is consumption that does nothing for labor. Most of the comforts of life are not necessary to support labor, but they are much enjoyed, nonetheless. Overall, the biological or physical tie between labor and consumption is not strong enough to explain their close social ties, any more than the biology of human sexual relations is sufficient to explain marriage and family life.

It is possible to view social relations, in this case the close tie between labor and consumption, as primarily caused by some physical ties, in this case the need to labor in order to consume. But this causality should be reversed. The nonphysical should be seen as "prior" to the physical. In this sort of analysis, the pairing of labor with consumption reflects the anthropological or metaphysical reciprocity between giving to and taking from the world. Following this philosophical logic, the direct physical ties between some sorts of labor and some sorts of consumption are only particularly vivid expressions of the underlying reality of these two human activities.

Emphasizing the metaphysical ties of labor and consumption has many advantages. Analytically, only a metaphysical approach can easily take into account the large amount of nonproductive labor, especially vast in complex industrial economies. If labor were to be judged only by its direct effect on consumption, then most of the labor in offices, schools, and hospitals and much of the labor in homes would disappear from view. The analysis of consumption will also be more accurate if it takes into account not only the labor it supports directly, but the whole economic organization of labor that coexists with the whole economic organization of consumption.

Morally, only a metaphysical view of labor and consumption can create an accurate hierarchy of the good of labor. If labor is the transformational donation of man to the world, then the best labor is that which gives the most, not that which makes the most consumption goods. A merely physical analysis of the tie leads to a preference for the most productive labor and a denigration of any labor that is far from the productive economy, particularly the labors of love and of the speculative intellect.

Sociologically, the metaphysical view of the tie between labor and consumption is also much more accurate than the physical. The close relations of the two are found in all human societies. Consumption goods are everywhere seen as a just reward for socially approved labor, whether or not that labor helps produce any consumption goods. Indeed, one of the rules common to all economic organizations is that the productive and nonproductive laborer must share all produced goods. Most obviously, mothers and children have a claim on the physical production or monetary income of fathers. On the other side, consumption allocations that do not reflect economic contributions from objectively valuable labor are usually given different social status and noneconomic names such as "charity," "benefits," or "unearned income."

At the most profound level of the economic aspects of human nature, the metaphysical tie of labor and consumption better reflects the human condition than the physical one. The two sides of economic activity express the two sides of men's place in the world—as giver and as taker. That symmetry is not simply physical, any more than human nature is simply material. Men share both a world of labor and a world of consumption. The two economic worlds are tied together, but the ties are not primarily physical—but rather metaphysical—between men's good but weak nature and the fruitfulness of the world and its resistance to men's efforts to master and humanize it.

Which Matters More?

Is consumption more important than labor? The conventional economists' say so, but their reasoning is ridiculous. In their inadequate vision of human nature, they argue that the satisfaction of the desire for more consumption goods is the basic economic good. At best, this is a poor observation; at worst, it is an argument in favor of the sin of greed.[13]

There are two better arguments for the priority of consumption. First, at the most physical level, consumption is clearly more basic than labor. Without food, survival is impossible, while life can drag on without any labor, even if that life becomes spiritually demeaning. Of course, the priority of necessary consumption goods cannot be extended to the many optional consumption goods (optional from the perspective of staying alive). The other argument is more theological—that consumption can be seen as more important than labor because it better expresses our essential dependence on the goodness of God. In particular, the Christian commandment to become like a little child, presumably like the infant who consumes the fruits of love at his mother's breast, is even more fundamental than the Christian commandments to labor at the various works of mercy.[14]

On the other hand, there are good arguments for the priority of labor over consumption. They start from the observation that labor is distinctly and almost purely human, while consumption is more closely related to men's animal nature. Labor helps define who men are, both as members of a species and as individual persons, in a way that consumption cannot. This philosophical observation is easily seen in practice. The answer to the open question, "Who are you?" usually includes something about labor—"I am a tailor," "a student," "a mother." Consumption replies—"I am an apartment-liver," "a smoker," "a fast-food fan"—are much less common, seem less adequate, and are more impersonal.

Similarly, in the pilgrimage of life, labor assists in the flowering of personality in a way which consumption cannot. Men both become and learn who they are much more through their life of labor than through their life of consumption. In the modern world, the importance of this process of self-discovery through the vocation of labor has perhaps been exaggerated, probably in response to the declining belief in the possibility of religious vocation. Still, even before the invention of careers, labor was seen as a significant part of man's spiritual journey, at least by the world-loving Christians.

Further, from that Christian perspective, the generosity of labor cannot be matched by anything related to consumption. Once the efforts of conventional economists to make labor seem selfish are dismissed, its basic *giving* nature shines through. Men wish to labor primarily for the sake of others—in labors of love for their loved ones, in productive labor for those who will consume what is produced, even in striving after success for the sake of their community's recognition. Human giving generally involves a sacrifice, an offering of time and a fight against labor's painful toil. In labor, men resemble the Christian idea of God the creator, who makes and guides the world in an excess of generous—and ultimately sacrificial—love.

These strong arguments for the priority of both labor and consumption suggest that a simple judgment in favor of one or the other is inappropriate. Rather, it is better to speak of a mutually reinforcing harmony. Just as exhaling and inhaling are equally important for breathing, the giving and taking dimensions of economic activity have equal importance. The full rhythm of life is not possible without full participation in the economic life, including both labor and consumption.

Part 4: Secondary Concerns

Production

Production is the intermediate step between productive labor and consumption. It is the process of using labor to transform the world into stuff for consumption. That path is often long and complex. It frequently involves labor at tasks that seem quite distant from the completed consumption goods. A chicken consumed at dinner, for example, requires many types of labor, including not only the breeding of the birds, but the production of fertilizer and feed; the operation of slaughterhouses, supermarkets, and trucks for shipping from slaughterhouse to supermarket; and cars for transport from supermarket to home. All economies have a good deal of production, and industrial economies have fantastic amounts of it.

Production is a sign of the harmony of men and the world. It would obviously be impossible for men to live if they were not able to coax from the world the things necessary for human survival, but the world and men are so well attuned that far more is produced than the merely necessary. One of the mysteries of economics is the way that the human intellect is able to comprehend and, to a significant extent, master the physical principles that guide the world. For example, prehistoric men understood the working of animal husbandry well enough to domesticate animals. The preindustrial Egyptians used their knowledge of the heavens to manage the floods of the Nile. And industrial-era men have gone so far as to bring such previously occult forces as electricity and magnetism into human service. It is equally mysterious how well these great forces are "attuned" to men. Just as wild animals have the potential to be made useful by domestication, electricity has the potential to be domesticated into such humanly useful products as light, heat, and computers. The modern worldview can be thanked for uncovering the extent of this metaphysical harmony.

While the ease of production is a sign of men's harmony with the world, its difficulty is a sign of the disharmony of men with the world. The curse of labor is found in the unwillingness of the world to be tamed just as much as it is in the toil men experience in taming it. The extent of the natural world's recalcitrance is often quite remarkable. For example, in order to collect a few ounces of gold, it is usually necessary to remove several tons of worthless rock. The disharmony is also generally persistent; without extensive labor at maintenance, most tools of production quite rapidly fall apart. However, the disharmony can often be overcome, at least temporarily, by men's effort. For instance, the production of airplanes shows that the occult force of gravity is not strong enough to resist men's desire to fly.

Production relies on tools, things which allow the man-world harmony to be put into action. (I use "tools" here in a broad sense, including not only hand tools but also sophisticated machines and what economists call "social capital.") Some of these tools are quite tangible, such as the machines of industrial factories. Some are quite intangible, such as the attitude and expertise of industrial laborers. The tangible and intangible tools involved in the massive production of an industrial economy are often quite sophisticated. They make labor more productive in every way—the yield from nature is greater, faster, and easier. These industrial tools are rarely freestanding. On the contrary, each factory depends so closely on many others that it is possible to think of the entire productive aspect of an industrial economy as a single gigantic tool of production.

There are also many standards of goodness for production. In practice, conventional economists often rely on a single, simple standard of quantity: more production is simply better. In preindustrial economies, where the production of food was generally insufficient, this crude approach would have been adequate, although the careful measurement of quantities of production was actually rare. In industrial economies, however, production is so abundant that no crude quantitative standard, even one adjusted for difference in qualities, can have much meaning. Efficiency—that is, the ratio between production and labor—is a somewhat more reasonable standard of goodness, since it involves both labor and consumption. The intrinsic satisfaction of laborers in their productive labor should also be considered part of the goodness of production. In addition, the beauty of the produced goods is a sign of goodness.

Social Arrangements

Economic activity always takes place within a social context. I do not mean that men never labor and consume alone, although such solitude is indeed rare, but that economic activities are always organized though structures or organizations that are not entirely economic. These socioeconomic structures are sometimes best characterized as men who are tied together by rules, such as the employees of a common employer, and sometimes as rules that tie men together, such as the contract system which regulates employment relations. Some of these organizations are predominantly social, such as religious or neighborly groups that provide economic services for their members. Others are predominantly economic, such as the monetary systems in industrial economies or "sweatshops" in poor countries. In most, however, the economic and social elements are thoroughly mixed. For example, modern corporations emerged from what would now be called sweatshops, organizations concerned almost entirely with production, but they are now complicated social entities made up of interlocking self-perpetuating communities and having their own "cultures" and "images."

Socioeconomic organizations are never perfectly harmonious. No matter how carefully their rules are drafted and no matter how limited or broad their membership, they are always scarred by men's moral weakness. The conventional economists' search for perfection in markets and monetary systems is doomed to failure for this reason (among others). On the other hand, bitter divisions in social organizations are certainly not unheard of.

Socioeconomic organizations vary in many ways, most notably in the degree of personal involvement. In industrial societies, the least personal organizations are the completely abstract systems of money and finance. Their impersonality makes them alienating to most participants, but they seem to be essential to both production and allocation. (No one knows for certain—all that can be said is that up to now such impersonal systems have been found in every industrial economy.) The most personal organizations are the complicated arrangements of property, which tie men to things in socially approved ways. Industrial property, however, can be quite impersonal, most notably in the ownership that is granted to abstract entities such as corporations or municipalities. Most socioeconomic organizations fall somewhere between these two extremes in their degree of personality. For example, contracts provide a formal structure for many personal economic relations.

Socioeconomic organizations generally have many purposes. Conventional economists identify two or three purposes of money, while anthropologists add several more. Similarly, corporations inevitably aim at a variety of goods, including profit, the quality or acceptability of what is produced, the durability of the enterprise, and the good of the employees. For any organization, the goals and their relative importance can change over time, often without the participants noticing. This shifting multiplicity of purpose is not distinctly economic. Rather, it seems to be a feature of all human social structures. It does, however, make social analysis in economics quite challenging. For example, it would be easier to understand the economics of regulation if regulatory organizations were always oriented to be either friendly or hostile to the regulated industries. In practice, however, they are both in different degrees under different circumstances.

The various socioeconomic organizations have complex relations. As the example of regulators and regulated suggests, organizations overlap and interact with each other in various ways—with hostility, friendly rivalry, or symbiotic support. The nature of these relations is sometimes clear and conscious, but sometimes it is unconscious or symbolic. This nature changes over time, sometimes after careful social reflection and sometimes almost by accident. Few relations are always friendly, but some are usually hostile. For example, monetary-financial structures generally have very tense relations with government organizations.

Allocation

The arrangements of labor and consumption within a society can be approached at various levels. At the most intimate level are the actual mechanisms of giving and getting—the exchanges of money, the privileges and encumbrances of inheritance, the various nonmonetary rewards for different economic activities. A too intensive study at this level tends to understate the social intentions that guide these arrangements. After all, the mechanisms are often changed when their results are judged to be undesirable—as when, for instance, they result in a too large difference in consumption between rich and poor. At the most elevated level, the motivations for actual allocations can be studied across a society by asking which men find themselves with what types of labor and consumption goods. This approach, which often leads to an economic study of social class and castes, is more revealing than the study of mechanisms, but it tends to overstate the intentional nature and solidity of current allocation arrangements.

The motivations for allocation arrangements are never purely economic. Indeed, the reasoning is often primarily social. For example, the allocation of consumption goods in feudal societies had relatively little to do with the effectiveness of different men's productive labor and a great deal to do with the social hierarchy. Similarly, in industrial corporations, social status, rather than economic contributions, best explains the particularly generous supplies of consumption goods allocated to senior executives. In the allocation of labor, such largely social indicators as family, education, accent, and friendship are usually quite important, sometimes more important than the purely economic indications of competence at particular tasks. This social bias in the allocation of economic goods and positions is probably an inevitable reflection of the relatively modest importance of economic concerns. Economic goods tend to be used to serve and reinforce other, more important goods. Unsurprisingly, the increasing centrality of economic concerns in industrial societies has led to closer ties between economic contributions and economic allocations.

The justice of economic allocations is a particularly difficult topic. It is hard to determine what goods are actually being allocated (for example, is it the use of a car, the ownership of a car, or access to the road network?), what the criteria of allocation really are (is employment awarded through impartial examinations or through a veiled system of inheritance?), and what those criteria should be (are impartial examinations better than veiled or naked inheritance?). The difficulty is augmented by the frequent use of economic distinctions for largely social purposes, such as in the sharply differentiated pricing of almost identical consumption goods. The debate on the criteria of justice is philosophical and heated. Some think allocation according to need should be the basic standard, while others argue for allocation according to contribution. In practice, industrial societies mix both standards. The oldest standard—allocation according to birth—is generally rejected in theory but has been extremely difficult to eradicate in practice.

The abundance of industrial societies should change the economic debate about allocation. Industrial prosperity has for the first time answered the most important purely economic question of allocation: who has to suffer from the indignity of absolute poverty? The new answer is no one. All other economic questions are secondary, although still contested. In the welfare states of rich societies, most of the economic questions of allocation justice would seem almost redundant. There is so much available and so few people go without. Although this universality does not seem to have stilled the debates, it may be better to think in more social and less economic terms about allocation.

Interactions with the Physical World

Men's special position in the world carries both an obligation and a responsibility. The obligation is to dominate, to do whatever is necessary to make the world our own. In economic activity, this translates into an obligation—not merely permission—to plough the ground, dig mines, breed plants and animals, and create new substances. The responsibility is to respect the world, to protect its mysteries—integrity, wildness, beauty. In economic activity, this translates into the monitoring of ecological systems, the minimization of damaging emissions, and the preservation of wilderness.

The two sides of this man-world relationship should be roughly balanced. The domination side is a largely accidental side-effect of economic activity. As economic sophistication increases, so does the scope and scale of domination. So agriculture alters landscapes more than did hunting and gathering, and industrial production modifies air and water more than does agriculture. Responsibility increases commensurately with domination, but that increase does not, as it were, come naturally. For responsibility to keep up, conscious attention and intention are required.

The balance between domination and respect can be lost in both directions. Inadequate domination, an excessive respect for an idealized nonhuman nature, can deprive men of economic goods that are more valuable than the preserved purity of nature. An exaggerated idea of the sacredness of nature sounds distinctly preindustrial. In industrial societies, an inadequate sense of responsibility is much more likely. The delayed effects of many sorts of environmental irresponsibility—the damage may not be felt for generations—make this vice particularly tempting. Without some conscience-raising, responsibility is likely to be left to heirs. And consciences have been raised, thanks to the environmental movement of the last half-century. Pollution, the economic heir to religious impurity, has been diminished greatly, at least relative to the increase in industrial production. Environmental responsibility has been integrated into economic management.

Is this enough? There is always room for practical arguments for greater responsibility, especially in relatively poor countries, but some radical environmentalists have a more philosophical objection. They believe that the industrial economy holds in its nature an excessive human domination of the world. This perspective is often associated with the scientific equivalent of millenarianism—a certainty that ecological catastrophes will eventually punish industrial societies for their massive disruptions of nature. In the modern spirit, the first place to turn to evaluate such complaints is to the scientific evidence. Unfortunately, while scientists can collect lots of evidence on particular issues, they are less able than philosophers to answer the basic question of whether men can or will solve all the environmental problems they cause.

The radical environmentalists' philosophy is only partly sound. Men are morally weak, and responsibility to nature requires substantial effort, so it is possible that men will systematically fall short. Environmental pressure, like any sort of exhortation to virtue, is helpful. The fight for good science is particularly helpful, since human moral weakness often reveals itself through misleading interpretations of the evidence. On the other hand, the underlying claim of the radical philosophy is false, at least if my claim of men's fundamental harmony with the world is accepted. That claim is supported by the history of the industrial economy—the natural world has stood up quite well to the expansion of population and industry.

This last discussion of economics and environmentalism made use of a nice set of philosophical words—nature, harmony, responsibility, domination. Indeed, labor and consumption are philosophical as well as practical concepts. They are parts of human nature that should be grouped with other traditional philosophical concepts—will, intellect, spirit, body, soul. Men ought to be seen as laborers and consumers in much the same way as they are seen as thinkers or political animals.

I can now turn to the next question—what are labor and consumption trying to accomplish? That moral analysis is philosophically necessary. The nature of anything human always includes the thing's purpose. Economic activity is no exception. It is a fully human activity that must be analyzed in the most basic human terms of right and wrong.

8

A Few Imperfect Ideas about the Economic Good

The first step in the economic method is complete. Economics has been defined as the study of men in the world, of labor and consumption, of the respiratory exchange of labor offered to make the world more human with the consumption received from the humanized world. It is now time to approach the next step in the method, the determination of the economic good.

As usual, conventional economists start out from the wrong ontological place. Like many contemporary philosophers, they do not like to talk at all about the Good—the transcendental, mysterious, divine ultimate that should be at the center of economics. When economists talk about goods—consumption, production, final and intermediate goods—they have nothing moral in mind, just terms for different varieties of what I have been calling stuff. But such language games are not enough to free them from the moral orientation of human nature.

Ordinary language shows just how ubiquitous the idea of the economic good actually is. Almost any economic actor—farmer, craftsman, mother, employer, employee, producer, regulator, or shopper—wants to be "good at" his or her economic activity. Any consumer hopes for consumption goods that are indeed "good." This everyday idea of economic goodness may not be totally transcendental, but like any sort of excellence, it has at least the rudiments of such nobility. The truest and best nature of anything, even of the humblest tasks and the meanest stuff, is a goal that stands apart from the more or less soiled examples of ordinary experience.

I will come back to this everyday sense of the economic good in the discussion of internal economic goods (in chapter 10). The present chapter deals with the rudimentary notions of the economic good—often understood as an amoral purpose rather than as actually good—that have been offered by economists of various persuasions. Some of these ideas are helpful, but they are both individually and cumulatively inadequate. A more satisfactory description of the economic good, with the requisite philosophical background, will be provided in the subsequent two chapters.

Utility

For almost all conventional economists, the one economic good is the utilitarian ideal, the maximization of subjective utility. Even self-professed non-utilitarian economists rarely stray too far from either the subjective or the calculative approach to the good. Yet their description of utility, or whatever is to be maximized, is hazy. Bentham's original notion of a physical measure of pleasure and pain now seems either primitive or futuristic (pending advances in neuroscience), but there is nothing obvious to take its place. So the quantity to be maximized is either left undefined or given a vague description such as "whatever people want." But the "whatever" is actually quite constrained, because it must be quantifiable if any sort of calculus is to be applied. This state of affairs is philosophically unsatisfactory, but it has caused economists remarkably little concern, largely because they make the completely unwarranted assumption that money is a reasonably good substitute for utility.[1]

I have already attacked utilitarianism as part of the discussion in chapter 2 of the conventional money-market-exchange model. The utilitarian scheme is unrealistic—men do not actually make choices primarily on the basis of calculations of expected pleasures or on anything remotely like that. It is also immoral. Pleasures are no substitute for the good, and ersatz pleasures, the "whatever" of conventional economics, can hardly help. No goal that is evaluated only subjectively—that is, without due respect for the errors of judgment caused by men's moral weakness—can have the absolute and objective nature of the truly good.

Conventional economists sometimes argue that neoclassical theory does not actually make any moral claims. The potential morality of utility is supposed to be irrelevant. Utility is just the thing that is balanced—the utility of sellers with the utility of buyers—in the economic equilibrium of a perfect market. However, this claim of amorality is unjustified. Equilibrium is desirable only because it is supposed to maximize utilities, so the maximization of utility must be the underlying good. But even if economists could somehow wriggle away from the idea of the good—which they most certainly cannot—utility would still not be a useful tool. As utilitarians from Mill onward have grudgingly admitted, utilities, whatever they are, cannot easily be compared. There is no obvious relation between the plus of pleasure (or positive utility) and the minus of pain (or negative utility). There is no obvious relation between utility now and utility later. There is no obvious relation between my utility and yours. There is no obvious relation between my utility and that of any group I belong to. In effect, utility does not do what its proponents say it does—provide a neutral and universally applicable standard for economic judgments.

For all of these crippling problems, men do sometimes seem to follow a principle of subjective monetary maximization, just as utilitarian economists say they do. We try to earn as much money as we can from our labor and try to spend as little money as we can for our consumption goods. This pattern of behavior lies behind some of the basic maxims of commerce: men use more of something when they do not pay for it directly; one good way to increase sales volume is to reduce prices; another good way is to persuade customers that prices have been reduced. These maxims, however, only work "on the margin" for relatively small increments and decrements of price and volume. More generally, the subjective monetary maximization principle only works when all other things are equal, and that happens so rarely that the principle is hardly a useful guide to overall economic behavior.[2]

Of course, the search for subjective monetary maximization is hardly a search for the good. The goal sounds suspiciously like a philosophy of "more for me, I don't care about you," a moral approach that reflects men's weakness rather than their virtue. The best that can be said for this motivational principle is that it can sometimes help make the production economy more efficient. And as will be explained in chapter 10, production efficiency is a relatively minor good.

Satiety

Neoclassical theory does provide one helpful hint about the economic good—the principle of "declining marginal utility." The intuition (ignoring all equations and spurious mathematical precision) is the following: the first bit of a useful thing adds a lot to life, the second bit adds something, but it adds less than the first provided; the third bit provides even less additional benefit than the second; and the pattern continues until the next bit adds nothing, or even makes matters worse. Food provides a clear example. A man on the edge of starving to death will respond to a crust of stale, tasteless bread with almost infinite appreciation. If he then receives an ample supply of bland food, that addition is also greatly appreciated, but contributes much less to his life than the initial supply of absolutely necessary food did. The addition of spices will make the ample but bland food more appealing, but does not do as much as the first addition, of ample food to barely enough food. By the time food improvements amount only to better frozen pizzas or increasingly exotic fruits, our formerly starving man will hardly care about the additional, or "marginal," improvements. He might not even notice them at all without advertising or some other effort to get his attention.

Declining marginal utility provides a good model for the pattern of benefit from many kinds of stuff, not only food. A room to live in is great, a house is very nice, a second house is fine and by the time you get your third or fourth holiday home it is probably more trouble than it is worth. It also works as a broad model for some lines of development of economic history. In the dissemination of knowledge, printing provided less additional good than writing. Computer search engines add even less. Like any conventional insight, however, declining marginal utility cannot be applied blindly. The second week of annual holiday time may add more to life than the first. The Internet probably added more than photocopying, the previous development in communications. Antisepsis probably improved health care more than all previous medical innovations put together.

For nonutilitarian economists, one aspect of the theory of marginal utility is especially useful—the concept of a maximum level of utility. If marginal utility declines to zero (or infinitely close to it), no more utility can be added. In some variations of the theory, the marginal utility can even decline to less than zero, so more of the stuff in question actually makes life worse. The notion of a finite limit to utility can and should be translated into more revealing language: some things are only good in certain limited quantities or to a certain limited degree. Up to that quantity or degree, more of these things are better, if only marginally. Past that quantity or degree, more of them are either worthless or actually harmful. Goods that can be maximized can be called "finite." Finite goods fit well within men's worldly state. Unlike transcendental goods such as truth or beauty, finite goods can only be fully realized in the world. Their worldliness makes finite goods less important to men, because nothing worldly can satisfy men's desire for more than the world can offer.

Many economic activities—in particular the production, allocation, and consumption of most types of stuff—aim at a finite good, the satisfaction of needs and all reasonable desires. That satisfaction can be called satiety (the two words are based on the same Latin word for "enough"). Few economists have taken the idea of satiety seriously, but they should.[3] Within its limits, satiety is a valid and helpful standard for the good. Men should only eat so much food, use so much soap, wear so many clothes, live in so much space, absorb so much entertainment or information, or be sensitive to so high a degree of comfort. The ethical standard of satiety is simple—enough is enough. If a man is sated in his food consumption, then it is wrong for him to expend effort to increase his food consumption. If a community is sated, then it is wrong for it to increase production. There might be some value in more choice or convenience, but the incremental gains are likely to be small. There are probably better uses for the individual effort and social capital in question.

It is impossible to identify the exact point of perfect satiety. For food, physiological experts may disagree with each other, or with a hunger-counseling spiritual teacher. It may be preferable to think of satiety as a range with fuzzy borders. Once the range is set, men will still want to exceed it or (for the excessively ascetic) fall short of it. That is the way moral weakness works. The actual prevalence of obesity or anorexia is irrelevant to the ideal good of food satiety.

For stuff such as food or hand soap, scientists can help define the satiety range. The body gives fairly clear signs of excess and deficiency. For many other kinds of stuff, however, the range will be determined largely by social expectations. There is such a thing as a full supply of clothing, but the social nature of the good of dressing well means that the "full supply" will always involve more than enough to keep warm and clean. How much more depends on the economic potential and social rules of each society. Compare a teenage girl in a rich community with an elderly man in a poor one. The old pauper will need far fewer clothes than the teenager to feel sated. Such subjective judgments can be wrong by the objective standard of the true human good. The clothes-hungry girl may already be supersated, while the ragged old man may have too little.

While satiety is truly good and is a reasonable description of the good of some economic activities, the identification of the idea does not exhaust the moral analysis of economics. To start with, the good of satiety does not provide enough information to make judgments between different finite goods. Is it more important to reach satiety in the consumption of food or of mobile telephones? Even within individual categories of stuff, satiety will rarely provide enough guidance to adjudicate economic disputes or set economic policies. An agreement that there are limits to the amount of information which men can absorb is not easily translated into rules for publishing or filmmaking. The judgment of satiety can be wrong. The wisest observers would probably have judged men's information capacity filled up well before the Internet was developed, but few wise observers would now consider the Internet redundant or harmful.

Satiety also does not apply to anything that is not strictly finite. Most notably, men do not have a clear limit to their need for and desires concerning labor in the same way they have a limit to their need and desires for food or even for communications. More profoundly, the concept of satiety loses its validity whenever economic activity participates in the search for transcendental meaning. More is often better when it comes to the labor of prayer, the consumption of beautiful art, or the production of richness in worship.

Industrial economies are so productive that satiety has been approached, reached, or even exceeded for many types of stuff. The spread of obesity has already been mentioned. If the moral weakness of "consumerism," an excessive desire for consumption goods, could be stripped away, a similar picture would probably emerge for most finite goods—clothing, housing, heat, transport, telephones, and media. Unfortunately, it is difficult to subtract consumerism, an economic evil to be discussed in chapter 11, from contemporary industrial economies.

Prosperity, More Prosperity, and Growth Rates

Satiety comes when everyone in a society has all they should want of some type of stuff. As an economic idea, it is moral, social, and modern. It is moral because "enough" is defined as what men should want, not what they actually want. It is social because the full-point only comes when everyone, not just some or most, has enough. It is modern because until the advent of the industrial economy, the idea of everyone having enough of any type of stuff was simply fanciful.

Prosperity is the amoral and preindustrial idea of the fullness of wealth. Satiety is having what is correctly judged to be enough; prosperity is having an abundance, or even a superabundance. The difference can almost be felt in the words themselves. Satiety cannot help sounding a touch dull, and the alternative descriptions—zero marginal utility and finite goods—are even less welcoming. In contrast, "prosperity" carries connotations of luxury, comfort, and even a most pleasant, if perhaps somewhat sinful, indolence.

The connotations suggest one of the major problems with considering prosperity to be the universal economic good. On its own, prosperity is not all that good. Most preindustrial moralists warned against the depravity that tended to accompany it.[4] Such blanket condemnations may have been excessive, but then industrial societies have seen a concurrent rise in prosperity and decline in social morality, a correlation that lends support to the moralists' case (although it is probably more accurate to say that both trends spring from the same source, the modern worldview). Satiety, the satisfaction of needs and reasonable desires, is good in itself because the desires are already defined as being reasonable. In contrast, the abundance of prosperity is only good when it is appreciated correctly, because otherwise it encourages unreasonable desires.

Another major problem is that prosperity, at least in its preindustrial form, cannot be universal. Before the advent of industrial technology, prosperity required a large number of servants who could not themselves enjoy prosperity. To judge by the striving for socioeconomic advantage in industrial societies, the individual goal of prosperity still seems to contain a sense of superiority or relative advantage. Since the highest economic goods should reflect the universally moral nature of economic activity, a prosperity that is exclusive by definition cannot be the central economic good. If these objections were not enough, prosperity also shares the narrowness of satiety—ignoring both the infinite and the good of labor, limits that disqualify both from serving as universal goods.

Conventional economists have too universal a worldview to endorse the premodern sort of prosperity as the goal of economic activity. They have, however, developed a modern variation of the idea, substituting crude quantity for the more subtle notions of ease, excellence, and social superiority. Prosperity is taken as a simple measure of the size of the economy, and the economy's good (or goal, in the amoral vocabulary of conventional economics) is simply to have more prosperity—to become bigger.[5]

This is a foolish idea. The notion that increase alone can constitute a good does intellectual violence to the conventional economists' own recognition that marginal utilities often decline. More need not be better at all, and the same amount more is unlikely to be the same amount better. In addition, "bigger is better" can only be applied to national economies if "bigger" can be quantified, if the size of economies can meaningfully be described by a single number. The chosen technique is a modified summation of the monetary values of everything purchased in a particular economy. This real gross domestic product (GDP) is a single number, but it is not a meaningful one. Rather, it is a hodgepodge of incommensurate stuff, services, and adjustments. The willingness of conventional economists to rely on such an obviously silly quasi-measure only shows how desperate they are to have some standard for the good.

Some economists have tried to address the narrowness of the implicit definition of prosperity through the creation of a broader notion: "welfare" or "human development."[6] Such efforts always magnify at least one of the conceptual weaknesses of the idea of prosperity. Any effort to decide what is truly important within or in addition to crude consumption quantity requires ethical questioning, exactly the sort of questioning that the use of "prosperity" or real GDP is supposed to avoid. Any list of additional elements is subject to criticism as either too exclusive or too extensive. Any effort to create a sum of incommensurate quantities—growth plus education plus life expectancy—will be arbitrary.

A further, and less attractive, variation on the prosperity theme is to find the economic good in having the fastest rate of GDP increase—not to be big or to become bigger, but to become bigger as fast as possible. The idea of looking for the fastest growth rate has only been around for a few decades, but it has become widely accepted as an economic purpose. It has even spread from economics into politics. National leaders frequently worry that their country's growth rate is too slow.

"Growth" has no moral meaning on its own, so faster economic growth can only be good if it brings good things. In poor countries, economic growth does bring many goods, so a focus on the speed of growth may serve as a reasonable, rough guide to economic policy. Alternatively, it may not actually be a reasonable guide, even a rough one, if the social dislocations and environmental damage that can accompany rapid industrialization are taken into account. In any case, as consumption satiety approaches, the goal of growth becomes senseless and the goal of fast growth becomes dangerous. In such an economy, growth hardly has any meaning. To the extent that it does, the most appropriate type of growth is slow or nonexistent.

Other Single-Minded Ideas

All of these suggestions of a single overriding purpose for economic activity have turned out to be inadequate. The utilitarian desire to reduce the economic good to a mathematical total of pleasure is unrealistic, impractical, and incomplete. Satiety is sometimes good, but far from universal in its application. The ideas connected with prosperity are too exclusive, too narrow, or just misguided.

Each suggestion fails for different reasons, but the multiple failures do suggest a general conclusion—that it is unrealistic to expect to find a single and simple good (or purpose or goal) that can encompass everything in the human economic condition. A brief survey of some other proposed single economic goals supports this negative hypothesis.

The most historically influential proposal has been Marxist: worker control of the means of production.[7] That goal has two severe problems, each enough to disqualify it. First, it is meaningless. The statement would only make sense if it were possible for some entity known as "the workers" to do something which can be known as "control" in reference to some distinct process known as "production." The sociology of organizations suggests that "workers" is an implausible single subject for a verb such as control.[8] Furthermore, a study of modern industrial capital makes clear that "control" is not a very helpful concept in the interdependent processes of production in industrial economies.

Second, the Marxist goal is much too narrow. The focus on labor is perhaps a healthy alternative to the conventional overemphasis on consumption, but the imbalance is only reversed, not righted. Then, too, the treatment of labor is inadequate. The model was developed in order to argue for a more just arrangement of unskilled and casual manual labor. That type of labor seemed crucial in the nineteenth century, but it plays a minor role in modern industrial economies. Neither agricultural nor skilled industrial labor is easily understood in Marxist terms, not to mention caring and domestic labor.

Catholic and communitarian thinkers have a better single idea for the economic good. "The common good" is similar to satiety in its generality, but it is distinctly ethical.[9]

Actually, the common good is proposed not solely as an economic purpose, but as a general orientation for all social policy. Unfortunately, the practical implications of the common good in question are hard to determine. That is hardly surprising, since the meaning of any purpose that is supposed to be so widely applicable is likely to be vague. As far as economics is concerned, the underlying ideas seem to be that we should labor in order to create a better community and that we should consume as a community, with concern for all of our neighbors.

If that is indeed what is meant by the common economic good, then it is an appealing goal. This definition, however, is hardly complete enough to provide any sort of guideline to economic action or policy. It leaves basic questions unanswered. What are the marks of a better, or of a good, community? What sort of consumption is truly communal, since so much of it is unavoidably individual? How does this common good relate to the individual good? How should the relevant community be defined? It looks as if the common good is a laudable idea, but can serve as only one aspect of the economic good.

Still, both "common" and "good" are polemically valuable words. "Common" provides a helpful counterpoint to the conventional emphasis on the individualistic good. Indeed, since labor and consumption both always take place as part of men's role in society, it can be argued that economic analysis should be primarily social rather than individualistic. "Good" helpfully emphasizes that the goal of economics is indeed the good, even if the description of that good must be left for later analysis.

Less developed, simple proposals of the economic good are even less satisfactory. The ideal of freedom of choice, usually including choice in labor, consumption, and production, is popular among some modern ideologues.[10] Freedom is certainly good, but freedom must be understood correctly, as a call to goodness rather than as a trivial ability to choose. In any case, free choice is certainly not the sole standard of goodness. It is not even high up on a list of economic goods. I am better off with an assigned good job than a wide choice of bad ones. Similarly, more efficient, safer, and cleaner production is more valuable than giving free choice to companies of what to produce and how to go about it. As for consumption goods, the modern abundant choice of virtually identical products seems hardly good at all.

A persistent theme among antimodern economists is the primacy of agricultural production and sturdy manual labor.[11] (To be fair, they might well countenance other goods, but their writing is too incoherent for a sure analysis.) Like free choice, good farms and hard toil close to nature are good things, at least at some times for some people, but they hardly seem to exhaust the content of the economic good.

Other one-idea men offer excessively vague single notions of the economic good—for example, minimal or maximal government or support of the family. Yet others offer extremely narrow notions—for example, appropriate taxation or equity in the allocation of consumption goods. While some of these ideas may indeed be good, all of them fall far short of encompassing all that is good in economic activity.

The search for a single economic good is best seen as a tribute to the unity of the transcendental good. Economists, conventional or not, all understand, perhaps only implicitly, that the Good must always be interchangeable with the One, but they err in assuming that this One Good can be found in a particular worldly arrangement. Economic goods are unified because they participate in (or partake of or support) the single transcendental Good, but individual economic goods are best treated separately. The economist can assume that these goods do have an underlying unity, but he should not try to describe the single economic good with any sort of precision. It is better to look for a hierarchy of goods—the topic of the next chapter.

9

Economic Goods for the World

The Hierarchical Idea in Economics

This chapter and the next are the intellectual center of this book. Everything up to here—the description of the industrial economy, the critique of the conventional model and its variations, the construction of a coherent vision of human nature, and the definition of economics in accord with that vision—has been a prelude to the discussion of just what economic activity is actually good for. The last chapter was meant to deal with some misleading and incomplete ideas on the topic. In particular, it was supposed to show that economists cannot rely on any single simple definition of the economic good, but must create some sort of hierarchy of specific economic goods. That creation is the task of this chapter. Once a hierarchy has been drawn up, the study of economics should take a more coherent shape.

The idea that goods can and should be carefully arranged in a hierarchy springs from the reality of order in the world and in all intellectual study (see chapter 4). Rankings from most to least important are standard in the Aristotelian-Thomistic philosophical tradition, but, thanks to the baleful influence of utilitarianism, are almost unknown in economics.[1] So before presenting the goods themselves, I will start with a few explanatory comments.

The conclusion of the last chapter was that "the economic good" is best understood as shorthand for a collection of different economic goods. In this chapter, I will list and rank those goods. A list without a rank would provide only limited information. It could proclaim the goodness of satiety in food and of satiety in mobile phones, but could not decide which good is better. That judgment, which has practical implications for production or consumption, requires some sort of hierarchy.

The hierarchy presented here is anchored in the Good—the one transcendental and mysterious good that stands above all individual goods, economic and otherwise. This Good can be thought of as a Platonic form, an Aristotelian nature, the Goodness of God, the apperception behind a linguistic unity, or in many other ways. The important idea for this chapter is merely that it provides a single and unchanging standard of comparison. One particular good is higher than another when it—depending on the philosophical vocabulary of choice—has more of, is a more perfect image of, or comes closer in meaning to the Single Great Good.

This transcendentally based hierarchy of goods is quite different from a utilitarian ranking—for example, the ordered preferences found in welfare economics. The most basic tenet of utilitarianism is that for each individual, at any instant, all utilities are ultimately commensurate; the value of X can always be expressed in terms of the value of Y. If a dozen cakes have the same price (or perhaps the same adjusted price) as one visit to the doctor, then they must have the same value. In a transcendental hierarchy, however, there is no such easy interchange, because the things to be compared are different in nature. In principle, higher goods should always take precedence over lower goods, whatever the quantities. The principle of incommensurability cannot be abrogated. No number of cakes, however tasty, can be as valuable as good health, because health is a higher good than gastronomical pleasure.

The next most basic tenet of utilitarianism is that utility is subjective; my ranking of values is different from yours, and mine can change along with my feelings. In contrast, in a transcendental hierarchy, the order is objective and unchanging, fixed in the nature of things. The list I am about to present does not reflect my fleeting and subjective preferences, but my best current understanding of objective, moral reality. I may change my list later, but that should not be because my preferences have changed. Rather, the pursuit of objective truth may lead me to a better understanding of the unchanging truth.

The hierarchy of external economic goods (I will explain the "external" in the next section) has a particular complexity—the ranking depends on both the value of the good itself and on the contribution of economic activity to that good. The consideration of the economic contribution changes the order from that which would be found in a straightforward list of all human goods. For example, in the complete list, beauty, which is transcendental and potentially eternal, might well be placed above physical life, which is always limited by death. In the merely economic list, however, life has been placed higher, not because economists are philistines when it comes to beauty but because economic activity is much more central to the promotion of life than to the promotion of beauty. On the other end of the scale, while economic activity plays a huge part in the promotion of the good of comfort, comfort's low position on the complete list of goods pushes it to the bottom of the economic hierarchy.

This sort of hierarchy of ideals cannot be used to provide recipes for economic action. In the world as it is—filled with moral weakness, marked by death and suffering, subject to futility, marred by ignorance, and divided against itself—it can provide only a framework for analysis. Actual decisions must indeed be made with due respect for the hierarchy of goods involved, but they must also take circumstances and intentions into account.[2] The debate on the relative value of food and phones starts with a comparison of the good of the two types of stuff, but it only starts there. It must also include the less philosophical and more technical questions raised by a concrete situation: How close is satiety for each type of stuff? How much effort would increasing each good involve? Are there evils or other goods that should also be considered?

Many of the circumstances that must be taken into account have little to do with economics. The economic good of feeding the hungry may be well served by migration from infertile terrain, but only if the potential migrants can find better land and a nonmurderous reception elsewhere. Economic analysis is completely unable to determine whether such conditions are likely to be met. Economists should be humbled by their inability to offer a complete practical analysis, especially as noneconomic considerations are often more important than purely economic issues.

The economist's intellectual impotence is not limited to great issues such as hunger and migration. It strikes in even the simplest situations. Consider the good of a family sitting down together to a good meal. Much of the action is or relies on economic activity—the labor of food production and preparation and the consumption of the prepared food. When it comes to one important good served by the family meal, the health of those who eat it, the economist has a great deal to say, even if he must rely on some noneconomic scientific expertise. But when it comes to the meal's contribution to the good of family togetherness, the questions become much less economic. Does a tastier or more nutritious meal make for better conversation? Does the ease or location of preparation make a difference? How much does the variety of the food from one day to the next matter? In such matters, the economist has little to contribute.

The hierarchy that I am about to present is liable to two sorts of criticism. The first is that it is a poor translation from the outline of human nature presented in chapter 5. I may have gotten lost, either in my broad understanding of the Good or in my analysis of the scale of economic contribution to the various goods. Alternatively, the starting point, the outline of human nature, may be dismissed as fundamentally flawed, whatever the accuracy of the intellectual translation. A follower of a world-abandoning religion, for whom worldly economic activity is only a distraction from men's true purpose, would likely argue that this list is distorted by an overvaluation of possible economic contributions to the good. A follower of a less spiritual view of human nature might make the opposite complaint, that I have undervalued the good of consumption and unfairly relegated the intrinsic good of success in labor to the next chapter, on internal economic goods.

The observation that other hierarchies of economic goods could be defended is not so much a concession as an invitation. The search for the true economic good will only be furthered by the presentation and discussion of alternative hierarchies. This invitation is offered to fellow travelers within the Christian worldview, who can improve my translation. It is offered to non-Christian nonutilitarians, who can articulate their own judgments of the nature of the good in this world. And it is offered to conventional economists and other utilitarians, who should move beyond their simplistic picture of economic man.

Finally, a reminder: economists should distrust common sense about economic appearances. In particular, the industrial economy has introduced a "false consciousness" about the nature of prosperity.[3] It is hard for us really to imagine a simpler consumption lifestyle—"How can they live without running water and toilet paper?" The lack of imagination easily leads to an overvaluation of the full panoply of industrial comforts. In a "true consciousness," the standard for the economic good must be universal, encompassing both preindustrial and industrial economies.

External and Internal Goods

The need for two hierarchies has already been alluded to. It comes from the observation that the economic activities of labor and consumption aim at two different sets of goods. The distinction can be expressed in several ways: external and internal; indirectly economic and purely economic; economically supported goods and goods of economic activity; goods for which the economy is a means and goods for which it is itself the end. I will generally use the internal/external vocabulary because it is more modern and perhaps clearer, but my philosophical preference is for the means/ends distinction. When economic activity is only a means to a basically noneconomic end, then the end is an external good. When the correct ordering of the economic activity itself is seen as the end, then the good, the correct ordering, is internal. The two types of good differ enough to justify separate rankings and separate chapters. External goods (ends) are discussed in this chapter, internal goods (means) in the next.

An example might help make the distinction clear. Consider the labor of the trumpet player in a symphony orchestra. His labor, the playing of notes, is, like all labor, a contribution to the world. That contribution supports several goods—beauty, the delight inspired by the music, the community brought together in the concert hall. The trumpeter's labor is necessary for all of these goods—the music would be less beautiful without his contribution, and so forth—but none of them are economic in their nature. In contrast, the internal good of the trumpeter's labor comes from the fit of the labor with the overall economy and with the whole society. The trumpeter should be in the right job, be able to do his best at his work, and be rewarded in a just way.

The existence of external economic goods should not be controversial. Labor and consumption always aim at being more than good labor and good consumption. Productive labor should produce good things. Nonproductive labor should make the human condition better in other ways. Even utilitarians think that consumption aims not at consumption itself, but at the consumer's pleasure. For the human economist, there is much more than things and pleasure at stake. As the musical example shows, economic activity supports such great human goods as beauty and community.

Philosophically, there is a problem with the idea of having both internal and external goods. Can there be a good in the means that is separated from the good of the ends? Certainly, in economics the two are intertwined. The trumpeter's labor is internally good in part because it gives him the satisfaction, and the society the benefit, of his contribution to external goods. Still, the internal and external are not identical. The good arrangements of labor and consumption are themselves significant parts of men's relations to the world, whatever goods they contribute to or partake of. There is something wrong with an economy in which a trumpeter is paid (or, more technically, receives social rewards which are) less than he deserves, even if the underpayment does not stop him from making beautiful music.

External goods are usually more valuable than internal ones, just as ends are generally more important than means. There are some important exceptions, especially in industrial economies, where an abundance of consumption and pointless labor has created a new economic situation. The internal good may predominate for an office worker whose labor of paper-shuffling and meeting-going contributes almost nothing to any external good. Still, the exceptions do not invalidate the general rule that external goods come first. If a sacrifice has to be made, it is usually the internal economic arrangement that should yield to the greater human goods. Mistreated trumpeters should keep on playing (although strikes may be justified if the internal economic good is served badly enough). This priority implies that the discussion of external economic goods should take precedence in both place and detail.

The Hierarchy

Life

Life, human life, is the highest economic good. Labor and consumption should support life before anything else. It is good to be alive, and men's economic activity has much to contribute to that goodness. It should aim to keep people alive by providing them with the basic stuff necessary for survival—the traditional goods of food, shelter, clothing, and fuel. It should also aim to keep people alive in their humanity by providing the basic care needed for human dignity—the love of a family and the support of a community. Finally, economic activity should aim to promote the multiplication of human life. If life is good, more life should generally be better.

The placement of life at the pinnacle of this hierarchy depends on both the special position of men in the world and the equal dignity of all men (see the third and seventh principles of chapter 5). The universal good of life is far from self-evident. While only nihilists would argue that no human life has any value, in many premodern worldviews and in many strands of the modern worldview, the claim that all lives are good in the same tremendous way has been denied. For some thinkers, while most lives deserve respect and economic support, a few do not, perhaps those of the weak or the old. For other thinkers, it is only a few lives, perhaps those of aristocrats or of holy men, which are truly valuable; the rest deserve less respect and economic support. Even when a society theoretically adheres to the universal view of the goodness of life, its economic organization never lives up to the theory. Rich or high-caste men are rarely willing or expected to make sacrifices that might keep alive more of the poor or lower castes. This disrespect is rarely active—"kill them" or "let them die." Rather, it is passive and insidious—a preference for goods that are less valuable than life.

All labor necessary for the preservation of life or for the nurturing of new lives has a meaning that more optional tasks cannot possibly provide. If my labor is literally vital—that is, if my life or the life of someone I love depends on it—then the labor is clearly good, and I am more likely to be more satisfied by it than by labor that supports lesser goods. The antimodern moderns' praise of preindustrial agricultural labor catches the appeal of this "working for a living." Their praise, however, tends to gloss over the great disadvantage of an economy that relies so much on absolutely necessary labor. In preindustrial economies, the combination of men's economic ignorance and moral weakness with the physical world's hostility often led to lives being snuffed out because of inadequate production. The good of necessity in labor was too easily accompanied by starvation.

In contrast, the good of life has been provided for in magnificent abundance in industrial societies. The threat of death from cold or hunger has been largely banished. Well-developed government welfare systems protect men's lives from economic ill fortune and from social or psychological incompetence. Parents can promise sufficient stuff to as many children as they may want to have.

The potential abundance of life has not been fully exploited. Indeed, birthrates are so low in prosperous countries that the number of the living is starting to fall. That pattern makes no economic sense. On its own, the abundant industrial prosperity ought to result in larger, not smaller, families, so the modern reticence about life must have more to do with some noneconomic, antilife aspects of the modern worldview than with anything directly economic. However, under the influence of the false consciousness of industrial prosperity, men often give economic justifications for their lack of interest in life. They claim that it is "too expensive" to have many, or sometimes any, children. These articulated fears are not about the risks to the greatest economic good of life, but about a possible shortage of lesser economic goods.

A misguided preference for the "quality of life" over life itself can be found in poor as well as in rich countries. Conventional economists often provide an economic justification for this antilife logic, arguing that too many people will get in the way of economic development. This justification is based on a profound underestimation of men's ability to master the world. There may eventually be some Malthusian population point past which more births stand in the way of more life, but estimates of that point have been receding for the last two centuries. Until it is reached, more people should be considered an economic accomplishment. Even if an "excess" population made it more difficult for everyone to have as many consumption goods as in a less fecund community—and nothing in the history of industrial economies suggests that a trade-off of this sort is actually necessary—that would not justify antilife economic policies. The good of life should take precedence over other economic goods.

When the mix of wealth and poverty in the modern world is set against the principle that life is the highest external economic good, a challenging practical and ethical syllogism emerges. The major premise is that it is inappropriate for a community to provide goods that are not required to support life as long as some members of that community do not have enough to live on. The minor premise is that knowledge and commerce are so sufficiently global that the only relevant community is the entire human race. The conclusion is that it is wrong to strive for increased prosperity in already rich countries. It is wrong, for example, to develop a more powerful mobile telephone technology largely for the benefit of about one-quarter of the world's population as long as 10 or 15 percent of the world's population suffers from the most fundamental sorts of economic deprivation—potentially fatal hunger, thirst, and easily preventable disease. The effort that is currently directed to the improvement of phones should be shifted to the improvement of agriculture, trade, distribution, and so forth in the countries where such improvements would better support life.

Although this syllogism is compelling, there is a good counter-argument. The development of phone technology in rich countries may not actually take away resources that could otherwise be used to promote life. Indeed, if the more powerful phones for the rich can also help spread less expensive phones among the poor, allowing them to share information more readily, then expending more effort to make cheaper phones might be the best use of resources. Perhaps that is what is actually happening. Certainly, the rapid spread of mobile telephones in poor countries does not seem to have increased hunger.

The example is typical of the ambiguity of economic history. In the economic history of life, the relations between intentions and results have been quite unpredictable. Many of the industrial developments that have helped support life—in metalworking, road-building, printing, mechanical and electrical engineering, organic chemistry—were originally aimed at some more or less frivolous consumption good or, quite often, at making war more deadly. Fortunately, men are good as well as morally weak, so they have learned to transform the trivial and the bad into the good. Going forward, more development of apparently pointless industry might continue to have other largely unintentional positive effects on the protection and promotion of life.

Health

The external economic good of life shades easily into that of good health, just as ill health shades easily into death. The two goods, however, are not identical. Health involves more than being alive; it means living life well in physical terms, fighting against the limits created by birth defects, accidents, and sickness of all sorts. Men are always subject to physical weakness, so good health is a precious and often fragile accomplishment. Both health and life are promoted by a combination of labor, consumption, knowledge, and social organization. The economic contribution to the mix is less significant for health than for life, but the economic role is still crucial.

The most important economic service to health is in its defense. There were hardly any effective efforts to protect health in preindustrial economies because so little was known about the causes of disease. In industrial economies, however, much knowledge has been acquired and exploited. The labor used to construct and maintain the infrastructures of sanitation—clean running water, cleaned wastewater, and the various technologies of personal cleanliness—is the most important economic contribution to health defense, followed by the consumption habits of cleanliness. Health is also defended by the provision of superior nutrition, universal immunizations, the use of temperature and humidity controls in living spaces, and the reduced use of dangerous types of physical exertion. All of these economic challenges have been met brilliantly. For example, industrial prosperity has converted the nearly universal practices of ritual cleanliness to a generally available economic good.

Economic activity can also be dedicated to the restoration of health. Labor aimed at curing the sick is found in every society, but in premodern societies such labor was largely vain in terms of practical effect, although not in social meaning. Modern medicine, however, has achieved a great deal. Antisepsis, antibiotics, and analgesics, to name only the most important categories, are perhaps not quite as important as immunizations (which are so beneficial that they are best classed as promoting life), but they certainly have made life much healthier for all who have been touched by them. The cumulative effect of modern medicine is that health can be restored, at least temporarily, for sufferers from most diseases and victims of many types of accidents. In industrial economies, health restoration has become an important industry.

Finally, for those who cannot be made whole, economic activity can help substitute for good health. The care of the handicapped requires great effort and great ingenuity, so it requires a significant amount of economic dedication. Preindustrial economies had neither a sufficient supply of available labor nor a sufficiently flexible collection of technologies to do much. Industrial economies, however, have achieved great things. The lame are moved in wheelchairs and special vehicles; the deaf can hear, thanks to hearing aids and sign language; the nearly blind can see, once they put their glasses on; computer technology can do many things for the dumb and the palsied; legal psychotropic drugs give some semblance of sanity to some of the insane.

In all three domains of health—defense, restoration, and substitution—the great achievements of the industrial economy are always vulnerable to the chaotic forces of the nonhuman world. The sanitation infrastructure requires a continuing economic effort if it is not to be rendered useless from decay or overwhelmed by an increase in population. The organisms of diseases change in response to medicine, so men must respond with new medicines. These accomplishments are also vulnerable to men's own moral weakness. The relatively easy cure of one generation of sexually transmitted diseases in the middle of the twentieth century encouraged easy acceptance of sexual promiscuity at the end of the century (although there were certainly important noneconomic and nonmedical causes of this change), which in turn led to an increase in other sexually transmitted diseases. The economy of health cannot rest.

As with the promotion of life and as is the case for all economic goods, both external and internal, the identification of health as an economic good provides a framework for analysis, not a clear resolution of any specific questions of allocation. Even when the likely effects of one sort of practice or treatment are fairly well understood, it is difficult to balance complementary goods. For example, is it better to dedicate labor to the defense of the health of many people through improved sanitation or to ameliorating the ill health of a few handicapped people through various modes of substitution? Should a new drug be prescribed if it improves the health of most who take it but causes dangerous side-effects for a few? At what level of "many," "improve," "most," and "a few" do these balances change? What should be the balance between the use of resources for research to find better remedies and for the application of already available technologies? Difficult economic questions of this sort must be answered at two levels—socially, by the organizations responsible for health policies, and personally, by each individual. There are few easy or obviously right answers.

Freedom

Freedom is only good if it is *truly* free, the freedom to follow the truth. The "economic freedom" of conventional economists is often not truly free. It is too broad to be free when it can lead to moral slavery, such as in the freedom to choose the labor of prostitution or the consumption of destructive drugs. It is too narrow to be truly free when it is restricted to "free markets." In practice, these are constrained by all sorts of rules, habits, and pre-existing conditions. Even in theory, the choices offered to most participants, those who do not wish to set up their own businesses or make grand change in their careers, are limited to trivial matters of consumption.

Once freedom is correctly understood, economic activity is not as central to its provision as to the provision of life and health. On a personal level, freedom comes far more from the respect and formation of conscience than from any consumption good or any type of labor. For a community, freedom does emerge from and in economic organization, but much more from and in the organization of government, culture, religion, and education.

Still, economic activity can make important contributions to the human search for freedom. The highest form of freedom relevant to economics is the search for knowledge. The freedom to know helps men fulfill their special position in the world. Economic activity does not directly produce knowledge, but prosperity enhances knowledge in various ways. It is prosperity which "pays for" formal and informal education. More precisely, the efficiency of industrial production makes it possible to direct more human labor to study and teaching and to maintain a physical infrastructure of knowledge in the form of books, schools, and technology for the transmission of information. The causality works both ways—education also helps develop the habits and skills that support the production of all sorts of stuff—but the greater human good is certainly the knowledge, not the stuff.[4]

Varied personal experiences offer another type of freedom. Experiences are not good merely because they are new or different, but when the variety is appreciated in a good way, it can add to the fullness of life. This sort of freedom is not hugely important for human flourishing—men can live fulfilled lives without ever leaving their villages—but it is a freedom that is extremely well supported by industrial economies. Cities, which both support and are supported by the hugely productive labor of industrial economies, provide all sorts of cultural opportunities. Travel for pleasure and for education, changing residences and keeping friends around the world can also deepen men's personalities. All of these are easy when labor is so productive, so little tied to the land and so well organized. The freedom of experience, however, is particularly easily turned to evil. With only a slight twist from the forces of moral weakness, the same economic activity that can provide good things can be used to support the crime, loneliness, and depravity of urban life, the mind-deadening and environment-destroying experience of bulk tourism and the vain escapism of empty consumer novelties.

The least valuable sort of economic freedom is a freedom often cited by conventional economists, the freedom of choice in consumption. If the ability to choose among hundreds of kinds of shampoo is a good at all, it is a trivial one. The ability to have a car in which to drive to thousands of different places is far more liberating than the ability to choose among hundreds of different types of cars. Choice hardly contributes to subjective consumption happiness. If anything, the blinding variety presented during any shopping trip in a prosperous country is often almost nauseating—if not in itself then in the contemplation of the vast effort expended for so minor a gain.

Community

Both labor and consumption help to define and support almost all sorts of communities—from families to global networks of telecommunications, media, and transport.

The family is the most basic community of labor. Until very recently, labor within the family was strictly divided according to gender, with women taking the lead in the labors of care and men in the labors of production and, in industrial economies, employment. That sexual balance has become less rigid, but the labors of children and childcare retain a special, community-defining position within the family. The family is also the most basic community of consumption. Families share houses and meals in all economies, with industry adding shared appliances, cars, and travel. The family consumption community extends through the generations, with parents passing down houses and furnishings, recipes and clothing. In industrial societies, unfortunately, the community of the family has been weakened. The attack is not primarily economic, but economic factors have contributed. For example, television, distant jobs, and ready-to-eat foods have made it easier to abandon family meals, once an important source of unity.

In preindustrial social organization, broader labor communities were frequently important sources of social definition. The shared work of the farm or food production cycle defined the community of labor for most people in largely agricultural economies. Guilds of craftsmen and other specialists were equally defined by their common labor. Membership in such labor communities had a social role, helping to determine who was eligible for marriage, for political leadership, and for help in times of need. After a rough transition period—as "hands" turned into employees—industrial economies have generated their own sorts of labor communities. Employees are bound by ties of friendship, hierarchy, and shared responsibility. The search for "a good place to work" is largely a search for a supportive community. Professional groups and unions cut across employment to provide a different sort of social support.

Consumption, as well as labor, helps to define larger communities. The specific clothing of a profession or social caste is a visible sign of membership. The common consumption of certain types or food or certain styles of domestic design helps designate neighborhoods. To the extent that these consumption bonds are merely economic, the communities they form tend to be weak. The weakness is found to an extreme degree in the shifting communities formed around the consumption of a common brand of soft drink or athletic wear.

Economic activity also supports more spread-out communities through the provision of the nonconsumed consumption goods of communication. Writing and roads provided some support in pre-industrial economies, but modern technologies have had a much more significant effect. With telephones and data communication, it is now easy to be in personal dialogue with almost anyone in the world at any time. In addition, the many dimensions of publishing and electronic media create and support a variety of more or less impersonal communities. As always, men are not strong enough always to use this technology for the good. Roads can separate as well as unite, e-mail can encourage superficiality, and television can all too easily bring isolation rather then identification.

Large corporations and economic agencies are distinctly modern sorts of community. Antimodern moderns often see these entities as new forces of evil, but their condemnations are excessive. Such global economic communities do generally work without much consideration of what is truly good, but this lack of reflection is only rarely disastrous. Usually, the goodness of human nature, a nature shared by corporate leaders, prevails. Such enterprises have many virtues: they bring many otherwise disparate people together for a common good purpose; they develop hierarchies based on merit; they find tasks for each employee that correspond reasonably well to his gifts and needs; they offer the talented a breadth of experience; they respond to other sorts of communities; and they even help in the broader economic development of some of the locations in which they do business.

Still, the antimodern moderns have a point. The social prominence and environmental influence of these industrial organizations give them historically unprecedented power and influence, an authority that should be accompanied by a historically unprecedented sense of responsibility. They should make their decisions for the benefit of all who will be affected by them, not only now but those who will live after everyone currently involved has gone, indeed those who will live after the corporations or agencies themselves have disappeared.

Beauty

Economic activity is neither the inspiration for nor the most important promoter of beautiful things, but it is certainly required for their creation. As the example of the trumpeter suggested, artistic labor is more than labor, but it is truly labor, and that labor must be integrated into the economy. More importantly, economic activity can be arranged so that its orientation favors beauty in all aspects of society, not only in the works formally designated as artistic.

In premodern societies, the creation and experience of beauty was usually enhanced by prosperity. All over the world and throughout history, rich societies generally made extensive, often magnificent, artistic efforts. If a society produced more than enough stuff to fend off absolute poverty for most of the population most of the time, it was more likely to allocate a most substantial share of its labor to the service of the divine, a service that could include splendidly beautiful buildings and extravagantly beautiful rituals. Such societies also had more rich men who were likely to engage in campaigns of aesthetic enhancement—landscaping, grand buildings, ornate interior decoration, elegant furniture, luxurious clothing, commissions of painting and sculpture.

This correlation extended into the first centuries of modern experiment. The development of oil-based paints supported Renaissance painting, and the development of printing supported the spread of great literature. In the middle of the nineteenth century, at the same time that the first antimoderns were complaining about industrial uglification, complex orchestral music reached a crescendo of beauty—thanks to the industrial skills that made it possible to design sophisticated instruments and to the industrial prosperity that permitted resources to be dedicated to the training of large numbers of professional musicians.

If the historical relationship between prosperity and beauty had persisted through the twentieth century, there would have been a beauty explosion, as the economics problem receded into history. Instead, the tie has been almost completely broken. The human world has not merely become less beautiful, but the goal of making it more beautiful has largely been abandoned, either unthinkingly or in a purposefully brutalist effort to reflect the supposed inner ugliness of the current human condition.

Of course, the judgment that the advances of beauty in domains such as photography and cinema have been overwhelmed by uglification in many others is a personal one, but I do not think it is peculiar. A review of the arts section of a newspaper, especially if it is followed by a drive around a suburban shopping area, would lead all but the most uncompromising fans of the modern spirit to agree that beauty has not been well served by the modern economy. When modern things are beautiful—as in the pure lines in suspension bridges or strips of highway across the wilderness—it is often by accident. When they are particularly ugly—as in garish advertisements which aim to shock potential consumers into paying attention—it is usually on purpose.

Many antimodern moderns blame the decline of beauty in industrial economies on the structure of industry. Their argument is not completely wrong, as there is some antipathy between efficiency in production, which is oriented towards the human minimum, and beauty, which is so closely tied to divine fecundity.[5] However, while efficiency is the internal good of production (see chapter 10), it is not the only or the primary good of the whole industrial economy. The decision to let one minor economic good predominate over other, objectively higher economic and noneconomic goods is much more social than purely economic. The Marxist fallacy that economic motivations can explain this large a cultural change should be resisted. It is not money but something more social that explains why electronic sound technology has not primarily been used to spread beautiful music, but to create ever louder and generally cruder musical noise.

Comfort

There is no single word which is quite adequate to the simple satisfaction produced by most consumption goods. It is partly physical, but not as intense as pleasure. It is partly intellectual, but not as elevated as delight. It is partly the proprietary passion of possession, but not base like greed or pride. It can be expressed as the "pleasure of having nice things" or as a sort of "at-home-ness" in a personal and social environment. I have used the word "comfort," but it should be understood to mean more than the physical comfort of, for example, sitting in a well-formed chair. Economic comforts include the good that comes from having a well-supplied kitchen, a well-furnished house, and a pleasant commute to a reasonably fulfilling job. As many women will testify, the economic comfort of fashionable clothes can be quite uncomfortable physically.

Comfort is the only economic good that is enhanced by almost every increase in prosperity. Indeed, comfort can almost be defined as the enjoyment of prosperity. In preindustrial societies, comforts were scarce. In industrial prosperity, they are everywhere. We can turn on electric lights, run hot water, sit in a heated or cooled room, look out clear glass windows, drive anywhere, call someone up on the telephone, buy new plates when the old ones break, put the clothes in the washer and then the dryer, and so forth through the hundreds or thousands of products and technologies that make up the distinctly modern consumption experience.

As comforts have increased in every possible dimension—type, spread, quantity, quality—they have become more important in various ways. Renunciation, once a fairly common mark of virtue and discipline in soldiers and monks, is now taken as a sign of mental derangement or antisocial behavior. Not only is the typical "middle class" lifestyle laden with comfort, but the refusal to want that lifestyle is seen as a rejection of a basic value of the modern world. The comfort culture pays particular attention to innovations and improvements. Consumers are expected to crave the next new thing, and most consumers seem to be quite ready to oblige.

On the other hand, there is a social undercurrent of disappointment with comfort. The innumerable little goods of modern consumption do not provide contentment, let alone virtue. Indeed, they often seem to inspire a jaded discontent. Men take the accomplishments for granted and notice the failings, however tiny. We complain about airline food and forget to wonder at the ability to fly. Our craving for the new and better is often followed quickly by indifference or even disgust.

The modern elevation of the social status and anticipated meaning of comfort reflect false consciousness more than any newly discovered truth about human nature. They deal entirely with men's desire to get more from the world, but have almost no bearing on men's desire to go beyond the world. The real value of comfort is modest indeed. This distance from the deeper and more important striving of human nature condemns comforts, however numerous and impressive, to spiritual near-irrelevance. If the desire for comfort is allowed too much sway, then comforts can become worse than irrelevant—distracting baubles, as traditional moralists always argued.

The desire for just a bit more comfort, so widespread in industrial societies, is misguided. As satiety approaches, it is foolish to expend much effort in the search for more, both personally and as a society. Prosperity is much better oriented towards the higher economic goods, to a life not lost or a sickness cured, or towards the noneconomic goods of freedom, beauty, and community.

Economic Goods and Human Goods

The hierarchy of external economic goods is complete. Before going on to the internal goods of economics, I would like to make some observations about the list as a whole.

The most obvious observation is that this list corresponds well to the description of human nature in chapter 5. At the top of the list are the economic goods that support men's nature as special, social, and capable of the transcendental, while comfort, the good that supports men almost entirely in the world, is at the bottom. The correspondence is hardly surprising, since I constructed both. Still, I hope that the description and the hierarchy clarify and support each other.

I also hope that I have kept my commitment to historical and cultural consistency. The description of the goods of economics could have been written in much the same words before the development of the industrial economy, if there had been any economists around to worry about such things. Even now, the goods listed are as relevant in poor as in rich countries. They do not change with the form of government, the size and form of economic organizations or the level of technological development. Such continuity should be a prerequisite for a description of the goods of something as universal and basic as economic activity. The sophistication of modern technology and the wide economic gap between the rich and the poor have changed some things, but not the fundamental economic goods.

The threat of moral weakness lurks throughout this hierarchy. To lose sight of the true nature of the goods produced by economic activity is all too easy (exactly as it is all too easy to ignore any of the highest human goods). The highest goods of life and health are easily lost sight of in the striving for social position and comforts. A slight shift is enough to contort the goods of freedom and community into the evils of slavery and alienation. Prosperity has been pulled away from beauty for no good economic reason. Economic evils will be discussed in chapters 11 and 12.

Although the list is meant to be historically neutral, it is hard to miss the industrial economy's profound effect on the search for the economic good. Industry has supported life in previously unheard of quantities, allowed many more people to die of old age rather than of sickness, supported many important sorts of freedom, created new and often helpful communities, and made possible the production of many beautiful things. On the other hand, it has also provided fertile ground for a complacent, even a hostile, attitude towards life, a sometimes destructive approach to the good of noneconomic communities and social uglification. I will discuss this balance more completely in chapter 17.

This hierarchy sheds some light on what is probably the most important question about economics—just what role should economic activity play in the good life? Of course, as an economist, whose detailed study takes in only labor, consumption, production, and the like, I am in a poor position to provide a rigorous answer to this question. Still, I can draw some lessons from the preceding discussion.

Consider first the highest economic good, life. Life is certainly high in the human hierarchy; otherwise murder would not be considered such a heinous crime. Still, followers of almost all ethical systems are supposed to be willing to sacrifice their lives for a variety of religious, political, or personal goods: men should be ready to die for the sake of truth, God, love, country, duty, and so forth. All of these goods must rank above life in a complete list of human goods.

Then consider the lowest good on the economic hierarchy, comfort. It is also the closest this list comes to an internal economic good. All of the other goods are essentially noneconomic. Life is biological or spiritual, knowledge is intellectual or spiritual, community is psychological or spiritual, and so forth. Comforts, however, are predominantly economic, made almost entirely with labor and enjoyed almost entirely through consumption. The correlation—the least valuable economic good is also the most economic of the economic goods—suggests that the economy is least valuable when it is most economic.

Putting the two observations together, it seems fair to say that economic goods play more of a supporting than a starring role in men's search for the Good. That conclusion accords with the statement (in chapter 5) that men's desire to get more from the world, a largely economic desire, often is, and perhaps more often should be, sacrificed for the sake of higher goods. These modest claims for the economic good are also in accord with the lessons of the history of revelation. The old dispensations of the great world cultures (Jewish-Christian, Greek, Indian) held prosperity to be an evident sign of divine favor, but that vision of goodness was then superseded by more "spiritual" notions. Indeed, the pursuit of prosperity can be as much a snare as a reward. As men get closer to the Good itself, they should care less about subsidiary economic goods.

The conclusion that economic goods are not at the center of the human condition does not justify a reversion to the premodern attitude, a complete disdain for economic activity and all of its virtues. The economic good is truly good. It deserves attention. It may have only a supporting role in the human drama, but the stars of that play—men's search for God, Love, Truth, Beauty, and the like—will shine more if the economic parts are played well. The internal goods of those economic parts themselves are the topic of the next chapter.

10

Economic Goods for the Economy

The internal economic goods are almost always less good than the external ones. This generally inferior status follows from the relatively modest direct role economic activity plays in men's highest calling—the striving for the good, true, and divine. The position of economic activity in men's life is comparable to that of sleep. Both are disproportionately time-consuming relative to their contribution to the good. A well-ordered economy is important to the good of a society in much the same way that a good night's sleep is important to the good health of an individual. They are both essential, but only in the negative sense that normal life is impossible without them. When they are functioning well, or even when they are mildly disordered, they do not deserve much attention. Both sleep and economic activity become pressing issues only when severely disordered, for example in the labor disorders of chattel slavery and early industrial destitution.

Allocation justice is the only possible exception to this relegation to the second tier of human concerns. A society as a whole cannot be considered just if money, labor, consumption, employment security, and economic-social status are allocated unjustly, so any study of social justice must include some economics. Still, economic arrangements usually contribute less to a society's justice than the allocation of such noneconomic goods as political and military power, social status, and religious honor.

Economists often pay too much attention to internal goods and too little to external ones. Practical economists, those employed in companies, government, and the financial markets, concentrate their professional labors on just one internal good, production efficiency (see below). The appeal of this narrow perspective is easy to understand—the work requires far fewer assumptions about noneconomic topics than does the analysis of external goods. Ease, however, does not lead to excellence. The inward-looking economist cuts himself off from what is best and most significant about economic activity.

Each type of economic activity—labor, consumption, production, allocation, and environmental interactions—has its own hierarchy of internal goods. The close relations among the different aspects lead to overlap and interactions, but the internal goods of economic activity are as distinct as its types. Ideally, each hierarchy should be studied separately and in detail, but a full analysis of all four hierarchies would probably require a book of its own. In an introductory work such as this one, these largely secondary goods deserve only secondary attention. I have chosen to provide only one open-ended term to characterize the overall internal good for each type of activity. Since labor and consumption primarily aim at external goods, the discussions of the internal goods for these two categories are particularly brief. The discussions of the internal goods of production and allocation are longer, in part because they have received so much attention from conventional economists—much of it quite sensible, some of it quite misguided. The discussion of the internal good of environmental interactions is particularly brief, largely because it has received so little attention from either economists or philosophers.

Labor

The internal good of labor is the *dignity of the laborer*, a dignity that should be understood in terms of men's good but weak nature.[1] Labor is fully dignified when it is worthy of the goodness and makes no concessions to the weakness. Just as men's sexual conduct is dignified when we do not give into the temptation to be "only human" in lust or adultery, our labor is dignified when we do not give in to the "only human" weaknesses related to labor.

Several families of labor weaknesses can be identified. There are the physical temptations of the body, both to strain too hard and to do too little. Dignified—that is, good—labor makes physical demands that correspond to but do not overtax men's physical strength. There are the temptations of intellectual laziness. Dignified labor calls for discipline, thought, and imagination. There are the temptations of moral degradation. Dignified labor supports and develops virtue. There are the temptations of greed and selfishness. Dignified labor supports and develops moderation, sharing, and healthy ambition. (This aspect of the internal good of labor is closely related to the external good of community.) Finally, there are the temptations to strive without any noble purpose. Dignified labor is objectively meaningful. Society also plays a role in promoting the dignity of labor. It should be organized in such a way that laborers are selected, trained, and rewarded in dignified, appropriate, and just ways. That internal good is more appropriately discussed under allocation.

Whether a particular labor situation—this worker engaged in that task—respects the laborer's human dignity is a question that usually requires close study and debate. Only a few types of labor are always undignified—notably prostitution, which assumes an inherently degraded view of the human body, and crime, which is structurally selfish and disrespectful of men's social nature. For the rest, circumstances and intentions have to be taken into account. Many types of labor promote human dignity in some circumstances and are undignified in others. Military labor is good when it is necessary for defense but bad when it aims only at disruption; good when it is disciplined but bad when it amounts to a frenzy of blind violence. Sometimes the analysis of dignity will focus more on the laborer than on the labor. Labor that entails heavy lifting is dignified for the strong but undignified for the weak or pregnant. At other times, a more complex social analysis is required. The dignity of different types of children's labor depends on the social arrangements of families, the educational system, and the available techniques of production.

Consumption

The internal good of consumption is *appropriateness*—consumption is good when it is appropriate to the consumer. Consumption goods necessary for the external goods of life and health are always appropriate. Once these necessities are assured, however, appropriateness is harder to determine, although it is still helpful as a standard of judgment.

Like any practical economic analysis, the identification of appropriate or good consumption must examine circumstances and intentions. Luxury foods might be appropriate for a sickly person but inappropriate for a healthy one. A particular cut of dress may be appropriate for a young woman but inappropriate for an older one. It may be appropriate for a member of a lower social caste in a rich country to own a car, but inappropriate for a person of a similar caste in a poor country.

The internal good of consumption is determined by what men should want, not what they think they want. Gluttony and greed are insidious varieties of moral weakness that seem to attach themselves especially to the life of consumption, so our own estimations of our needs and desires for, and of our responses to, different sorts of stuff must be treated with caution. The difficulty of mastering consumption desires leads to a variety of common evils—including the traditional disorders of avarice and miserliness and the newer one of consumerism (see chapter 13).

Conventional economists dimly recognize the good of consumption, but generally ignore both the limit of satiety and the possibility of distortions of judgment. Instead, they usually make the simple assumption that more consumption is better, so that the good in this economic domain is approached as a fairly straightforward matter of quantity. This moral abdication easily slips into immorality when economists work to ensure the smooth operation of organizations that encourage consumption beyond any appropriate human measure.

Production

The internal good of production is *efficiency*, which can be thought of as the ratio of consumption goods produced to the labor and raw materials (or given capital) contributed. Greater efficiency means that more comes out of less—more consumption from less labor and given capital. Antimodern moderns have often denied that efficiency is good at all. Rather, it is castigated as a mean-spirited thing, a way to squeeze the world and one's fellow men as tightly as possible without even a hint of generosity or abundance. Besides, there is something bleak about the relentless functionality and inhuman scale of the factories and warehouses necessary for efficient production.

These objections have some validity; production efficiency is indeed a minor good that becomes unattractive when it is sought excessively. Industrial efficiency seems especially hard to separate from some economic evils. Nonetheless, it is a good. Production efficiency indirectly supports many external economic goods. Efficient food production supports life, the highest external economic good. Efficient medicine production supports health. More generally, the less labor that is needed for production, the more that is available for the pursuit of higher goods. Also, efficiency reduces the need for undignified, back-breaking labor and can ensure that appropriate consumption goods are produced.

Efficiency is a "ratio," but it is nevertheless more a rough idea than a precise measure. Conventional economists use the concept correctly but miss the imprecision. Of course, some steps on the long path from given capital to stuff can indeed be measured in a meaningful way—the step from energy to electricity, from iron ore to iron, from burned coal to airborne mercury (an undesirable step) or even from hours of human labor to the production of a car. The last is particularly tricky, since it is never appropriate to think of men solely as tools, but almost all of these measures are less precise than conventional economists assume. The conventional effort culminates in a single index of a whole economy's manufacturing "productivity," which is mostly a meaningless compilation of incommensurate relations. The conventional effort actually goes further, claiming to measure precisely the productivity of nonproductive labor, for example the labors of care or the useless bureaucratic labors that blight industrial economies. Such claims only provide support for the view that economists have dismal ideas about the good.

Both the possibility of measurement (if only for some aspects) and the ultimate reliance on given capital make the study of efficiency sound more like a hard science than most other aspects of the human study of economics. However, as an economic-social phenomenon efficiency is almost completely human. The overall level of efficiency of any particular economy depends only slightly on the configuration of given capital. The crucial consideration is the overall social approach to economic activity. In comparison to a hunter-gather economy, a more efficient agricultural economy requires a great deal more discipline in labor and a greater commitment to repetitive and regulated actions.[2] In turn, the yet more efficient industrial economy requires much greater social commitment to many types of efficiency, such as a willingness to organize labor in huge factories and networks with carefully timed tasks, a desire to explore science and develop technology, an acceptance of economic change, and an expectation that the world will always yield more from less if only we work at it.

These attributes can be thought of as coming together in what Max Weber called the "Protestant work ethic"—although dropping the denominational adjective is preferable, as the mindset has turned out to be available to followers of all creeds.[3] The work ethic is one part of the modern worldview. It is not a guide for everyone in industrial societies, but it shapes the labor lives of more than enough people to keep the industrial economy running. Development economists, who long hoped that industrial economies would spring up in preindustrial societies as soon as factories were built and "markets" were introduced, have discovered that these factors are secondary. Such societies get more prosperous exactly to the extent that they adopt the work ethic (now often, and largely misleadingly, presented in terms of "institutions"). Where the ethic is lacking, the factories quickly rot.

Perhaps because industrial efficiency makes such a bad initial impression, conventional economists were initially somewhat doubtful. Adam Smith praised the specialization of labor, and Marx praised the power of machines, but neither considered production efficiency as either a unified ethic or as especially good. Indeed, both thought that efficient production reduced laborers to dullards. Not until the beginning of the twentieth century did the research of Frederick Taylor and the practical philosophy of Henry Ford lead economists to see efficiency as a clearly internal economic good.[4] Both before and after it was identified and praised, the search for the good of production efficiency has been one of the most successful social endeavors in human history.

The utilitarian search for more from less (see chapter 8) fits in reasonably well with the internal good of production efficiency. More efficient production allows customers to pay less and laborers to work less. Conversely, the desires to work and pay less encourage and reward increased efficiency. The modern industrial economy, however, depends much less on such hedonic cravings than on the work ethic, which has more to do with stoic and Christian virtues than with anything utilitarian.

Efficiency is always an instrumental good, so its value depends entirely on the final good that is being served. The highly efficient death factories of the Nazi concentration camps provide an extreme example of this means turned to a bad end. Similarly, although infinitely less horribly, the overall good is not served by the increased efficiency that the Internet brings to the distribution of escapist video games.

Allocation

The internal good of economic allocation is *allocation justice*, the just distribution, or rules of distribution, for labor and consumption within a society. Justice is a moral virtue of the highest order—a transcendental, divine attribute, one of the four cardinal virtues of St. Thomas, found not only in society but in all sorts of physical and metaphysical harmonies. Economists should approach their little corner of justice with humility, since justice is not primarily an economic concept. Indeed, just economic allocation is so completely entwined with a broader understanding of social justice that it is almost impossible to talk meaningfully about this internal good without also considering the largely noneconomic good of social justice. Just economic allocation is primarily social, while just social allocation is only secondarily economic.

My caution in discussing just economic allocation is unusual among economists, who often dedicate a great deal of attention to the topic. Their analysis generally suffers from a series of flaws. They tend to disregard the broader social context; emphasize monetary measures rather than actual labor and consumption; focus on either the allocation of labor or the allocation of consumption goods while ignoring their interaction; attend excessively to the rules of distribution (for example, free markets or administrative procedures); focus on either individual economic relations (commutative justice) or on socially determined rules (distributive justice) without any effort at integration; and assume, naïvely, that economic equality is both easily defined and obviously desirable. All these flaws lead to debates that frequently generate more heat than light.

At the risk of falling into a philosophical pit, I will simply mention three standards of economic allocation justice that are widespread and, in my judgment, truly just. There is allocation according to contribution—to each according to his contribution to the economic good. This is one underlying principle of wage structures within an economy (other social judgments also play an important role in wage-setting). There is justice according to need—to each according to his legitimately determined needs for labor, consumption, and economic security. This is the underlying principle of the tax-and-benefits system of welfare state economies. Finally, there is justice according to social position. This is the standard that is hotly defended by parents who wish to pass on their economic status and possessions to their children, and also by young adults who expect certain education qualifications to lead to certain types of employment. It is equally hotly attacked by liberal philosophers.[5] For all three standards of justice, the actual justice of a particular society depends on how the relevant principles are applied. What has this man contributed? What does this man need? What is this man's correct social position?

Interactions with the Physical World

The good of men's relations with the physical world is responsibility. All economic organizations, whether or not they are large and sophisticated in their production techniques, are responsible for their use of the world.

There is a both a deep unity in the whole physical world, human and nonhuman, and a radical difference between the human calling, with its need to cultivate the world and its freedom to transform it, and the rest of nature, which is totally constrained by unchanging laws. Economic man has the responsible position of steward or shepherd of the nonhuman world. That responsibility leads men to use nature for the human good, but it also leads men to respect nature's integrity and beauty. In both use and respect, men are responding to the inner nature of the natural world. The two are not in fundamental conflict, but they are not always in obvious harmony. Legitimate disputes are possible about which aspect—use or respect—is more applicable in particular situations.

Advice

As I said at the beginning of this chapter, some of the internal goods of economic activity are the home territory of most conventional economists. Much of their analysis is intelligent and some of it is quite useful. Still, there are problems almost everywhere.

Efficiency is probably the most natural center of interest in the conventional approach. If the assumed good of utility is translated into the maximization of the quantity of production, and if that good is translated into the unquestioned praise of economic growth, then greater utility comes from greater production efficiency. There is now within economics a well-placed emphasis on innovation, but the typical analysis is flawed by economists' failure to recognize that coordination and regulation do more to promote efficiency than competition. Macroeconomics—which is dedicated to another aspect of production efficiency, the alignment of the monetary system with the organization of production—has been more successful, although it, too, has been distorted by a strange notion of economic rationality.

When conventional economists worry about allocation justice, their efforts are marred by inadequate philosophical study. They mostly do no more than apply some unquestioned assumption about justice. These range from one extreme, that whatever men earn in a fair economy is just, to the other, that justice has almost nothing to do with men's actions. Methodologically, the assumption that cash income provides an adequate measure of economic position leads to many ethical confusions.

Environmental economics is a newer field. In this domain, economists must rely heavily on the expertise of scientists, who in turn must rely on economists to understand the logic of industrial production. At present, many environmental economists seem to start from an antiindustrial position, trusting the most dolorous scientific estimates of the damage wrought by men's economic activity. Their proposals for the promotion of environmental responsibility usually involve less industrial activity. The historical record of successful pollution abatement suggests that a better starting position is a belief that industry can solve the environmental problems that it causes.

I would give all inward-looking economists several pieces of advice. To start with, they should reconsider most of their assumptions. The dysfunctional conventional market model of how the economy should and basically does work cannot be repaired. It must simply be jettisoned. Economists should also remember that economics is not primarily a study of impersonal forces, but of persons. If the internal goods of labor and consumption were given due regard, there would be much less dismal advice. Renewed attention to men rather than things should lead economists upward towards the greater, external economic goods. Finally, professional economists should remember that there are many other ways for an economy to be bad other than through inefficient production, unjust allocation, or environmental destruction. To these economic evils I now turn.

11

Evil in Economics

Evil is a philosophical mystery and an economic reality. The reality is readily recognizable—greedy consumers, lazy workers, rapacious and heartless corporations, corrupt governments. The philosophy is, well, mysterious.[1] As seems so often to be the case, the pseudo-amorality of conventional economics makes the job harder for the human economist, forcing him to disentangle a philosophical mess. It would be trouble enough to replace supposedly nonmoral terms such as "imperfect," "irrational," and "inefficient" with what they actually mean in the necessarily moral human understanding—"bad" and "evil." That clarification, however, is only a first step, as it does not deal with the distorted morality of the market model. The enthusiasm for the motivation of self-interest brings that model perilously close to calling evil good.

This chapter aims to provide a quick reeducation in applied moral philosophy. I have no intention of musing on the pure philosophical question of just what evil really is. For economic purposes, it is enough to accept only two things—that in the moral realm whatever is not good is bad (or evil), and that men do evil when their moral weakness distorts their understanding of the good. For the record, however, I should say that this discussion is supposed to be compatible with the Augustinian-Thomistic understanding that evil does not really exist in itself but is only a sort of shorthand term for the moral and ontological vacuum that is created by the absence of good.

Good and Evil

Men have evil desires and do bad things. But men always want to do the good. The unending coexistence of the universal will to the good and the perpetual temptation of the bad (in this life, in any case) is part of the mystery of evil. The persistence of evil may be inexplicable in theory (at least without heavy doses of theology), but it is unavoidable in practice. It marks economics as it marks all human activity.

Because men do not desire evil for the sake of evil but for the sake of an ill-considered or misunderstood good, the spread of evil is often insidious. Economic evils creep in behind good intentions and in moments of intellectual, emotional, or spiritual weakness. Here are some examples. Corporate leaders rarely notice that they are becoming drunk with power or that they are less competent than their sycophantic aides tell them they are. Managers who decide to sell infant formula may notice that the product is beneficial for many babies but ignore the possibility that it harms more babies than it helps. Rich people often neglect to help poor people who can and should be helped, while poor people neglect to help themselves, a shared neglect that amounts to cooperation in the subtle evils of indifference and inaction.

Evil is alluring as well as subtle. The "glamour of evil" is found when men crave morally destructive luxury, physically destructive drugs, or the excitement and defiant autonomy of criminal labor.

Evil is all too often too closely entwined with the good. The tie is so close in economic matters that economic evils must sometimes be tolerated for the sake of greater, noneconomic goods. An argument along these lines used to be provided as a justification for preindustrial slavery—without it, it was said, great spiritual and artistic works would not be possible. Slavery has disappeared in industrial economies, but it has been replaced by new sorts of labor evil, most notably the alienating jobs apparently required for production efficiency. Factories cannot function and stores cannot be stocked without some tedious labor (or so it seems; no one has ever really tried to eliminate it). The evil of labor alienation must be set against the good of efficient production. Similarly, the evils of environmental depredation must be set against the good of the consumption goods produced by the humanization of nature.

Economic evil is often as much social as individual. To be sure, vice, like virtue, is ultimately personal, but social structures, which should support and protect the good, sometimes work as "structures of sin," corrupting instead of protecting.[2] The social acceptance of unnecessarily cruel conditions for labor is always structurally sinful. More subtly, the social protection of "private property" is structurally sinful when such property "rights" help to perpetuate unnecessary and absolute poverty. Structures of sin can also arise when evils are condemned only halfheartedly, as in the common response to illegal drugs—easy money for the sellers and infrequent penalties for buyers and sellers alike.

How Bad Are We Really?

How easily do men slip away from the good? This question, hotly disputed by philosophers and theologians, is crucial for the determination of economic policy.[3] If men are very weak, then they will need numerous social structures to provide economic miscreants with firm deterrents and fearsome punishments. Conversely, if men are hardly weak at all, then social structures will need to provide nothing harsher than gentle discouragement and mild correction.

One extreme view is that men are bad by nature. They seek only to get their own way with no thought for virtue. Utilitarians believe something like this, although they are interested only in pleasure or utility, a particularly drab sort of willfulness. (Of course, they also do not consider this self-concern actually to be bad.) This extreme view is wrong. Virtue and goodness, not evil and selfishness, are at the center of men's moral condition. Men generally want good things, and they only want bad things because they mistake them for the good. The great accomplishments of industry would be impossible if men were cutthroat by nature. Cities and factories require numerous large, enthusiastic, and generous organizations in which all members work together for good goals. Such communities would not function unless trust and economic goodwill predominated. These virtues often fail here and there, but these local difficulties only show that men are good but weak, not that that they are not good at all.

At the other extreme is the utopian claim that men are not really weak at all; it is only that their virtuous nature has sadly been corrupted by the injustices of society. Eliminate the injustice and their natural virtue will once again show through. Since Rousseau first blamed all social difficulties on the institution of property, the social problem has often been considered primarily economic. Most notably, Marx blamed class selfishness, which would disappear when the Communist economy arrived. Other economic utopians offer different purifying reforms—a libertarian minimization of government, land reform, the return of small businesses, better management practices. The utopian view of human nature is just as wrong as its opposite. Men are morally weak; any hope of eliminating this weakness (at least in this life) will prove futile. The elimination of sin is a task for redemptive religion, not social policy.

The rejection of the two extremes leaves a broad middle ground of susceptibility to evil. Men seem to fill it all up. Some men seem extremely good, some extremely bad, and some everything in between. Philosophers can debate where the weighted average is found in human nature, to what extent nurture can change that average, and whether societies have as broad a moral range as individuals. The economist needs only to know that the potential for economic evil lurks in all men, no matter how virtuous, and in all societies, no matter how well organized.

Dealing with Evil

The acceptance of the persistence of evil does not imply that the struggle against it is pointless. It implies the contrary—goodness is constantly under threat, so it must be protected energetically. In economics as in any other human endeavor, there are basically only two alternatives in the battle against evil: vigilant defense and ignominious retreat.

The insidious nature of evil makes the defense hard work. The elimination of one evil all too often seems to allow another to thrive. The recent history of the response to the notion of property provides a good example. In the nineteenth century, radical socialists observed, correctly, that property was used in evil ways by the rich to exploit the poor and to frustrate the common good. They claimed, with substantially less accuracy, that in history and in theory "property is theft." They called, disastrously, for the abolition of "private" property in favor of universal non-ownership. In Communist Russia, a property-free society was established. The results were bad in almost every way, including the domination of all economic activity by an unjust clique.

On the other hand, nineteenth-century liberal thinkers theorized, correctly, that the existence of property supports personal dignity. They claimed to observe, with much less accuracy, that "private property" was the source of economic progress and contentment. They called, foolishly, for the elimination of all government property and the subordination of government interests to the claims of private property. The liberals' intellectual descendents briefly held sway in postcommunist Russia. Their attempt to establish a society with strong property rights and a weak government led to the domination of all economic activity by new and possibly even more unjust cliques.

Both the socialists and the liberals underestimated the persistence of evil. No type of possessive relationship between men and things—not private property, not communal property, not government property, not no-property—can eliminate men's greed and irresponsibility. Rather than search for a complete cure, it is best to look for the most effective techniques of countering temptation and abuse. A single system is likely to be less effective than a hodgepodge. Such a pluralistic therapy can be seen in the wide variety of property relations found in contemporary welfare states—private, semipublic, corporate, inherited, taxed, expropriated, entailed, contracted, and so forth.

Once the economist unburdens himself of belief in the possibility of a total victory over economic evil, he should be a very effective strategist in the fight against it. His analysis of the underlying workings of different economic organizations should help clarify the deep sources of evil. His knowledge of history and of possible alternative arrangements should give him helpful ideas about reform.

Of course, specific decisions will still be difficult. For example, the construction of a large dam brings substantial benefits—improved irrigation leading to increased food production, the generation of beneficial electricity, the reduction of devastation from seasonal flooding, and the satisfaction of taming the forces of nature. It also brings substantial evils—accidental deaths during construction, the destruction of animal habitats and natural beauty, the disruption of flooded communities, the eventual silting of the dammed river. Other evils, most notably the misuse of the dam's economic benefits, are not necessary but may be difficult to avoid. Since these goods and evils are not commensurate, they cannot simply be set against one another. Indeed, there can never be a simple rule for deciding whether to build a particular dam.

At least dam planners can benefit from extensive historical evidence and scientific knowledge. Much less aid is available for most economic decisions, both small and large. For example, many residents of industrial societies agonize about their careers. Some of the questions that are asked, or should be asked, relate to evils that are possible but far from certain. Will this career path make me greedy? Will it distract me from my responsibilities to my family and community? Will it eventually make me a collaborator in an evil economic activity? The evidence required to answer such questions is simply not available.

False consciousness can aggravate the problem. A man may not feel greedy or hostile when he desires greater consumption rewards for himself. On the contrary, he may well feel that he is fighting against an injustice—pay that does not reflect his real contributions. In practice, however, in an economic organization with a fixed supply of consumption goods (a reasonable simplification of normal reality) more for one inevitably means less for another. The subjectively nongreedy desire for greater consumption can inadvertently but objectively be equivalent to an evil desire to make others poorer.

The Fallacy of Self-Interest

When the devious persistence of evil is fully considered, the conventional economists' view that self-interest is a sound basis for economic organization seems either evil or naïve. Which of the two it is depends on how self-interest is defined.

The evil praise of self-interest is based on a crude belief that it is legitimate for me to pursue my goals without any respect for my neighbor's pursuit of his. If that is self-interest, then men are not actually very self-interested. Such completely selfish men would not and could not come together to form any sort of society, but would be stuck in the war of all against all that Hobbes postulated as men's state of nature.[4]

The problem of how such brutes could become civilized hardly bothered Hobbes, but at least he believed that a strong government was necessary to keep men's destructiveness in check. Crude economists who want to justify weak government and who see the market as a constant struggle in which only the fittest survive do not give the organizational question much thought. They simply explain cooperation and community as the result of humans' cunning calculations of their ultimate selfish advantage.[5] These calculations may be hidden by some socially approved pieties, but acts motivated solely by genuine concern for the good of others are considered abnormal. And so they would be, if victory in the market struggle actually did require unremitting dedication to crude self-interest—a belief that "greed is good."[6] This argument for the good of selfishness is almost never presented in moral terms. That avoidance is not surprising, as a translation into moral terms leads to an endorsement of evil—the bad means of selfishness are recommended as the best way to obtain the good ends of prosperity.

It is perhaps worth saying one more time that the conventional claim that the economy is based on selfishness is simply nonsensical. Crude self-interest is an obstacle to, not a support for, economic success. Trust makes possible specialized labor, shared technology, and commerce with strangers. Industrial economies rely on blind trust, both in the knowledge of the thousands of experts who develop technologies and in the goodwill of the millions of people involved in the long chains of production.

The naïve praise of self-interest is based on a more sophisticated and less objectionable definition. Self-interest is a moral sentiment (to use the vocabulary of Adam Smith) that combines good and evil. It is good in its striving for excellence, its demand for just rewards, and its almost instinctively generous desire to share the benefits of knowledge or experience. It is bad in its selfishness and destructive greed. In Smith's theory, in a well-ordered society the good aspects of everyone's self-interest can flourish while the bad aspects of each individual's self-interest can be thwarted without too much effort. The social process is almost automatic, working like an "invisible hand."[7] As long as no single man or organization is allowed to get too powerful, each is prevented from realizing his own evil intentions by the contrary greediness of all the others.

While less objectionable, this proposed social mechanism is unrealistic. Evil is much too insidious to be warded off simply by other evils. Rather, the fight against evil requires a continuous effort to be good. Without a social effort to combat the evils of selfishness, one set of self-interests will always gain a quite visible upper hand. Markets, no matter how perfect, cannot keep economic evil in check. Only a wide variety of intentionally moral rules, structures, and enforcement mechanisms can do that. Even conventional economists implicitly admit as much in their recognition of the ubiquity of "market imperfections."

Each of these rules, structures, and mechanisms has a target, or perhaps several targets—particular distortions of the good. The next chapter provides a list of these economic evils.

12

Economic Evils in the World

It is more difficult to order evils than goods. All goods point towards a single unity, the transcendental Good, while evils deviate from the good in many different directions. Goodness goes together with reason, which is inherently ordered, while evils by their nature are irrational and disordered. Evils tend to intoxicate those who get too close, so students of evil easily lose their objectivity. A good is as good as it is, while the badness of an evil has two dimensions—the goodness of the negated good and the distance from that good. These difficulties do not make a hierarchy of internal economic evils impossible, but I prefer not to make the effort. What follows is a more modest arrangement, a simple list of internal economic evils. The order was chosen for narrative ease and does not imply either increasing or decreasing magnitude.

Like economic goods, economic evils can be divided into external and internal. External evils, the subject of this chapter, are those which are not directly economic but are broader evils created by excessive, inadequate, or misdirected attention to economic activity. Internal evils, the poor arrangement of the various types of economic activity, will be discussed in the next chapter. This chapter separation maintains the book's symmetry, but the division between external and internal is less clear for evils than it is for goods.

Underestimation

Since economic activity has a significant role to play in the human search for the good, the failure to recognize and cultivate sufficiently economic contributions is an evil. It occurs when too little time or effort is dedicated to worthy economic activity, when economic excellence receives too meager social rewards, and when economic goods are abandoned for the sake of lesser noneconomic goods. Underestimation can affect everything economic—the whole complex of labor, consumption, production, allocation, and man-nature relations. It can also be partial, affecting only particular corners or domains of the economy.

Underestimation can take many forms. When men act as if the economic goods of life and health were worth less than arbitrary social traditions or religious rituals, the great good of life is undervalued. When the fear of social discontent leads to social rules that discourage the poor from seeking prosperity, the goods of human knowledge and experience are insulted. When the search for otherworldly enlightenment is considered to be in direct opposition to the search for daily bread, the dignity of labor is rejected.

Historically, economic underestimation was ubiquitous before the development of industrial economies. We now know that the poor were always and everywhere condemned unnecessarily to wretchedness, and that the many potential goods which can be promoted by a better organization of economic activity—knowledge, community, and beauty—were left almost completely unexplored. Of course, most of the men who perpetrated this evil cannot exactly be held responsible. Before the coming of the modern worldview, the potential good of economic activity was unknown and unsuspected. To accuse men of economic neglect for failing to try to do something that they thought—reasonably enough, in the prevailing intellectual and cultural climate—to be impossible is anachronistic. Just as a doctor working any time before 1945 could not be blamed for not prescribing antibiotics, a premodern society should not be blamed for its collective lack of technological competence. Perhaps Christians should have known that the doctrine of the Incarnation—God's endorsement of the full gamut of human experience—held a latent praise for the application of human ingenuity to labor and consumption. In practice, however, this doctrinal development was a response to the discovery, in large part made by unenthusiastic Christians or atheists, of the potential scope of the economic good.[1]

The evil of economic underestimation has not been eliminated, despite the global spread of industry and greatly increased interest in prosperity. Any individual can neglect the work ethic for no good reason or can unreasonably fail to promote or profit from some aspect of the economic good. As a social phenomenon, underestimation is most obvious in the widespread indifference to the persistence of absolute poverty. In some countries, the slow resolution of the economic problem could perhaps be motivated by a virtuous concern for the preservation of greater noneconomic goods—the real goods of prosperity do seem to arrive along with such modern evils as family breakdown, social alienation, and the loss of faith. But that is a generous interpretation.

Overestimation

The economic evil of overestimation occurs when the contribution of economic activity to the good is thought to be higher than it really can be. This evil can take the form of unrealistically high expectations about the external goods that economic activity can provide. It can also be related to the internal goods of economic activity in the form of an unjustifiable dedication of time and energy to their attainment.

When it is believed that prosperity is potent enough that in some way it can trick death and relieve men of its terrors, then the genuine goods of prosperity have been fatally corrupted by exaggeration. Such a false belief does not need consciously to be fully accepted in order to be dangerous. It merely needs to be adopted, however unconsciously, as a guide to action. When the marks of prosperity are deemed, either in words or in deeds, to be more important than the marks of virtue, prosperity serves to undermine rather than to support the good social and ethical order. When the search for prosperity is confused with the search for true happiness, then prosperity turns men away from their proper goals.

These signs of an exaggerated valuation of economic activity are hardly a modern creation, but they seem especially relevant to, even prevalent in, the socioeconomic organization of industrial societies. The increased importance of economic goals in the modern world has been a theme of this book from the first chapter. Some of that increase is a merited correction of the preindustrial underestimation, but there seems to have been an overcorrection. Too much is expected from labor and consumption, too many higher human goods are sacrificed for the sake of comforts and internal economic goods, too many questions of social policy and personal conduct are analyzed in shallow economic terms. It seems that the shift to the modern worldview has gradually led to a shift from an insufficient to an excessive interest in economic objectives.

In both the premodern and modern periods, intellectuals and cultural leaders have generally been on the wrong side of this debate. Most premodern thinkers did not push for greater prosperity, but warned that men and societies should not become too attached to the goods brought through labor and consumption. Although it took some time for modern thinkers fully to endorse the economic agenda, the conversion is now complete. Mainstream contemporary thinkers may vaguely lament the "materialism" of modern society, but they rarely call for more poverty or even for spiritual crusades against an excessive interest in worldly matters. Rather, they generally urge dilatory governments and social leaders to work harder at the promotion of prosperity, even in rich super-satiated economies.

To a Hegelian, the historical shift in the valuation of economic activity—from underestimation to exaggeration—looks like a move from an erroneous premodern thesis to a slightly less erroneous modern antithesis.[2] The next step should be the resolution of these contrary errors in a synthesis—a more correct valuation of economic activity within society. That prediction may eventually come true, but such a happy day is a long way away. The history of industrial prosperity is far too short, and the analysis of its goods has been far too skimpy, to suggest that a sure middle way between the two evils of false valuation is in the offing.

False valuation, in the form of both under- and overestimation, is a broad error. All but one of the other economic evils on this list can be considered, at least in part, as an example or effect of some sort of false valuation. Only destruction stems almost entirely from another, particularly grim, part of human nature.

Greed

Greed is the craving for more than is appropriate. It is not necessarily economic but rather extends to all the many ways in which a selfish understanding of needs and desires cuts men off from the human community and from their natural communion with the divine. Humans can be greedy about political or military power, sexual pleasure, social status, professional reputation, personal popularity, holiness—indeed about pretty much everything that we put our minds to.

Economic greed is typical, perhaps even archetypical, of the vice. It seems to be especially difficult to moderate economic desires, especially our desire for the stuff of consumption. The greed for land and financial assets is also strikingly widespread, although it is as much social as directly economic. A man is greedy when he wants more stuff or property than he can justly be allocated ("He is so greedy that he would steal from a baby"). He is greedy when he considers the acquisition of this stuff a good that justifies spurning other, higher goods ("He would lie and cheat, even sell his grandmother, to buy that car"). He is greedy when he places comfort, the lowest of the external economic goods, above higher economic goods ("She'd sacrifice good care for her baby rather than give up on buying that house"). He is greedy when he thinks too much or wrongly about the goods of consumption ("For him, everything is a matter of money").

Greed is also common in labor, although perhaps less obvious. It takes the form of disproportionate ambition ("I don't care if I deserve the promotion, I want it anyway"). It lurks in the desire to gain something from labor that labor cannot offer ("I want my job to make me happy"). It emerges in the jealousy of the labor of others ("If only I had his job"). It underlies the desire to do less than is expected ("The boss will never notice if I don't do this") or to ask for more esteem than is deserved ("The boss doesn't appreciate me"). Greed also finds a home in the relations between labor and consumption. When people think they are underpaid, it is often because they unjustly value their labor more highly than that of their neighbors.

In general, greed is an especially insidious vice. The violent or lustful man may be unable to restrain himself, but usually, perhaps some time after the fact, he can admit that he has done something wrong. In comparison, men rarely feel greedy—before, during, or after the fact.[3] Their greedy desires almost always seem reasonable and just. "I just want—a good life, a quiet life, what my neighbors have, recognition for what I have done, a fair share, a tiny bit more, to be comfortable, to take care of myself, something worthy of what I have to offer. . . ." Economic greed does not escape this self-delusion. The resident of a large house tends not to notice the many smaller houses in his neighborhood, only the few bigger ones. A man who has a good job frequently does not concern himself with the many worse jobs, only with the few better ones. A consumer rarely thinks that his desire for "just a few" more goods might be harmful to anyone.

The situation is similar from a social perspective. In discussions of the global distribution of economic goods, the rich fiercely resist any suggestion that they are in some way greedy, but no more vehemently than the poor dismiss the suggestion that greed plays a part in their desire for nearly instant equalization. Similarly, advertising has its value, but when a "special price" or "more for your money" is offered, greed is almost always present. Shopping centers offer convenience and choice, but the abundance easily slips into an environment of greedy hysteria. Both personally and socially, the self-righteous denial of the presence and dangers of greed only encourages greed's further development.

Absolute Poverty

Among conventional economists, the evil of poverty is almost always taken for granted. Its undesirability is considered so great that almost any other sort of economic disorder—pollution, income disparity, harsh labor conditions—is frequently excused as an unavoidable byproduct of the all-consuming fight against poverty. Unfortunately, the conventional definition of poverty is generally too rough to be morally useful.[4] There is a tremendous moral difference between absolute poverty (not having enough stuff to support the basic external goods of life and health) and relative poverty (not having as much stuff as some neighbors).

Absolute poverty is an evil for everyone involved—those who suffer it, to be sure, but also for those who actively promote it or passively countenance it. It will be discussed in the discussion of internal economic evils (chapter 13) as a variety of inappropriate consumption.

Relative Poverty

As a social category, relative poverty seems to be inevitable. Both "the poor" and "the rich" are socially meaningful groups in almost every society. In all societies, almost everyone has, and is aware of having, less stuff than someone else. The relationships of relative poverty and relative wealth are frequently central to the social order. Of course, apparent inevitability does not imply goodness—murders and hatred are also ubiquitous but are quite clearly evil. Still, relative poverty is not evil in the same absolute way as absolute poverty. The moral value of any particular example of relative poverty depends on many factors: facts—how much stuff I actually have, relative to what my neighbor has; value—what goods I am deprived of by relative poverty; feelings—how poor that deprivation makes me feel; and social values—what counts as poor and what poverty counts for in a society.

The facts, the objective content of relative poverty, change along with the economic background, in particular with the wealth available to the rich. Where only the rich attend any school, the poor are those who remain uneducated. Where everyone goes to school but only the rich attend universities, the poor are those with only secondary educations. Where good housing is scarce, the poor live in hovels. Where housing is more plentiful, the poor lack some token of housing status, perhaps private bedrooms or a second bathroom. For the last two centuries, the direction of change in the objective content of relative poverty in industrial countries has been uniform—the poor have been getting richer, so much so that the industrial poor now enjoy consumption satiety for many important categories of stuff.

One of the motivations for the creation of welfare states was the desire to reduce the scope of relative poverty. In rich societies, it is now generally accepted that everyone should have access to all of the most valuable goods of prosperity—the stuff necessary for survival, basic health care, education and access to the roads, telephones, and the other grids of the modern economy. As prosperity increases, the list of things thought to merit universal availability lengthens. It now includes not only telephones but electricity, televisions, broadband Internet, and, in Europe, lengthy paid holidays. In addition, legally guaranteed minimum wages, socially accepted employment protection and "redistributive" income and estate taxes ensure that the poor are not too poor and the rich not too rich.

Welfare policies have worked remarkably well. Within rich societies, they have eliminated almost all the vestiges of absolute poverty, except perhaps among the socially or legally marginalized. They have also sharply reduced the objective differences between the relatively poor and the relatively rich. In a preindustrial society, the rich man had servants and education while the poor man lived in ignorant squalor. In a contemporary rich society, the rich man drives a new car that rarely breaks down while the poor man has to get by with an old clunker.

What neither the welfare state nor the resolution of the economic problem has managed to do is eliminate relative poverty. Objectively, the consumption desires of the poor may in affluent communities be almost as sated as those of the rich, but the "almost" is subjectively and socially significant. The poor still feel poor and are considered to be so. The idea that the lack of a second house or the inability to travel regularly to other continents would qualify someone for relative poverty is bizarre by historical standards, but it is a social fact in contemporary economies.[5]

Relative poverty is coextensive with social inferiority in every society, but in premodern societies that inferiority was usually accepted as almost incontrovertible, a socioeconomic status that was inherited and could only be changed by good fortune or great effort. (That statement is, of course, a simplification or even an idealization.) In modern societies, however, both relative poverty and relative wealth have lost their inevitability. The relatively poor often strive to improve their relative position, while the rich often strive to maintain or increase theirs. The modern fight against relative poverty seems to be morally unhelpful. Both rich and poor too often take meaningless jobs for the sake of higher pay. Both spend recklessly for the sake of having some status-laden consumption goods. Both too often snub the good of the family, community, or church for the sake of climbing, or maintaining their position on, the socioeconomic hierarchy. Both are too often persuaded that they "simply must" live in a certain neighborhood, drive a certain sort of car, or wear clothes with a certain label.

An economist can easily recognize and regret the moral damage of the socioeconomic jostling in socially fluid modern societies, but he lacks the intellectual tools required to evaluate fully any particular example of relative poverty. That task requires the combined effort of moralists, sociologists, and social philosophers.

I would suggest that Christianity is a good source for a more complete moral teaching on the goods and evils of wealth and poverty. Conventional economists, who wish to drag men down to their own dismal morality, have rejected the old insights, but the tradition of seeing wealth in poverty and poverty in wealth has lost none of its wisdom.

The Christian sees moral evils on both sides of the socioeconomic divide. For the relatively poor, there is the psychological risk that a subjective sense of deprivation will incite an unmerited feeling of personal inferiority and bitter desires for more stuff. There is also the sociological risk that relative poverty will cut off the relatively poor from full participation in the goods of community. The moral dangers are probably greater for the relatively rich and include the temptation to pride and to an overvaluation of economic advantage. In other words, the rich all too easily believe that their superior economic position gives them a privileged position with God and a spiritual superiority over their poorer neighbors. Sociologically, the communities of the rich tend to be much more closed than the communities of the poor. In addition, the rich frequently use their wealth to exploit the labor of the poor.

From the Christian perspective, the most potent remedies for the evils of both relative poverty and relative wealth are spiritual. The rich should learn that material wealth is often accompanied by spiritual poverty. They should interpret their relative advantage as a call for greater generosity to the poor and for service to the community and the divine. Relative wealth should be a means to make neighborly love more concrete and to reinforce men's mutual responsibility. The poor should be encouraged by the spiritual riches of poverty. A willing acceptance of poverty leads to a virtuous dependence on neighborly love and divine providence; it allows freedom from the worldly cares that tend to accompany wealth; it should awaken the conscience and solidarity of the rich; and it models the Christ-like self-emptying necessary for the totally God-dependent Christian mission. In theory, the Christian call for the rich to relieve poverty may conflict with the call for the poor to accept it. In practice, however, men's moral weakness will keep that conflict from becoming a socioeconomic problem. There will always be plenty for the rich to forsake and plenty for the poor to accept.[6]

Ugliness

Just as economic activity can and until very recently generally has made the world more beautiful, it can (but should not) make it uglier. The struggle to ensure that economic activity not cause uglification was not particularly difficult in preindustrial economies. The production of stuff could never involve much more than scratching the surface of the earth, and there was little to be gained, even in the purely economic domain, by the sacrifice of beauty for the sake of efficiency, simply because the available efficiency was so limited.

The struggle is much more difficult in industrial economies. It is often "costly" in terms of labor or materials to build beauty into mass production. It seems much easier to suggest that efficiency has its own beauty—the "less is more" of modern architecture and the Bauhaus lines of modern design. In addition, the startling and the shocking are often more seductive than the beautiful, at least at first. A glance at a shopping center or a contemporary TV commercial suggests that the substitution of attention-getting for beauty is as common in economic activity as it is in other parts of modern culture.

This attack on the beautiful is an example of the misdirection of economic activity. Like any transcendental good, the beautiful would only be pursued more avidly if it were correctly valued. The willingness to sacrifice it for the sake of the internal good of production efficiency and of trivial additions to the level of comfort shows so great an imbalance relative to the hierarchy of human goods as to almost constitute a preference for evil over good.[7]

Alienation

Economic activity should strengthen the human community. When it works in the opposite direction, it creates an economic evil. The traditional economic word for the evil of community-weakening is alienation. It was first used in this sense by Marx, who argued that if factories were not the property of the workers, they necessarily separated, or alienated, the laborers from the full fruits of their labor. This alienation was embodied in the impersonal and exploitative money ties of wages and prices, the "cash nexus." While many of the details of Marx's theory are doubtful and some are dead wrong, he was onto something. Working for someone else's money is less personal—and in some way less satisfying—than working your own land to produce your own consumption stuff. Contractual employment relations do not sever completely the close ontological tie between labor and consumption, but they do obscure it.[8]

Since the time of Marx, labor and consumption in industrial societies have become much more widely separated. The processes of production are now so complex and mechanized that most workers find their labor-lives almost completely separated from their consumption-lives. Furthermore, consumption goods have become so sophisticated and so well finished that consumers rarely feel any connection to the laborers who made them. The increasing use of money is probably alienating in itself. The extensive tax-benefit system, which keeps wages and prices far apart, and a speculative financial system, which creates monetary gains and losses out of thin air, add more alienation.

Yet Marx's separation of labor from consumption is only one type of modern economic alienation. Three others are probably more significant.

The first is the draining of meaning from much labor in industrial societies. Instrumentally neutral labor, which both feels and is meaningless, is distinctly modern (more on this in chapter 15). Then there are modern jobs that have a good purpose which is hidden from the workers. A man toiling in a factory may feel like no more than a cog in a gigantic and uncaring machine, even if his labor actually supports some good. Other types of labor serve the good and are felt to be good by the laborers but are dismissed as nearly meaningless by society. Mothers, along with other unpaid and poorly paid caregivers, are in this alienating social position.

Next is the separation of labor from all other aspects of life. This process starts in childhood, when the labor of schoolwork almost always takes place in isolation from families and often from friends. Later, employees find their jobs totally detached from their lives in the home, neighborhood, and church. The demands of quite meaningless professional careers often include marriage-breaking hours, family-damaging moves around the world, and close personal relations based on narrow and unimportant shared interests.

Finally, industrial mass consumption is also alienating. This idea was already hinted at in the description of the dazed indifference that many consumers feel in the face of the cornucopia of modern supermarkets. That alienated response is not limited to well-stocked stores. It can also be felt at home, where standardized products are felt to come out of nowhere and to have no obvious connection with, or meaning for, the consumer. One of the principal purposes of advertising is to reduce or gloss over this consumption dullness.[9] Advertisements can achieve some modest successes—such as the brief excitement stimulated in response to genuine or claimed novelty and the shallow meaning that some brands seem to accrue—but consumption alienation never seems to be far away.

Marx, who thought everything was economic, believed that economic alienation would inevitably cause social collapse. His proposed solution was communism, which was to be a property-free, nonalienating way of organizing economic relations.[10] In a curious irony, the Marxist evaluation of the danger of alienation has been shared by some of the most virulent anti-Marxists, the antimodern moderns. These thinkers, however, do not propose to put factory workers in control, but to demolish the factories and return workers to a largely agrarian, family-based preindustrial economy. The proposed proletarian and agrarian revolutions differ in many ways, but both start from the same basic fear, that economic alienation is a severe enough problem to justify radical changes in most current economic structures.

That fear is based on an incomplete vision of the modern economy. Certainly, economic alienation is an evil because it takes away human meaning and fractures communities. This evil may even be an inevitable byproduct of the efficiency and complexity of industrial economies. In that case, the evil of industrial alienation must be evaluated along with the corresponding goods—the abundance of life, health, knowledge, community, and so forth that industrial economies have supported. From that broader perspective, economic alienation looks like a much less serious problem. In addition, the relatively minor role of economic activity in men's search for the good suggests that even a highly alienating economy is no more than a minor irritant to that search, as long as the higher aspirations—truth, goodness, love, the divine—are well served.

Even if industrial alienation cannot be avoided fully and even if it is not a great evil, it remains an evil that should be resisted. The techniques of resistance are not obvious, but injecting meaning into industrial practices and organizations should be possible. Already, the tribal loyalty found in many corporations offers a crude sort of meaning to both employees and customers. Finding other sorts of nonalienating economic communities that do not demand unacceptable sacrifices of economic goods should be possible.

Destruction

Economic activity makes the world more human. That humanization is supposed to serve the goodness of human nature. Humans, however, are not merely good. They are good but weak. Economic activity can support men's weakness with the same effectiveness that it supports the good. The economic contribution to greed has already been mentioned. The economic contributions to war and destruction are more indirect—men are greedy in their economic activity while they are destructive through it—but more evil.

The skill of labor and the efficiency of production can be turned against others. It is a simple matter. Instead of employing young men to farm, work in factories, and build cathedrals, they can be sent off to kill other young men and to destroy as much as possible of their neighbors' farms, factories, and cathedrals. The result is certainly human, all too human. Consumption is disrupted, men are killed, the human world is filled with ruins. There may be something noble and glorious about the sacrifices of war—that was the nearly unanimous judgment of premodern thinkers and remains a common view.

The economist must see things differently. Destruction is directly opposed to all external economic goods. It is a drain on prosperity, not only in the ravaging of crops, houses, and productive hard capital, but also in the deviation of labor from more constructive purposes. Victory in war does not change that judgment, even if the victor suffers little economic damage. The human economist must recognize the equal dignity of all men, so he has to consider victors and losers indifferently. In total, war always destroys.

Modern industry has had the same magnifying effect on destruction that it has had on most economic goods. Almost exactly the same tools—technology, organization, trust—that have been used to solve the economic problem can be used to create destruction on a scale that is equally unprecedented. Modern explosives have made destruction almost effortless, and nuclear weapons have created an entirely new dimension of potential damage. It is technically possible that all the economic goods supported by industry will be swept away by the destruction made possible by that same industry.

Will this technical possibility be realized? Optimists have long argued that prosperity promotes peace because richer societies have more economic goods to lose in war, while the poor should realize that destructive labor mitigates against their own potential prosperity. The limited importance of economic goods suggests that this hope is misplaced. The desire for war comes from aspects of human nature that are quite far from the economic realm. It was glory, not plunder, that motivated most premodern wars. If great modern wars are to be avoided, the brake will not come from the joys of prosperity, but from a strong desire for peace.

One peculiar caveat to this economic condemnation of destruction was already mentioned in chapter 9. The direct economic result of war is always poverty, but the indirect results can be economically more desirable. Some of the technologies of destruction can later be converted to serve the economic good. The desperation of warfare, especially of modern warfare, can encourage an energy and openness that stimulate economic innovation. The economic reconstruction of a war-damaged or war-destroyed territory is often an opportunity for improvement, as has been shown in Germany, Japan, and Korea in the last sixty years.[11]

All these external economic evils need to be kept in perspective. They are never desired—as with all human activity, labor and consumption always aim at the good. Many of them are relatively minor, as when men are a little bit greedy or respond churlishly to relative poverty. Even when they are serious, as in both the preindustrial undervaluation of economic activity and the industrial overexpectation of economic joys, the evils are often committed as much out of ignorance and mistaken idealism as out of deep moral corruption. The only economic evil that deserves unremitting and serious condemnation is the conversion of industrial ability to destruction.

As far as these external economic evils are concerned, the economy itself—a society's arrangements of labor, consumption, production, and allocation—is more of a means than a direct cause. Societies and individuals determine their economic valuations and orientations as part of the broad human effort to find the good. Economic activity plays only a supporting role in that drama, for evils as well as for goods. Economic failures should be blamed primarily on social structures and individual values that provide inadequate economic guidance. The fight against external economic evils will certainly include changes in economic behavior, but the main battle will be fought elsewhere, in the effort to establish an appropriate place for labor and consumption in each individual's life and in the organization of society.

Internal economic evils are different. They can be addressed entirely by changing the way the economy works. It is to these that I now turn.

13

Economic Evils in the Economy

Evils may be harder to order than goods, but they are often easier to identify. The good, after all, is ideal and transcendental, while evils are all too present in the here and now. Internal economic evils are especially obvious because they confront men in their everyday lives. Everyone knows about hunger, bad jobs, and all sorts of stupid economic arrangements. There is no point in simply restating the obvious, so in the following discussion I try to provide some philosophical depth. By using the internal economic goods of chapter 10 as a template, I hope to keep the evils solidly linked to the goods that they distort.

The pairing with the internal goods is asymmetrical. While the internal economic goods were all judged to make relatively minor contributions to men's good, some of the internal evils—particularly absolute poverty and extremely undignified labor—are grave insults to human dignity. This imbalance is a manifestation of the mystery of evil. It is puzzling but true that the lack of a relatively minor good can be a major evil.

A purist might complain that most of the internal evils really belong in the preceding chapter. They look like manifestations, in the purely economic domain, of the misevaluation of economic activity, the first three items in the list of external economic evils. My justification for the separation is that in that chapter I was particularly interested in the social effects of a misevaluation of economic activity, while in this one I am dealing with the directly economic effects—especially on labor and consumption—of various misevaluations. Still, the division between external and internal is admittedly less clear for evils than it is for goods.

Undignified Labor

The internal good of labor is found in the dignity of the laborer (see chapter 10). The internal evil is the deprivation of that dignity. It takes various forms. Labor should be a source of life, but men can be worked to death. Labor should help people find the fullness of life, but the forced labor of children and the overwhelming labor of adults can take away the very possibility of human development. Prostitution and crime are demeaning because they violate moral laws, violations that do more damage to men's dignity than any sort of consumption rewards, social position, or subjective satisfaction can repair. Selling useless goods and performing repetitive and monotonous tasks are more insidiously demeaning, but intellectual gifts should not be stunted, misused, or turned from the good.

The lack of dignity in labor can be more social or subjective than objective. For example, most societies consider it undignified for members of a privileged social group to labor at menial tasks, and many consider it undignified for the nonprivileged to take on too elevated labor. Individuals often have precise subjective standards of dignity for their own labor. Moral and social philosophers can debate how seriously these slights should be taken. Possible answers range from "ignore these imaginary wrongs" to "the judgments are more important than the facts." Christians believe that both social and subjective indignity can be removed by converting any stigma into a "redeeming" or ennobling offering.[1]

Before consumption satiety became a plausible goal, the protection of objective labor dignity was rarely a significant factor in economic decisions. Perhaps the prevalence of absolute poverty—and of desperate labor aiming to ward it off—led to the assumption that degradation and wretchedness were inextricably woven into men's life of labor. Whatever the rationale, the result was clear. Few mines or factories were not developed because the labor involved was necessarily inhuman. If scrupulous men stayed away from such ventures, unscrupulous men took their place. When willing labor was not readily available, slaves or convicts could almost always be found and forced. Not only the worst scoundrels collaborated in this evil. Indeed, the temptation to make labor undignified was so great that aristocrats have been regarded as saintly merely for not working their peasants to death in times of shortage.

In industrial economies, many varieties of undignified labor have become unacceptable. Employers are not supposed to offer and employees are not supposed to accept excessively dangerous jobs, whatever the consumption reward. Hours and effort are carefully regulated, the ill are not forced to work, and employees can gain redress for poor treatment on the job. While moral weakness, which of course has not been eliminated by prosperity, ensures that these standards are not kept perfectly, increased prosperity has certainly been associated with less indignity in labor. Technically, this improvement has relied on more efficient production, which has eliminated the need for desperate and undignified labor, and more thorough regulation of labor, which has ensured that much of this potential good of prosperity was actually realized. The underlying change, however, has been in social expectations—what was previously accepted as a necessary evil is now seen as an avoidable disgrace.

On the other hand, the advance of industry has been accompanied by the development of some new varieties of undignified labor. Alienating labor has already been mentioned. Modern executives who die of stress-related illnesses are another example. They are just as dead, and probably got no more out of their labor, than the nineteenth-century factory workers who died of exhaustion or after an unnecessary industrial accident. Also, the tolerance of prostitution seems to be increasing, spurred on by some noneconomic aspects of the modern worldview. In poor countries, undignified labor has diminished as industry has entered, but it remains absolute poverty's apparently inevitable companion. The moral scandal of such indignity in a rich world is discussed in the next section.

Inappropriate Consumption—Too Little

Men suffer from absolute poverty when they are not sure to have enough of the basic consumption goods—food, clothing, shelter, and fuel—to stay alive. The absolutely poor man is not certain to die from want, but he is always in danger of death and rarely has much more than is absolutely necessary. Like satiety, absolute poverty is best seen as a range rather than a precise condition. Conventional economists, who usually define absolute poverty in terms of cash income—one or two dollars a day—are basically on the right track. Another rough approximation is the pervasiveness of malnutrition. Food is the most basic consumption stuff, so men are absolutely poor when they routinely cannot get enough of it. (See chapter 17 for more on the definition of necessities.)

Absolute poverty was almost universal in preindustrial economies. It was always close to the poor members of a community and never too far from the rich. (Indeed, by modern standards most of the relatively rich were poor in absolute terms—their limited height was a sign of intermittently inadequate nutrition.) Like the common indignity of labor, the universal nearness of death from want was accepted as a sad but inevitable part of the human condition. Until relatively recently, it seemed obvious that starvation and high infant mortality could no more be eliminated from human society than could jealousy, lust, war, or social injustice. For Christian thinkers, want and demeaning toil, like illness and death, were physical manifestations of men's moral inadequacy.

To be sure, men were supposed to fight against absolute poverty as much as against jealousy and injustice. But it was believed that victory was in practice impossible. The fight against absolute poverty was thought to be vain in much the same physical way that it now seems obviously impossible to construct a perpetual motion machine. The poor, the absolutely poor, would always be with us. In a well-ordered and peaceful society, absolute poverty might be warded off for a while, especially if the society had a temperate climate and access to fertile soil, but no land could be wealthy and peaceful enough to avoid famine forever, just as no man could ever be wealthy enough to buy eternal life. An ample supply of the most basic economic stuff remained among the many human desires that stretched well beyond the human grasp.

The advent of industrial society has changed the moral position of absolute poverty. Since this evil is easily curable, all—rich and poor alike—are responsible for curing it. The rich have the time and ability to help, and the poor have access to the necessary physical, psychological, and social tools. Shamefully and unnecessarily, absolute poverty persists, probably the worst aspect of the contemporary global economy.

The rich should be the most ashamed. Much has been given to them, so much is expected. Residents of rich countries should not enjoy the many benefits of prosperity without taking on the less obviously gratifying obligation of eliminating absolute poverty wherever it is found. A merely passive goodwill is insufficient. It is not good enough for rich countries merely to be "open" or "fair" in their trading patterns, any more than it is good enough to be willing to sell food to a starving neighbor at a "fair" price. As in any fight against evil, action is necessary and sacrifice is likely to be required. There are many possible techniques: less supersated consumption or less economic growth for the rich, more openness to poor immigrants, a willingness to make "unprofitable" investments of time and labor in initially unwelcoming poor countries. Such techniques have been tried with enthusiasm by a few of the rich, but at best halfheartedly by most.

The poor should also be ashamed, since they could so easily turn the little they have into much more. Thanks to the easy flow of information, money, and people, the wonders of the industrial economy are readily available. No longer must the poor struggle through the degradations of factory life experienced in the nineteenth century. The poor of today may have to start working in sweatshops, but the prospect of ergonomic factories, a service economy, and mandatory vacations is neither distant nor doubtful. Nor must the poor struggle to develop and adopt troublesome new technologies. They need only follow a well-worn path out of absolute poverty.

Inappropriate Consumption—Wrong Stuff

The global elimination of absolute poverty would not ensure a morally ordered life of consumption. There are two other directions of disorder—inappropriate consumption (wrong stuff) and excessive consumption (too much stuff). Both have flourished in industrial economies.

An undignified dependence on harmful substances is the most prominent sort of inappropriate consumption. Substance abuse is certainly not a new economic problem—in the Bible, Noah is said to be the first to get into trouble with too much wine-drinking (Genesis 9:20–23). The prosperity of industrial societies, however, has made all types of wrong stuff more readily available. Modern alienation, noneconomic as well as economic, may have increased the temptation to turn to them. The principal culprits are alcohol and psychotropic drugs, but pornography is also flourishing. Some would argue that tobacco, caffeine, and other softer drugs should be on the list. Real killjoys might include reckless recreational activity and even excessively mindless "relaxing" holidays.

Other, less obviously pernicious types of inappropriate consumption have clearly increased along with consumption comfort. More clothing and beauty aids are available, so there is more room for vanity and the insecurity of fashion-consciousness. In small doses, new styles reflect the eternal newness of life, but in large doses they reduce the wearer to serving an arbitrary master—to becoming a "slave of fashion." Men may not be as desperate as women for socially accepted beauty, but they are more likely to be slaves of consumption fashion in cars, physical fitness equipment, or spectator sports. Victims, both female and male, of this sort of dehumanization often do not understand the deleterious effects of their desires, but their false consciousness only compounds the evil.

Prosperity has also brought some totally new varieties of inappropriate consumption. The stupefying rhythms of modern music serve as a mass-produced narcotic. The endless electronic clutter of television pollutes almost all homes in prosperous countries, often reducing viewers to a mental dullness that can only be broken by ever more shocking images. The design of electronic toys seems to aim at inducing an addictive response in children and adults. There is something distinctly undignified about the influence of brands on consumption.

Inappropriate Consumption—Too Much

Industrial economies offer consumers a dazzling abundance of stuff. There are various possible responses. The morally sound one is discussed in chapter 16. The despairing response is alienation, the dull sense of loneliness in the face of so much stuff offering so little good but presented with exaggerated and artificial enthusiasm. A distinctly modern response is a sort of addiction that is sometimes known as "consumerism."[2]

The consumerist is always discontent with his current consumption. He is always looking for more and better. His desire is not deterred by satiety. Indeed, many consumerists have more stuff at their fingertips than they can possibly consume. Even if they have everything—houses, cars, clothes, home entertainment system, leisure activities, travel—in quantity and quality, they are always on the lookout for still more and better. Whether the starting position is excess or mere sufficiency, the consumerist approach is not defined by the stuff that is possessed or desired but by the endless inappropriate desire itself, an insatiable craving that is akin to the drug addict's ever deepening dependency.

The consumerist's mentality is clearly a sign of the overvaluation of the economic good, particularly of the most modest economic good of comfort. Less clearly, it seems to show an unconscious confusion of love and stuff, of being and having. There is also a social aspect to consumerism, the desire for conspicuous consumption to assert a social position. Morally, consumerism is a variety of the external economic evil of greed, but it is a particularly flamboyant variety that is uniquely suited to the stuff-filled industrial economy.

Consumerism is an easy target for moralists. Every expensive wedding, every gift-fest at Christmas, every teenager with a desperate desire to head for the shops—the mix of ostentation and triviality is quite obviously unbecoming. Such attacks are easily overdone. While most consumers in industrial societies make some intemperate judgments, few of them are totally obsessed consumerists. It is probably better to think of the typical consumer as over-indulged and self-indulgent than as a victim of an economic addictive disorder. The consumerist may best be understood socially—as making the response that fits best with the untrammeled production and culture of advertising found in industrial economies. In this case, we are dealing with a structure of sin rather than an individual weakness.

Inefficient Production and Too Efficient Production

Efficiency is the internal good of production (see chapter 10), so the corresponding evil is inefficiency. The evil is greatest when the need for stuff is greatest. Until absolute poverty has been eliminated, inefficiency in the production of food and the other basic goods that ward it off cannot be justified.

When no such great good is created by the stuff to be produced, the evil of inefficiency must be evaluated in a broader moral context. To waste labor or natural resources is bad, but what is truly wasteful is not always clear. The loss of potential consumption and the potentially unnecessary humanization of nature must be set against the possible alienation and social disruption required to make production more efficient.

That evaluation is likely to lead to a different conclusion in modern than in premodern economies. There is now a huge surplus of productive labor relative to men's needs and their virtuous desires for stuff, so further increases in the efficiency of labor may lead only to the creation of more pointless labor or to more undesired and morally unhelpful leisure. There is also a huge surplus of available stuff relative to absolute poverty and even, in many categories, to satiety, so the ability to produce more with the same amount of labor may be an ability that should not be exploited. Certainly, inefficiency that forces men to toil at machine-like or dangerous tasks is evil. For other types of production, greater inefficiency may actually be desirable because it would promote more important economic goods. As antimodern economists point out, less efficient farms might provide more dignified labor for those who wish to till the earth.

When it comes to the production of stuff used for destruction or degradation, it is efficiency, not inefficiency, that is evil. The efficient production of weapons of mass destruction or pornography only aggravates the evil involved. It is also often evil, although not to the same degree, to aim for greater efficiency in nonproductive labor. In labors of care and education, slower and more laborious is often better than faster and more efficient. There may be aspects of these tasks that are close enough to production to benefit from the logic of efficiency—for example, in the application of medical technology—but a mechanical logic has no place in human relations. That technically sophisticated and statistically successful medical care is often alienating to patients and caregivers alike is no accident.

Unjust Allocation

Justice is the good of economic allocation, so injustice is the corresponding evil. Some allocation injustice is inevitable in a society made up of morally weak men. The difficulty is increased if my overlapping criteria—need, contribution, and social position—are accepted. Any balance of the three considerations will be liable to merited attack from various sides—too much or too little attention to need and so forth.

Within modern industrial welfare states, however, economic allocation is never tremendously unjust by any of the three criteria. In terms of need, no one is allocated absolute poverty, while everyone is allocated access to electricity, clean water, sewage, education, police protection of property, and many other goods of prosperity. In terms of contribution, consumption rewards are differentiated, generally in rough accord with well-understood indices of labor excellence. In terms of social position, parents are allowed to pass down to their children much but not all of their economic-social status.

This moral amelioration often passes unnoticed. On the contrary, the modern mix of an excessive interest in economic matters and a broad and worldly understanding of equality often leads to an exaggerated concern about unjust allocation. Conventional economists of the political Left are particularly prone to worry that the poor have too little and the rich too much. They sometimes add worries about the unequal distribution of economic insecurity, the unequal wages of men and women and inequality in intergenerational socioeconomic mobility. Some or even all of the worries may be justified (I have my doubts about sex-related inequality—see chapter 14), but economic fervor about these relatively minor moral distortions is inappropriate in satiated economies.

Of course, there is always room for less unjust allocations in rich societies. Any remaining pockets of absolute poverty should be eliminated. There is much more room for improvement in those poor societies (most of them) in which the rich are few and very rich, and the poor are many and often suffer from absolute poverty.

However, the greatest current allocation injustice extends over the entire world—the unequal distribution of economic goods between a few rich welfare states and many predominantly poor countries. Economic fervor is quite appropriate in the face of this injustice.

Environmental Irresponsibility

The environment should be treated responsibly. The corresponding evil is environmental irresponsibility, either excessive respect for inhuman nature or excessive exploitation of the given world for the sake of creating a useful human environment. In both directions, the determination of excessive is made more difficult by the tension between men's two types of responsibility to nature—use, for the sake of the good, and respect, for the sake of the beautiful.

Excessive awe in the face of a divine nature probably disappeared from the economy with the decline of hunter-gatherers, although some radical environmentalists seem to be trying to revive this evil. On the other hand, while the border between the good of respectful use and the evil of excessive exploitation is frequently disputed, no one would deny that modern technology can seriously damage the natural environment. The labor of men is now powerful enough to reshape and redistribute the chemicals of the earth so as to poison the air, the water, and even the earth itself. It can eradicate the beauties of nature. It can create materials that are durably dangerous, lingering, and damaging for millennia. It might even be strong enough to tip over one or another of the most fundamental balances of the natural world—for example, to so damage the atmosphere that the global climate becomes hostile to men.

The economic evils of environmental depredation, actual and potential, have several causes. Some are the result of miscalculation—humans do not know how great the effects of their efforts will be. Some are the quite avoidable side-effects of industrial production—humans should pay more attention. Finally, some are the unavoidable "costs" of the goods of industrial production—humans cannot be so well fed and so well informed without somewhat mistreating the earth. The relative importance of these three causes is debated. The greatest ideological controversy concerns what is inevitable, while the greatest practical debates concern what should be avoided. As yet, environmental economics is too undeveloped and too biased against industry to provide much guidance.

This skimpy discussion of environmental evil concludes the directly moral part of this book. I now return to the two most important aspects of economic activity, labor and consumption. The goal of the next four chapters is to move tentatively into the third and fourth parts of the economic method described in chapter 6: description and evaluation. Chapter 7 provided a first glance; I can now try to integrate that basic description with the moral discussion of the subsequent chapters and with some less strictly economic concerns. The goal is not to provide a complete analysis, but a first step towards a truly human economics.

14

The World of Work

This chapter and the next are dedicated to labor, men's generous effort to make the world more human. The next is about the different types of labor, but that typology needs to be set into a broader human context. The economic good is too modest and too dependent on other goods for any aspect of economics to be studied as if it were self-sufficient. This chapter is my effort to avoid the distorted and solipsistic conclusions that inevitably emerge from such intellectual isolationism. I will place labor in the context of two other social sciences: sociology and psychology. The goal is not a comprehensive study but a sketch of a few of the most important connections between labor and the rest of the human condition.

Neither the sociology nor the psychology presented here is exactly conventional. Both academic disciplines are marred by the same antitranscendental bias and overly quantitative methodology that so distort conventional economics. The sociologist and psychologist rely on descriptions of human nature that are less inadequate than the economist's, but weak enough to force me into some intellectual improvisations.

Confusions

Before getting underway, a few common confusions about labor should be cleared away. The first is the idea that wages should be trusted to indicate the value of labor. This error comes from what should by now be a familiar problem, the misleading implications of using a "market" model of economic organization. According to that model, labor is always traded for money, and money is the only standard of value. These assumptions leave no room for the value of unpaid labor, most notably the highly valuable labor of "stay at home" mothers. They also leave no easy way to state that wages are often much higher than the value of the labor would justify, most notably for the vast amounts of useless (or instrumentally neutral) labor in industrial economies.[1] The result of these errors is truly dismal: the mildly harmful labor of a soft-drinks advertising executive is considered highly valuable because it increases market output, while his wife's truly valuable labor of taking care of home and family is counted for nothing, if it is not castigated as a lost economic opportunity.

Economists are not solely responsible for all labor confusions. Sociologists bear more of the blame for the assumption that the standard or natural type of labor relationship is employment—the organization of labor through the binding of men, employees, to socially approved organizations, employers. It is certainly true that employer-employee relations are widespread in industrial societies and that they achieve two important economic goals—they create communities and, through wages, they express clearly the metaphysical tie between labor and consumption. In addition, the voluntary and arbitrary nature of employment relations corresponds well with the modern worldview's enthusiasm for autonomy, although the ties are not arbitrary enough for purist market economists.[2]

However, employment is by no means the only or necessarily the best way of reaching either goal. Labor communities can also be organized around family, land, or hierarchical social caste, all of which have more social resonance than employment and some hint of a transcendental meaning. The labor-consumption tie can also be created through direct production, family obligations, community traditions, charity, investment income, welfare systems, pensions, and government grants. Most of these are less alienating than wage employment.

The confusion about employment relations leads easily into a confused belief in the primacy of employment contracts. Again, the economists are aided in their error by another group. In this case, it is the political philosophers who endorse the "social contract," a distant, hostile, and reductive model of government and human relations. In the economic contract model, employment is fully expressed as a simple contract—an exchange of specified amounts of labor from the employee for specified amounts of money from the employer. Ideally, the two sides negotiate the contract freely.[3]

In industrial reality, most employees do sign contracts, although usually not very freely. The written agreements, however, largely serve to provide limits to the behavior of both employers and employees. In a well-functioning organization there is no "working to rule," that is, to precise contractual terms. Rather, there is a cooperative effort that demands excellence, sacrifice, and justice. The signature of a contract is not, as conventional economists would have it, a sign of men's underlying economic autonomy, but a sop to men's moral weakness. The relation between employee and employer is much better described in terms of mutual commitment or symbiosis.

The last confusion—the exaggerated emphasis on the personal meaning of particular jobs, careers, and vocations—is sociological. Indeed, the reductive psychology of conventional economists, which leads them into many errors, helps them avoid this one. Their "economic man" does not expect "meaning" from his labor; he only wants money and the things money can buy. However, for too many sociologists, not to mention psychologists and workers, the job is supposed to provide meaning roughly in proportion to the time and effort dedicated to it. Each person should strive to find a "right job," a type of labor that fits his personality perfectly. This craving lies behind the job-hopping, the employment personality-testing, and the constant meditations on career planning and development that are so common in industrial societies.

There is nothing wrong with the idea of trying to match the laborer's personality with his labor. Unfortunately, the effort is doomed. Men's moral weakness ensures that all jobs are felt to be harsh and boring and that all workers are tempted by greed, pride, and sloth. The world's imperfections ensure that fundamentally unfulfilling labor will be necessary to keep the economy functioning. There is no way to make the tasks of street cleaners or parking inspectors interesting, satisfying, or soul-expanding. Rewards may placate workers, but they do not change the jobs' content. More substantially, the good of labor is too limited to satisfy more than a small portion of the human craving for meaning. Indeed, the greater the striving for meaning from labor, the more likely the end result will be disappointment and alienation. The social effort spent on finding fulfilling professional vocations would be better dedicated to developing both a spirit of sacrifice and generosity in labor and a more fulfilling noneconomic life.

Labor in the Context of Sociology

Sociology is the broad study of the human community. The subject overlaps with economics in various ways, so economists have much to offer sociologists and much to learn from them.

Labor and Social Experience

Economists should be interested in how men socialize their labor and how labor fits into social structures. Marx thought these relations could be fully explained in economic terms, particularly in terms of the control of labor. He was wrong. Labor (along with the other economic activities) fits into society in both subtle and complex ways. If anything, Marx's dictum should be reversed. Labor (along with the other economic activities) plays a supporting rather than a starring social role. Many goods take precedence over the dignity of labor and efficiency in production, including the relevant internal economic goods. Consider families. A labor-based analysis leads almost nowhere because families are not primarily communities of labor. They do sometimes labor together, but labor relations are less important to the meaning and functioning of a family than are the nurturing of children, the projection of continuity over generations, the conservation of mutual love, the promotion of common honor, and even shared consumption. Families may be an extreme example, but it is the same for social structures of worship (adoring and placating the divine takes precedence over religious labor), governments (external honor, domestic order, and citizens' welfare takes precedence over employee welfare), media (content over stars or producers), and schooling (education over teachers or students).

These examples suggest that the upper bound of the social importance of labor is low—on its own, a community of labor is rarely important enough to serve as the binding principle of an organization. Still, some social structures are primarily organizations of labor, and there are more of these in modern than in premodern societies. In particular, the factories and workshops that produce consumption goods can be seen as anchored by the arrangement of labor. The usual modern form of such an organization is the corporation. Even there, though, labor is not the sole corporate anchor; customers, machines, and money also provide unity and purpose, so that the good of the labor community is often sacrificed for some other corporate purpose.[4] Similarly, radical labor unions were once communities of labor, but they lost their way once absolute poverty and deeply undignified labor were eliminated. They have had to try to find other, less labor-oriented purposes—social, political, or religious.[5]

While the upper bound of the importance of labor in organizations is low, the lower bound is quite high. Social organizations cannot exist without laborers, and their good is often an important consideration in the organizational structure. The labor of priests, soldiers, bureaucrats, and teachers helps define the structures of churches, armies, agencies, and schools. This contribution gives economists the opportunity to help out sociologists. The economist can offer the same sort of supporting analysis that an engineer provides a theologian who is trying to understand the meaning of cathedrals.

Labor and Social Categories

Each man expresses his own thoughts, but his expressions are limited by the shared social structure of a common language. He may be able to modify the language to express new thoughts, but the grammar and existing vocabulary of his native tongue help shape even these new thoughts. Similarly, each man offers his labor as his individual gift to the world, but the labor-gift is formed and limited by his social position. He may be able to change either some aspects of his own social position or of the position's labor-meaning, but existing social categories help to shape the labor and give it meaning. This partial social determinism goes against the romantic individualist strand of the modern worldview, but it is in accord with a philosophically sound view of freedom. Labor is most free when it best reflects the true nature of the laborer, including his social position.

Biology is the most basic social category relevant to labor. Of course, biology is originally a physical rather than a social category, but physical characteristics—sex, strength, dexterity, and intelligence—are projected or reflected in social structures.

Nearly everything about sexual differences is highly controversial, but philosophy, theology, culture, biology, and history all suggest that these differences should be reflected in the social organization of labor. That conclusion would hardly have seemed problematic in premodern societies or in modern societies before about 1960.[6] Always and everywhere, the primary labor of women was maternal, caring, and domestic. Always and everywhere, men hunted, fought, built, made, grew, mined, forged, governed, traded, studied; their labor dealt with most things outside of the home and anything that required physical strength, aggressiveness, and quantitative analysis. Some tasks were assigned to different sexes in different societies, and some were assigned to both, but the use of sex as a discriminant in labor was assumed to be socially beneficial—women's work helped women feel and be more feminine, while men's work helped define masculinity.

The easy acceptance of sexually determined labor has disappeared. Such labor differentials persist in industrial economies, but they are often resented. Indeed, sex-neutral employment is generally accepted as a goal of public policy in rich countries. Labor, however, is just one battlefield in the war between human nature and modern androgynous thinking.

Sexual differences are perhaps the most controversial, but they are not the only biological factors relevant to the social organization of labor. Before the development of machines, physical strength was an important source of labor categories. Only strong men could be blacksmiths or teamsters, for example. The use of strength as a determinant of labor has faded, but dexterity remains a prerequisite for a wide variety of tasks, from sewing to surgery. Industrial production and complex government have greatly increased the importance of intellectual ability as a discriminant in labor.

Sex is fixed, and strength, dexterity, and intelligence are consistent through most of a person's life, so membership in the socioeconomic structures associated with these characteristics tends to be permanent. Age, which is also used as a determinant of social structures, changes constantly, so humans move through a series of age-related labor structures. Children are best suited to childish labors, young adults to energetic tasks, and the old to labor that requires the wisdom of experience. In preindustrial societies, age divisions were often quite formal. Stages of maturity were marked by initiations into certain types of labor, frequently in conjunction with noneconomic initiations into specific roles in family, community, and cult. In modern societies, age discrimination is often illegal, but it is still practiced. Indeed, some new age-related labor stereotypes have been created—the dynamic young leader, the disoriented mother returning to paid labor, and the lazy old man waiting for his pension.

Caste, class, status group, and social order are all names given to social structures that have no real biological foundations.[7] Caste structures mark out patterns of, among other things, consumption, civic responsibilities, social hierarchies, and rules for marriage. Caste-specific labor is only one element of caste, but it is often an important caste marker. For preindustrial peasants, craftsmen, and religious, caste membership and labor-type were almost identical. In modern societies, members of each caste have access to many types of labor, but there is a broad consensus that certain jobs do or do not belong to the "lower class" or "middle class."

Premodern castes were frequently believed to be hereditary, for reasons of tradition, law, and the spurious biology of noble or common "blood." Landowners' children were expected to own peasants' children; the blacksmith's son might not become a blacksmith, but he would likely take up some sort of caste-typical craft labor. The modern belief in labor vocation is deeply inimical to such social determinism, but moderns are still born into socioeconomic castes. Children imbibe caste distinctions and expectations, including those of labor, as part of their upbringing. To be sure, caste is less socially constraining than sex or age. The latter are immutable, while the ambitious and the feckless can sometimes change their own labor and their children's caste.

The Social Ontology of Labor

In the next chapter, I will give a typology of labor that is based on what the laborer is actually doing—simply being, working with things, working with people, working for no purpose, working to destroy. For the sociologist, an ontological approach is more relevant. Labor can be divided according to the way that the laborer's being is oriented to his society—as a servant, aristocrat, controller, or social "free agent."

In serving labor, the authority and power of the laborer is considered to be less important than, or subservient to, the authority and power of the person labored for or the thing labored on. The labor of domestic servants is clearly serving, but the category is much wider. Working the ground is serving labor as long as the farmer is considered primarily as the servant of the ground and its powers of fertility, rather than as their master or proprietor. Craft labor is serving when the craftsman thinks of himself primarily as following given rules rather than as expressing the power of his individual genius. Caring labor is serving when the good of the caregiver is subservient to the good of the person cared for. Service does not require blind obedience, but rather attention to the true good. The farmer shapes the ground that he serves, and the mother directs and forms her child.

Serving and controlling labor (described below) differ more in attitude than in practice. The serving laborer approaches his tasks with humility and diffidence, perhaps even with a religious awe at the wonder of the world to which he is contributing. The controlling laborer is confident in human ability, particularly in his own. In the distinction between the premodern and modern worldviews, serving labor is predominantly premodern and controlling labor is predominantly modern. That division brings with it symmetrical ideological risks: controlling labor will appeal too much to enthusiastic moderns and serving labor too much to antimodern moderns. Still, serving labor has the advantage of corresponding well with the timeless Christian praise of fraternal service.[8]

The premodern enthusiasm for serving labor helps explain the almost unquestioning acceptance, by Christians and non-Christians alike, of labor castes that now appear to exemplify social oppression—serfs, slaves, and indentured servants. Marx said that only false consciousness could explain the lack of revolt by the downtrodden, but service was often seen as noble in its own way. (In addition, the belief that the social order reflected a divine dispensation provided the whole arrangement with a sense of naturalness and an aura of transcendence.) Of course, this noble creed was badly served. Men's moral weakness ensured that serving labor was often corrupting for the served and unnecessarily bitter for the servants.

The modern worldview's endorsement of individual autonomy leaves little space for virtue in service. The coming of industry has made it possible for that belief to take social form. In the labors of production, the serving approach has largely been replaced by a controlling one. Some types of premodern serving labor, most notably many forms of personal service, have been made redundant by automation. Where serving labor remains, as in "service industries," a professional and mechanical approach has frequently created a controlling or impersonal sort of quasi-service.

Everything about aristocracy is premodern. Economically as well as socially, the modern worldview has swept away the radical distinction between aristocrat and commoner, a distinction that was long assumed to be immutable and universal. In consumption, the distinction between castles and hovels has been leveled by the universality of the welfare state and the ubiquity of the "middle class." Similarly, most of the distinctive labors of aristocracy—hunting, falconry, pomp and display—have disappeared almost without a trace. Although aristocracy and aristocratic labor are gone, perhaps they should not be forgotten. Notions that were once considered self-evident may yet find their way back into our social structures.

Aristocratic labor is best seen as a consequence or manifestation of the aristocratic caste worldview. That worldview was centered on the social reality of caste superiority and a spiritual ideal of perfection. The combination of real exclusivity and aspirations to excellence can reasonably be called "nobility." Of course, the behavior of many individual aristocrats was far from noble, but the ideal was clear enough to all: aristocrats were supposed to be social leaders in their labor. They were expected to set the standard in government, war, social mores, justice, and education. Indeed, one of the few domains in which aristocrats did not "naturally" take a preeminent social role was labor connected with production. The richest and most powerful merchants and craftsmen were often not aristocrats. Similarly, while aristocrats were intimately connected with agriculture, they generally considered the actual labor of tilling the soil to be ignoble.

In their labor as in their lives, aristocrats were expected to be in some sense representatives of the whole of society. A king or lord did not simply own his land; he represented it and its inhabitants to God and to other kings and lords. I believe that the labor responsibilities of this representative position—to defend the inhabitants, to pursue glory, to administer justice, to lead in learning and worship—had a certain nobility (in the noncaste sense of the word) but aristocratic representative labor is so premodern a notion that it is hard even to explain it. Sports teams, which are believed to represent the excellence of their home cities, provide a rare contemporary example.

The representation before God was particularly important. Aristocratic labor was supposed to bring transcendental excellence into society. In all cultures, the aristocratic idea of nobility was always imbued, or at least tinted, with a striving for something higher than could be found in the commonplace world of weakness, fragility, and change. While the great mass of servile serving labor was turned submissively towards the harsh authority of nature, the few aristocrats were supposed to look beyond, toward immutable goods. Soldiers searched for glory, scholars for wisdom and knowledge, and religious for holiness and the will of God. (The same pattern can be seen in other domains, for example in the aristocratic quest for refinement in manners and beauty in décor.) The representative nature of aristocratic labor allowed nonaristocrats in some way to share in this transcendental glory.

Controlling labor is almost as modern as aristocratic labor is premodern. It is an economic embodiment of the modern worldview's endorsement of man's autonomy in the face of God, nature, and his fellow men. It aims neither to serve a superhuman nature nor to search for a transcendental truth. Rather, it is organized and oriented to overpower anything that gets in its way. The distinction between serving and controlling labor is found primarily in social attitudes, not in the labor itself. The premodern hunter and the modern slaughterhouse employee are engaged in the same economic task—making animals useful for men. The social understanding of the two types of labor, however, is quite different. The hunter was to serve nature, to be dependent on its whims; the laborer in the industrial abattoir has precise control over the life and death of animals.

Each individual controlling laborer usually has many masters—other men and manmade rules. These controllers of the controlling are not, however, masters in the nature of things (as aristocrats were thought to be), but masters only for the sake of convenience. The relations between employees and their employers in controlling labor are very different from the relations between servants and their human masters in serving labor. In serving labor, the service was unconditional and almost fated. In the controlling relationship, nothing is considered God-given. The labor can be improved, the bosses can be challenged, and the rules and relationships can be changed. The power of human reason (thought to be unlimited) is available to all.

The advent of controlling labor has contributed significantly to the economic good, both by providing a cornucopia of consumption goods and by tempering nature's disorders. The internal good of labor has also been promoted by the willingness to take control of the organization of labor. When labor was approached primarily as serving, there was little interest in pushing for such industrial accomplishments as safer working conditions, pensions, disability insurance, and abundant holidays. However, controlling labor also has disadvantages. Sociologically, the accidental nature of its hierarchies can lead to vain striving for advancement as well as dissatisfaction among those who find themselves controlled. Environmentally, the controlling approach to nature tends toward a dangerous arrogance. Spiritually, the replacement of aristocratic with controlling labor has brought a lessened interest in the striving for transcendence. Even economically, the controlling approach to caring labor can lead to a disrespectful attitude to the cared-for.

The labor of social free agents is what might be called a postindustrial category. Its existence is doubtful, but the idea is interesting in a depressing way.[9] This labor is built on the foundation of economic alienation. The free agent is not a permanent member of any labor community. He works for himself, coming and going as he desires. He feels no need to do anything beyond what is laid out in his contract and is in no way responsible for the good of any labor community—after all, he is not a member. The free agent scorns serving labor and takes control for granted. He looks only for individual fulfillment and freedom from responsibility.

A few freelance laborers who diffuse their specialized skills as selfishly as possible might genuinely be called "social free agents," but labor still takes place largely in communities, communities of control rather than of service, but communities nonetheless. It can only be hoped that free agency does not become too popular, since this approach is just as antieconomic as it is antisocial. All economies rely on communities built on trust and sacrifice. The pursuit of "what I want when I want it" is particularly antithetical to the complex modern industrial economy, which needs consistent effort in many domains.

The Ideal Job

The ideal of labor has shifted along with the predominant worldview. In premodern societies, thinkers generally agreed that the best sort of labor for a man was whatever was noblest in both spirit and social caste; the only debate was over the relative nobility of the tasks that take men beyond this life—the labors of war, of government, and of the transcendental (worship, contemplation, and philosophy). Maternal labor, which protects life and serves the transcendent good of love, went almost unnoticed, although the feminine and masculine ideals were rarely compared directly. The shared ideal of nobility both reflected and helped to form the predominantly aristocratic arrangement of premodern societies and preindustrial economies.

Economists have been agents for the modern worldview's revolution from the start. The physiocrats, who first used "economics" in its current meaning, dismissed all the noble premodern ideas of ideal labor as "sterile," meaningless, and impoverishing. They idealized the productive labor of agriculture.[10] As the productive potential of industry became clearer the Marxist successors to the physiocrats turned to the hard manual labor of the factory for idealization. By the time machines came to do most of the work of production, even the idea of an ideal labor had been exposed as unacceptably premodern in its requirement for a universal judgment. Still, economists have maintained a hierarchy of value in labor. At the top is "management," those who organize production and distribution, especially "top management," the leaders who shape corporations.[11] The illusion that finance creates wealth has gained credence, so some gullible economists now also praise the labor of speculators, dealmakers, and financial investors.

Antimodern moderns have not abandoned ideals. They put farmers at the pinnacle of labor, but their thinking is quite different from the physiocrats'. The antimoderns argue that the necessity of food production makes agricultural labor most natural to the human condition. That claim confuses the human condition with the unfortunate—and, as it turned out, temporary—preindustrial need for vast quantities of exhausting, monotonous, and often desperate labor on the land. The antimodern moderns also claim that the closeness of agricultural labor to the created world allows men the greatest possible contact with the divine. That claim is also confused, although there truly is something wonderful about helping nature serve men. But the beauty of nature is best appreciated by urban intellectuals, not ignorant peasants who must also endure its cruelty. Agricultural labor offers limited intellectual challenges and is socially isolating. On modern factory farms, it is much more industrial than ideal.[12]

Should the human economist suggest an alternative, ideal type of labor? My fondness for premodern thinking pulls me toward an affirmative answer while my appreciation of the diversity of men's gifts and the complexity of economic excellence pushes me in the other direction. A partial answer is provided in the typological hierarchy in the next chapter. At its pinnacle is the mere labor of being (or of being alive), a labor so minimal that it is usually thought not to be labor at all. As far as more conventionally economic activity is concerned, it is the humble labors of love—mothering, caring, teaching, and worshiping—that are the most valuable. The labor ideal: men best serve the economic good when they are best able to receive and to give love.

Labor in the Context of Psychology

The previous section discussed the social importance, categories, and meanings of labor. Its external view should be supplemented by an internal, psychological analysis. Of the many aspects that could be considered, I have chosen those that seem most important or most commonly misunderstood: the role of compulsion in labor, the centrality of the search for excellence, the complex relations of labor and leisure, and the social and personal meaning of the rewards that are allocated for consumption. All of these can be seen as variations on a single theme, the mysterious effect of men's moral weakness on their labor. That weakness makes the compulsion of labor troubling, the search for excellence easily obscured by self-interest, the relations of labor and leisure complex, and the craving for rewards urgent and unsatisfactory.

Compulsion

Labor is marked by compulsion. The human need to labor could have been included in the description of human nature in chapter 5—it is a specifically economic manifestation of men's unending desire for more from the world. Like any other attribute of human nature, it cannot really be explained, just observed.

There is a biological basis for this compulsion. As a species, men are compelled to labor by direct, external, and physical necessity. If some men did not hunt, gather, or till, then all men would die of hunger and cold. This external compulsion was felt by many people much of the time in preindustrial economies, although the pressure of need should not be exaggerated—it was not fear for individual physical survival that motivated women to care for their children or priests to worship the divinities. In modern industrial economies, the motivation of physical necessity can explain the labor of only a few people, the 5 or 10 percent of the adult population that keep absolute poverty away. The rest us must labor for other reasons.

Some nineteenth-century utopian thinkers could see no good reason for universal labor and expected the arrival of industrial prosperity to eliminate the compulsion. The utopians were wrong. Labor compulsion is not merely a matter of contingent physical need, but of human nature, something that prosperity cannot change. Labor is a necessary part of being human, like speaking or friendship. Men certainly can live without speech or friends, but at the cost of some of the fullness of their humanity. Similarly, men can live without much labor, but "doing nothing" is dehumanizing.

Of course, when the alarm goes off on any given morning, I may not feel much like going to work. I may feel that a life of leisure is what I want or even deserve. If I am lazy or rich, I may try it out for a while, but eventually I will follow that inner compulsion—to labor at something, to have some project, some tasks to fill up the day, some accomplishments to strive for. (The individual's compulsion is to labor in the broad sense used in this book, not necessarily to labor in a paid job.) The combination of the compulsion and curse in labor is part of the mystery of evil. Economists must simply accept it, observing that the compulsion is stronger, at least for most men in most societies, but that sometimes the battle is closely fought.

Society often helps out when internal compulsion flags. It provides penalties (negative rewards) for failing to labor. Of course, social disapproval falls not only on complete indolence but also on some types of labor that individuals may find satisfactory. This communal compulsion to socially approved labor was universal in preindustrial societies. Not even aristocrats were exempt, although what was socially approved for them was often inadmissible for commoners. It is almost as universal in industrial societies. The advent of industrial prosperity has changed some of the types of labor that receive social approval, but not this economic criterion of social acceptability. In modern societies, the very small child tries to do what pleases his parents; the older child labors to please his teachers; what adults do "for a living" is a basic part of their social definition. Social validation for adults is increasingly restricted to paid labor, so both men and women feel compelled not only to labor but to have a paying employer.

Excellence

The desire for labor is not usually just for "any old job," and it is not usually satisfied if the labor is performed "any old way." On the contrary, the compulsion to labor is always directed toward excellence.

Like the compulsion, the excellence is part of human nature. Men wish to be good in everything they do, including their economic activity. They strive, or at least should strive, to labor well.

The definition of excellence for any particular sort of labor can be approached either subjectively, in accord with the laborer's own sense of accomplishment, or objectively, in accord with some higher external standard of what the labor should accomplish. Subjectively, all types of labor offer the same sort of excellence—all people can do their best, whether the result is a mediocre picture or a masterpiece, a delinquent child or a fine young woman, the hungry fed or the papers shuffled correctly. Even if the result is unimpressive, the striving itself has value, like any effort at perfection. Indeed, all tasks, no matter how humble, can be a source of real good for the laborer if they are undertaken as spiritual exercises in dedication and excellence.[13]

The objective standard of excellence is more helpful than the subjective in two ways—it avoids the distortions of subjective judgment introduced by men's moral weakness and reflects the social goal of labor, the good of the world. Mediocre artwork and the wild child should be criticized, no matter how content the artist and mother might be with their labors. Indeed, there is something unsatisfactory or even futile about an artist or mother who is happy but bad at the job. Still, in some circumstances—when the laborers are children or mentally retarded adults—the objective standard of excellence must take the laborer's potential contribution into account. The objective standard of excellence varies over time and between societies. A contemporary painter who produced works technically similar to those of an excellent painter of a millennium ago would likely be considered inept. A modern Californian mother who raised her children in the style of an excellent Spartan mother of the fifth century B.C. would be considered a lunatic.

Each of the ontological dispositions in the sociology of labor comes with its own objective standard of excellence. Unlike the standards for painters and mothers, those dispositional standards do not change, since the dispositions reflect ways in when men approach the world, not the details of time and place.

The excellence of serving labor is found in the appropriate use of reason. Service is quite different from blind or mechanical obedience. The serving laborer must both understand what is being asked and determine how best to obey. The search for understanding is challenging. When serving nature, the commands are often hidden; when serving men, the commands often have to be purified of the master's moral weakness. The serving laborer must also use reason to restrain the passions of his own moral weakness. Without the use of reason, the laborer is likely to follow the wrong commands or follow the right commands badly.

The excellence of aristocratic labor is found in the single-minded search for "the best" (in Greek, *aristos*). The aristocrat is always supposed to come as close as possible to human perfection. If he is fighting, he wants to be the best equipped, the bravest, and the most skillful. If he is studying, he wants the best masters and the highest wisdom. If he is religious, he wants to achieve the highest level of holiness. If he is leading some sort of government, he wants to be the most just leader (or the most powerful, depending on the social vision of excellence in government). Aristocratic excellence is particularly impressive when it is maintained, but particularly pernicious when it is distorted. Aristocrats have sometimes searched not for the best, but for the most license. They have labored at being the most cavalier, cruel, and dissipated.

Controlling labor is excellent when it is perfectly oriented toward control. The most obvious expression of this excellence is efficiency, the wonder-working internal good of production. Control can also be expressed through various sorts of power—being the boss of a large number of people, directing a large industry, or making far-reaching decisions. Persuasion is another sort of control, so success at sales, especially against the inclination of the purchaser, is often thought to be an excellence in controlling labor. All of these excellences of control are easily perverted from moral to immoral. Without a moral framework, what subjectively may seem to be excellence in controlling labor often turns out to be objectively evil.

Finally, the excellence, along with the existence, of free-agent labor is not yet clear. These workers seem to feel they are excellent when they least rely on anyone or any social structure. That is certainly an error; the promotion of any form of alienation is evil. Indeed, if there is an objective good in this sort of postmodern labor, I have not been able to discover it.

Men do not always want to be good at their jobs, any more than they always want to get out of bed for work when the alarm sounds. The muted or absent desire for labor excellence sometimes reflects moral weakness, a distorted wish to get out of something hard or to take advantage of others. Shirking is wrong, but evil is rarely overcome solely by correct philosophical arguments. The social organization of labor should help men respond to their sometimes hidden desire for labor excellence, just as it should help men respond to the sometimes faltering compulsion to labor in the first place. Sometimes, however, a lack of striving for what is supposed to be objective excellence is a sign of disagreement about what is really excellent. An unambitious woman in a corporate hierarchy is likely not to be drawn to the controlling excellence of power. The objective excellence proposed to barely skilled workers in a supermarket often seems insulting rather than realistic. In these cases, it may be the social organization rather than the laborer that is disordered.

Labor and Leisure

Labor and leisure are a pairing, but they are not directly opposed to each other. The relationship is more subtle, in part because leisure itself has several dimensions.

Leisure sometimes takes the form of total nonlabor, the leisure inactivity of lounging on the beach or the "at leisure" of an off-duty soldier. Men's need for complete inactivity, however, is modest. Just as we sleep in order to wake up refreshed, we rest in order in order to labor again, so the compulsion to do something, to labor, is rarely absent for long.

What men, especially men in modern societies, seem to crave is not so much nonlabor as labor stripped of social compulsion. This sort of leisure is not necessary for human survival or dignity, but modern men often claim to "live for the weekend" or holiday. They alternate between socially compelled labor, the job, and what might be called internally compelled labor—leisure activities that are just like labor except that the leisure-laborer, not the employer, makes the decisions about what he is going to do and when he is going to do it. The result is often hard work—the home gardener who does just what the market gardener does; the tourist who is exhausted after his sightseeing; the marathon runner who seems to be searching for a sort of labor excellence not available in her day job. Perhaps these leisure activities are taken up so enthusiastically because so much of the socially compelled labor in industrial societies is alienating.

"Leisure" is also used in industrial societies as a marker for activities that are excluded from the socially approved economy. Leisure-time goes for anything outside of the job—family, friends, travel, study, celebrations, physical exercise, hobbies. Indeed, consumption is considered a leisure activity. Leisure in this sense is as much a necessity as labor; both are required to play out the full drama of existence. The need for leisure-time is sometimes expressed, with more force than accuracy, as a need for a "work-life balance." In fact, labor is also a necessary part of life, but one that does need to be balanced.

The most profound understanding of leisure is transcendental. The Judeo-Christian story of creation includes a Sabbath, a day of leisure to be dedicated to worship, sacrifices, feasts, and celebration. Not all cultures have a Sabbath, but they all seem to have some sort of holy time during which men abandon the everyday and worldly toil of labor and turn to human-divine relations with thanksgiving, penance, supplication, and wonder. The socially representative labor of the aristocratic caste can be seen as an example of transcendental leisure—the nobles are freed from worldly necessity in order to engage in noble activities.

The organization of labor and leisure should provide all three of these types of leisure. Industrial societies have done this reasonably well. In particular, they have vastly expanded the time available for compulsion-free labor. Workweeks have been shortened, holiday allotments increased, and the expected years of schooling and retirement lengthened. Whether the work-life balance has been helped or hindered by industrial prosperity is a more disputed question. As for transcendental leisure, it seems to be in decline—aristocracy has disappeared, and the Sabbath has lost out to the resolutely secular weekend. But the system of economic organization cannot be held responsible. The shape of the working week is certainly influenced by the outcome of the modern fight between God and Mammon, but these battles are fought primarily on other, higher fields of human endeavor.

Rewards

Societies use rewards to organize and reinforce the compulsion of labor and the striving for labor excellence. Men work in order to earn wages or salaries and to acquire titles, prestige, perks, holidays, and pensions. They are rewarded by pleasant social environments, educational opportunities, travel, job security, and adventure. Society also imposes punishments—low pay, public shame, and, in extreme conditions, prison—on labor that strays too far from socially approved standards. Rewards are social by definition—they are part of the relations of men with their communities. Indeed, rewards provide something like a social commentary on labor. Conversely, the satisfaction of the reward is personal by definition, since something has to be perceived as a reward in order to function as one. The mix of social and personal provides a rich field for economic observation.

The economist should not forget to consider each reward. Consumption allocations are familiar and obvious. These can come in kind, ranging from flour to personal service, or in money. Part of the value of monetary awards is directly related to consumption, the stuff the money will buy. Part is social, as is seen in the habit of comparing stated salaries rather than take-home pay. Consumption allocations have to be set in the context of labor conditions—job security, opportunity for promotion, or a prospective pension.[14] Then there is social status within the labor environment. Outsiders recognize some labor-status symbols, such as the special costumes of master chefs, surgeons, and prisoner-workers. Insider symbols include job titles, office size, and the location of parking places. There is also social status in the broader society, such as the exalted social positions of priests and lawyers and the denigrated positions of waste-collectors and executioners.

Comparing the personal meaning of rewards is hard, because so many factors must be considered. The socioeconomic context matters. A salary or a consumption lifestyle that is considered affluent in a poor country might well be thought of as miserable in a rich one. A title such as executive vice president has no meaning out of its corporate context. Also, the definition of the context matters. To a worker without any title, executive vice president might sound good, but to a chairman or president, it might sound like a mark of failure. Finally, personal history matters. A house or a title will likely have one meaning for a man who receives them in recognition of his own labor and another for his son who receives them in recognition of his father's accomplishments.

Systems of rewards will always be perceived to be more or less unjust by all participants. The complexities of the definition of justice and the determination of context make an objectively just system virtually impossible. The moral weakness of all participants, both those who grant and those who receive, ensures that even if a system were reasonably just, few members would perceive it as such. This inevitability has a practical implication—there is always room for improvement in any reward system, but potential reformers should realize that moral weakness cannot be eliminated. That realization should lead to fewer calls for drastic reforms.

Systems of rewards both protect and weaken social order. They protect by providing a clear social meaning for each person's labor. In preindustrial societies, the reward system ensured that everyone— peasants, craftsmen, and aristocrats—knew what to expect from his labor. The rewards for labor reinforced other signs of social status. In industrial societies, high pay gives a clear social signal of approval for certain types of labor, and the lure of higher pay provides a clear social incentive. On the other hand, the nearly inevitable reality of injustice in reward systems, amplified by the even greater and completely inevitable feeling of injustice, encourages social ill-will. Millionaires struggle for an extra few inches of beach at an exclusive resort, and monks fight over the distribution of cutlery.

Whatever the system, however just it manages to be, there is one consistent psychological-spiritual truth about rewards for labor: they tend to be disappointing. Whatever the initial or expected personal evaluation of a reward, the subsequent evaluation tends to be lower. Wealth and honor are often sought diligently, but when they actually arrive they usually provide less happiness or satisfaction than anticipated. This disappointment springs from men's transcendental orientation, which limits the value of any ephemeral and worldly token. And though this disappointment is universal, it is probably particularly sharp in industrial societies, which suffer from individuals alienated from all social structures, including reward-granting ones.

The response to disappointment should be philosophical reconsideration, but it rarely is. More often it is the answer of the jaded addict, which is to ask for more rewards in the vain hope that a higher dose will make the crucial difference.

The consistent effort of conventional economists to flatten human nature enough to make economics into a mathematical science has worked all too well in the study of labor. Some of them worry about measures of "unemployment," but often without much conviction and almost never with any serious thought given to the social meaning of that state. Some worry about just wages, but they rarely consider how justice should be determined. Mostly, however, labor is treated as no more than an impersonal force, an aggregated input to economic activity to be juggled with capital and natural resources.

I hope that this chapter has shown how inadequate that approach really is. My technique has not been to elaborate the criticisms of earlier chapters, but to make a positive effort to show a few of the many ways in which labor is much more than an impersonal force leading to production. It is a meaningful expression of the richness of human nature—a way in which men are tied to each other; an expression of each man's and each group's particular place in society; a field for cooperation and rivalry; a way to express each society's and each group's response to nature and necessity; a means of self-expression; a driving force in each person's life; an opportunity for excellence; a moral stumbling block; a source of personal satisfaction and discontent. Much more is to be said, by economists and by other students of humans and society, because labor supports every aspect of the human endeavor. Politics, pure science, the arts, religion, education—the ties of labor within each of these human disciplines deserve full attention. But I will stop here, in order to leave enough space to present a hierarchal typology of labor.

15

A Typology of Labor

The notion of a single ideal type of labor was rejected in the last chapter. A lack of perfection does not, however, imply a lack of order. This chapter provides a morally meaningful ranked division of types of labor. The division is introduced here; the moral ordering is based on the discussions in chapters 9–12 and on the definition of labor (in chapter 7) as a contribution to the world. The list is presented from most to least important. It is divided into four sections: the basic labor of man simply being; the unmediated labors of man-to-man and man-to-transcendental; the mediated labors of man-to-thing; and the pointless and destructive labors of doing without doing good. I believe that this division, which is largely new, is a fertile one. Each type of labor has its own logic, excellence, and temptation, all subjects which deserve more attention than is possible in an introductory book.

The definition of labor as contribution helps explain why the highest good on the list is the simple labor of being. The contribution of life should be considered more important than whatever labor contributes to life. The logic of contribution also helps explain why the labor of being is followed by men's direct labors for the benefit of their fellow men—the contributions of love, care, and service. These spiritual and human labors come before all thing-labors because they (the spiritual labors) contribute to man's highest quest, the search for something more than the physical world can offer.

Still, labor with things has much to recommend it, especially in comparison to the remaining two types of labor.

Basic Labor

Nothing is more basic in the human condition than life itself. There is also nothing more elevated. Man is not man before he comes to life, and his most fundamental transcendental aspiration is for life in its fullness, whether that fullness is to be found in the heavenly eternity of Christianity or the unchanging All of Buddhists and Hindus. In the more worldly domain of economics, life—its protection, promotion, and propagation—is the highest economic good. The labors that support the good of life could be ranked in various ways. From a materialist perspective, the toil of supplying food and shelter should be given priority. That approach is certainly defensible; basic stuff is certainly necessary for life. But I am writing in the Christian tradition, in which human life is understood to be above all a manifestation of God's love, something immortal that transcends the needs and decay of the body.

This spiritual perspective leads me almost to reverse the materialist ranking of types of labor. The most important labors are those which make possible a life that is distinctly human—a life with meaning, a life that is lived in love. For economists, this love is articulated in many ways, in the labors of care, study, and worship as well as in the productive toil of humanizing the physical world. But the first and most basic articulation comes in the pure offer of the self—the very little spark of life that is given to the world and to the human community to be nurtured and supported.

The Labor of Being Alive

The gift of life, no stronger physically than a breath or a heartbeat, makes men most in the image of God (to speak in Christian terms).[1] The simple labor of living is literally vital for everyone, but it is almost always completely overwhelmed by more active sorts of labor and leisure. Still, economists should not forget.

This most basic labor of being becomes a matter of economic concern in the exceptional periods of life when the functioning of the body and the control of the brain are not completely automatic. Then, the simply being person, whatever his age and however long he remains in this condition, is making a basic but vital contribution to the world—being alive. The crude labor of life against death is sacred, an expression of the transcendental nature and supreme value of human life. Such a judgment may seem extreme, metaphysical, or sentimental, but it is endorsed by most of those who love and care for the barely alive or the almost dead. These caregivers do not merely support life but are themselves sharers and beneficiaries of the pure and basic labor of being. It is also the judgment that was disputed in the eugenic campaigns of the early days of the Nazi government.[2]

The labor of a newborn infant—all of us at the beginning of our lives—is the most universal example. He simply is. He can do almost nothing for himself, has almost no control of his body and but a minimal ability to express his intelligence and emotions. Yet to his mother and his community, he is the most wonderful of beings, one whose labor of life is a sign of hope and a joyous responsibility. Moral weakness (and sleeplessness) may sometimes tarnish the joy, but the desire to see the flourishing of this hard, initial labor of being is almost never lost completely. Especially weak infants need help in this labor; industrial medicine has been most obliging.

At the other end of life, the very old and the extremely handicapped are often able to do little more than cling to life. For the most part, caregivers testify that they cling quite hard. This labor of being is accompanied by less joy than the hopeful penumbra that surrounds the newborn, but the genuine grief at the death of a senile parent or a "vegetable" sibling shows how much that labor is appreciated. Again, moral weakness enters in—the very old and the very ill can seem disgusting and difficult. And again, here the accomplishments of the industrial economy are tremendous. Not only are there many new powerful tools and techniques with which to help the very weak, but the resolution of the economic problem has allowed far more of the labors of the healthy to be dedicated to the good of totally dependent men than was possible in even the most generous preindustrial economy. The decision to make that tremendous commitment to the fundamental labor of these weakest members of the human family is one of the finest uses of modern prosperity.

The Labor of Illness

Illness is sometimes only an involuntary leisure activity. But when the illness is both prolonged and severe enough to limit men's abilities, it becomes a sort of labor. Psychologically, illness takes up time and requires effort much as other sorts of labor do. It also comes with the same sort of pain and necessity as labor, although without any obvious excellence. Illness has its own sort of rewards, rewards of recovery or enduring. Socially, its labor status is recognized in government welfare systems, which consider disability and serious illness to be almost like occupations.

The contribution that illness makes to the world may be obvious only to Christians, who see the willing acceptance of illness as an offering, a participation in the sufferings offered by the crucified Lord.[3] In that analysis, the labor of illness plays an extremely important role in the work of salvation. A non-Christian might be able to point in the same general direction, seeing the struggles of the ill as valuable testimonies to the preference for life over death and to the willingness to suffer for the sake of the fullness of life.

No amount of prosperity can eliminate the labor of illness, any more than it can eliminate the death to which illness eventually leads. However, industry has altered the social patterns and typical individual experience of illness. It has become more common. Modern medicine has been successful both at delaying death and at curing illness, but more successful at the former. Men live longer lives with more times of illness, especially in their last years. Illness has also become less physically challenging but more psychologically or spiritually burdensome. While pain can now be kept under better control and special arrangements can be made to compensate for many enduring physical weaknesses, men seem to be more sensitive to their physical weaknesses and less able to see any spiritual value in the suffering that illness still entails. As is so often the case, the practical improvements come from prosperity while the spiritual difficulties come from some other strands of the modern worldview.

Unmediated Labor

Labor is men's humanizing offering to the world, both to the physical world of given capital—earth, air, energy, plants, animals—and to the human world, the fragile yet resilient communities of men who live, strive, and die together. The labors that reshape the physical world support the human world of society, so such stuff-labors of production are secondary (in a philosophical sense) to purely social labors, which do not merely support but actually constitute society. I call these social labors "unmediated" because the laborer works directly with the beneficiary of his labor, not with some sort of mediating stuff. The unmediated laborer may require stuff to do his labor correctly—the doctor's medicines or the teacher's textbooks—but the stuff is only a tool, a means. The purpose, the end, of the labor is the person. In contrast, the purpose of mediated labors is the transformation of stuff; any personal relations—among fellow workers or between a salesman and a customer—are only means to that material end.

Reproductive Labor

In English, the word "labor" is used to refer to the process of giving birth. This linguistic accident aids economic understanding.[4] Parturition provides a nearly perfect example of all the characteristics of labor. The goodness of this labor is tied up with the greatest economic good, of life. The "curse" of this labor is felt in the physical pains of bearing and the emotional pains of raising children. The compulsion of this labor is manifold: it is unavoidable once pregnancy starts; there is no relief until the child can take care of himself; it is required for the basic good of mankind, the community, and the family; many women feel fundamentally "unfulfilled" without it. The drive to excellence in this labor is clear in any conversation with a mother about her children. The psychological status of this labor is so important that it is virtually indelible. Few women think of themselves as "ex-mothers," even when their children are independent or dead.

Pregnancy and giving birth, the central biological labor of reproduction, are of course entirely feminine. The subsequent reproductive labor of nursing is almost as biologically constrained. Nursing is accompanied and then superseded by nurturing. Women and men both nurture, but women generally seem to be better at providing this sort of love. Even in increasingly androgynous modern societies, childcare remains predominantly "women's work" (in practice if not always in theory).

Reproductive labor, understood to include both bearing and caring, is among the most important and most transcendental of human labors, but we seem incapable of consistently appreciating it, either personally or socially. In both preindustrial and industrial societies, the labor of mothers has almost universally been slighted. The excellence of their love and sacrifice is all too often dismissed, undermined, or ignored in social and economic arrangements. The huge affluence of industrial societies has not helped, at least in the economic treatment of this labor. On the contrary, children are increasingly seen as an economic burden and their care as an economic drag, because they take mothers out of the paid workforce.[5]

Caring Labor

Psychologists and artists can try to explain why men need love and its labors (I use "caring labor" to avoid the romantic connotations of "labors of love"). Economists need only notice that they do, that men are very needy indeed. The need for labors of care extends through all phases of life and takes many forms.

The need for nurturing labor has just been mentioned. Mothers and now fathers provide what the young cannot manage: coordination and dexterity, protection from the hostile world, the interpretation of experiences, the wisdom of age. As the child grows, nurturing labor is increasingly shared, first with fathers and relatives and then with teachers and other educators. In preindustrial economies, neither studying nor educating labor was often a specific responsibility; it was just part of growing up for children and part of the job for parents and apprentice-masters. In industrial societies, education is one of the many aspects of the labor-life that has become more specialized. Educating labor is a profession, and the academic labor of young people lasts for years. Nurturing and educational labors continue until adulthood, which used to arrive around the time of puberty, but in modern societies seems not to arrive fully until children are twenty-five or even thirty years old.

The need for care does not disappear with adulthood. Some adults need care always, and all adults need care sometimes. Nursing labor includes both the care of the weak—the blind, deaf, lame, frail—and the "tender loving care" of the ill. As with educational labor, the move from preindustrial to industrial economies has been a move from unselfconscious and almost anonymous family care to a nursing labor of many distinct professions. The ill also benefit from curative labor, the more technical medical effort to stave off decay and death. This curative fight is ultimately doomed, but the spiritual and practical value of the labor is not really diminished by its final failure. Curative labor follows the typical historical pattern of caring labor—from preindustrial simplicity to industrial sophistication, from something in large part intuitive and folkloric to something highly analytic and technical.

Humans also need care to help them overcome the various disruptions and distortions of life in society. As a category, social care labor hardly existed in preindustrial economies; it was largely something women just did. Now, there are specialists for almost any problem group: delinquent youth, prisoners, former prisoners, single mothers, confused taxpayers, new residents, substance-abusers, the emotionally distraught, the lazy, the sexually deviant, the dangerously fat, the dangerously thin, the recently rich, the recently poor, the over-indebted. Each social caring profession has its own private vocabulary and most have complex administrative structures.[6]

Finally, there is the labor of personal service. This labor responds to a preference rather than a need, but it is indeed pleasant to have someone else to do the cooking, wash the clothes, clean the house, or help you with your toilette. The industrial transformation of personal care labor has a unique twist. In the home, it has not followed the typical pattern of expanding and becoming more specialized. Rather, domestic service has declined and become less specialized. Today's cleaner or nanny is expected to have a wider range of skills than the typical preindustrial house servant. That shift reflects the greater ease of housekeeping, but the main causes are the egalitarianism and individualism characteristic of the modern worldview. Modern men would rather work for organizations than for other individuals or families. Outside of the home, however, personal care labor has flourished and become specialized in a fairly typical industrial way. Many jobs have been created by restaurants, resorts, and other various modern forms of regimented relaxation.

Transcendental Labor

Men want more than the world. I call the labor of getting and transmitting that more "transcendental." The contribution of transcendental labors can only be expressed imperfectly, because it goes beyond both the world and men's words. It aims at the superhuman ideals—the beautiful, the true, the good, and the One. It aims at immortality. It never exactly reaches its targets, but men so treasure the transcendental that even hints and fragments are welcome.

Economists are in a particularly weak position to study transcendental labor, since its supernatural domain surpasses the highest economic good of life. Still, they can observe that transcendental labor is different from all other types of labor in the potentially vast scale of its effect. The influence of Homer and Plato has been felt on many continents for millennia; the glory of the Roman Empire is a durable testament to the transcendental labors of the famous leaders and anonymous soldiers who established it and of the historians and poets who immortalized it. Economists can also observe the mania of artists, the holiness of religious men, and the death-defying discipline of soldiers. The striving for perfection or a sort of immortality seems to be accompanied by a distinct formation (perhaps in some cases a deformation) of the transcendental laborer's character.

Besides observing, economists can also divide this labor into categories, starting with artistic labor.[7] Poets, painters, sculptors, musicians, photographers, actors, directors, cameramen, lighting technicians—all seem to combine the meticulous toil of craftsmen (whose tasks are considered under mediated labor) with what might be called "inspiration" or "enthusiasm." The evaluation and interpretation of their labor depend on which side is emphasized. If it is the craft, then artistic labor is seen as providing little more than the utilitarian pleasure of entertainment. If it is the inspiration, then the labor is essentially connected to—comes from or strives towards—the transcendental ideal of the beautiful.

Intellectual labor is oriented toward another transcendental: the true. Thomas Aquinas divided the search for the true into three parts.[8] Knowledge, the lowest, is pursued by the intellectual labor of scientists and researchers; understanding is the concern of philosophers; wisdom, the highest, is the aspiration of theologians. Under the influence of the modern worldview, there is more interest in knowledge, especially the technical knowledge that leads to the machines and medicines which serve nontranscendental economic goods. In contrast, theology has been relegated to the fringes of intellectual life, and often of spiritual life as well.

The transcendental good is served by governing labor, which encourages virtue, and by protective labor, which discourages vice. At least in premodern societies, governing—the authority of men over men—was seen as transcendental, especially in its power over life and death and its responsibility to administer justice.[9] Some of that transcendental aura may have been lost in the transition from the kings, nobles, and court officials of premodern governments to modern democratic politicians and professional bureaucrats. Indeed, many bureaucrats toil away at technical tasks that belong in some less elevated category of labor. Still, I would argue that the duty of public service cannot fully shake off its connection with the transcendental. Governing labor is also found in some nonpolitical organizations: religious institutions, charitable organizations, and perhaps even some corporations.

Protective labor used to be almost exclusively the task of soldiers, whose principle job was to fight wars. Not all of the labors of war can be considered protective; they are often destructive and of no economic value.[10] In modern societies, specialization has also found its way to protective labor. Police and related professional disciplines have been created to protect the public order in peacetime. Among all laborers, the protective laborer is most noble in his willingness to risk his life, but probably also most likely to succumb to the temptation to use his authority and power for evil purposes.

The labors of the One, or God, are spiritual. Many forms of purely spiritual labor have fallen out of favor in modern societies. Soothsayers are discredited, contemplative monks are rare, and the bodies of the dead are disposed of with the scantiest of rituals. Even priests often see their labor primarily as caring or ministering rather than as purely transcendental. The shift has nothing to do with the advent of the industrial economy. On the contrary, industry has freed up vast amounts of labor from the necessity of toiling to satisfy consumption needs. Some of this labor "surplus" has gone to care for the ill, some has gone to create huge industries of leisure and tourism, but less than none of the surplus has gone into spiritual labor. The choice to deemphasize directly spiritual labors is social, not economic. The antitranscendental bias of the modern worldview is responsible.

Some labors of play should be included in the transcendental category. Play is sometimes no more than a leisure activity, but play can involve much more—the intellectual labor of learning, a generic labor of love, and, most profoundly, a transcendental labor of wonder at being itself. Few men sacrifice their lives for the sake of play, but the Christian is certainly mindful that "unless you become like a little child, you shall not enter the kingdom of heaven."[11] That admonition suggests that play, the most typical activity of children, is a quite serious responsibility.

Mediated Labor

Mediated labor is the labor of things—tools and material, force and dexterity, planning and physical transformation. Mediated labor is less important than unmediated labor, but it is certainly valuable, indeed invaluable, production absolutely required for the preservation of life. It is also as distinctly human an activity as loving, learning, or praying. Only men can turn the raw stuff of the world into things that are useful, desirable, or meaningful. Birds may make nests, but the human ability to convert a tree into something as different as a chest of drawers requires a different dimension of skills and ideas. Such labors even hold a hint of the divine, for they transform raw stuff so radically that it becomes a sort of quasi-creation.

The objective inferiority of mediated labor certainly does not imply a denigration of mediated laborers, a denigration that was almost universal in premodern societies. Whatever their objective contribution or caste, all mediated laborers should feel the universal satisfaction of subjective labor excellence. Many of them can also take pleasure in knowing that they are contributing to real economic goods. In particular, the labor of agriculture is a prerequisite for the highest economic good: life. Christians and others might add the praise of humility—the laborer who knows himself to be bound to the dark and dumb earth or to the hard physical struggle of making the world work for men is in a particularly good position to be open to the infinitely rich world of heaven.[12]

I have divided mediated labor into two categories, direct and indirect. One is not better than the other, but the division reflects other distinctions. Sociologically, indirect laborers have generally enjoyed higher status than direct laborers. Grain merchants are generally more highly esteemed than farmers; office workers usually rank above factory workers. Psychologically, most men seem to prefer indirect to direct labor, although that preference is not universal and may be influenced by sociological conditions. Historically, a helpful way to describe the development of productive labor in modern industry is as a decline of direct labor and a concomitant increase in indirect (as well as in instrumentally neutral) labor.

Directly Mediated Labor

Conceptually, the first phase of humanizing the world is the gathering of the elements that are to be made into actual consumption goods. This labor of crude production and extraction is typified by farming, which was by far the most common sort of masculine labor in most preindustrial economies. The labor of agriculture, herding, forestry, and beekeeping employs few men now, but it will always remain archetypal, the most basic offering of human strength and knowledge to the most basic productive economic effort—turning the wild fecundity of nature to men's advantage. The basic nature of the labor is reflected in the close correlation between the sophistication of agricultural labor and the sophistication of a whole society. Preagricultural hunting and gathering supported only nomadic communities; the organized culture of agriculture first supported refined cultures of art and learning; the move to industrial agriculture has made possible the great cities of industrial civilization.

As might be expected of so basic an activity, agricultural labor is both good and bad for the laborer. It is not the ideal labor suggested by antimodern moderns, but it does offer a satisfying necessity, a lack of Marxist alienation, a unity of labor with family life, and closeness to the wonders of nature. On the bad side, it tends to be physically demanding and socially isolating. Both the advantages and disadvantages have become less extreme with the coming of industrial agriculture. The labor is now less harsh, less necessary, less wonderful, and more alienating.

Other types of labor also serve to gather treasures from the world. In fishing, men use their physical strength, tools, and intelligence to take advantage of nature's fecundity. Except for fish-farming, which is essentially just another variety of industrial agriculture, fishing is effectively aquatic hunting—exciting and metaphysically satisfying, but relatively inefficient.[13] In mining, men extract mysterious materials from the reluctant earth and then engage in the almost magical work of smelting and refining. Mining labor is harsh—isolated locations, bad health, frequent accidents, occasional disasters—but it seems to encourage particularly close communities, both inside and outside of the mine.[14]

The second conceptual phase of production is the centralized shaping of the gathered elements into useful stuff—the operation of mills, breweries, workshops, and factories (including factories that only make goods for other factories). In preindustrial economies, these facilities were typically workshops, and the laborers were typically craftsmen. For most types of stuff, workshops have yielded to more efficient factories and craftsmen to more efficient machines. Construction laborers are the only significant group to retain most preindustrial craft habits. From the perspective of consumption, the change to factories is an improvement—more stuff for less labor. From the perspective of the laborers, it is largely a loss. Craft labor was often skilful, imaginative, challenging, and sociable. Fortunately, some new forms of craft labor have sprung up in industrial economies—including the many varieties of machine maintenance and software development.

For the first century or so of the industrial age, observers thought that it was not machines but assembly-line laborers who were replacing craftsmen.[15] Men performing monotonous tasks to an almost inhumanly fast mechanical rhythm in superhuman scaled factories became a symbol of the industrial age.[16] That perception proved erroneous. Tremendously efficient factories are indeed typical of the modern economy and society, but men basically get in the way. Compared to the simplest mechanical device, human laborers need more expensive fuel, break down more often, and require more precisely controlled working conditions. Compared to sophisticated modern machines, men are weak, slow, imprecise, and careless. Unlike machines, men have to be cajoled and closely supervised if they are not to lose interest and dedication. When they are no longer useful as productive devices, men require much more complex and long-term disposal techniques than machines, a responsibility that often falls on the factory operator.

The error was caused by a misreading of the historical trend. As long as the available machines were not very efficient, the development of new industrial processes led to an increase in the demand for factory labor. When the increase in the efficiency of machines caught up with the increase in the number and size of factories, the proportion of the paid workforce working in manufacturing started to decline, from about 40 percent in 1910 to less than 20 percent today in rich countries. The proportion that directly works the tools and machines, as compared to doing the craft labor of repair and the indirect mediated labor of monitoring, has declined much more.[17] The decline should be welcomed, because in the logic of factory production the direct laborer is merely a more or less effective machine. The men get in the way of mechanical efficiency, and the deadening routine of efficient production gets in the way of men's dignity. The laborer is dehumanized and his alienation—from the total process of production, the final products of his labor, the natural world, and the labor community—is almost complete.

After agriculture and manufacture, the third conceptual phase of production is the household labor that comes right before consumption and makes consumption possible and pleasant. In preindustrial economies, this domestic mediated labor included a large amount of production of stuff that could not efficiently be manufactured in a centralized facility. That included growing vegetables, raising poultry, keeping fires lit, gathering water, preserving food, weaving, sewing, and mending. Consumption life was simple by industrial standards, but the available tools and materials were even simpler, so the labor was varied and complex. All of those tasks have been centralized in industrial economies; heat, light, clothing, cleansers, and many foods are bought ready-made, and domestic appliances have simplified the remaining labors. The industrial homemaker is left with only a lot of shopping to do, a larger house to clean, some meals to prepare, and perhaps a little mending.

This was, and mostly still is, women's work.[18] The gender-based assignment of domestic mediated labor seems to be universal, but there is no unanimity on the underlying relation between domestic productive labor and femininity. Sociologists tend to focus on the convenience of mixing house-care and childcare. Feminists tend to see oppression. Antifeminists tend to see a deep connection between caring for the things of the home and caring for the people who live there. Whatever the explanation, women at home now have much more time to focus on caring labor.

The final phase of production is disposal. In preindustrial economies, most of the labor of cleaning was undertaken without much consideration by farmers, craftsmen, and housewives. There were only a few specialists in disposal—of corpses, rags, and sometimes excrement. This labor was vital, but the laborers almost always belonged to the lowest social castes. The development of industry has done to cleaning labor what it did to caring and indirectly mediated labor; it has created more skilled and interdependent specialties. There are operators for all of the systems that take care of human waste, fouled water, exhausted industrial materials, and used-up consumption goods. The coming of industry has made this labor more skilled, but no less vital. It has not, however, much improved its low social status, which is presumably related to a noneconomic notion of impurity.

Indirectly Mediated Labor

In preindustrial economies, indirectly mediated labor was rarely distinguished from directly mediated labor. The farmer took care of most of the labors that surround production—barn-building, obtaining tools, trading excess production, negotiating relations with the landlord. It was much the same for craft laborers. A brewer rarely divided the actual beermaking from training apprentices, selling the beer, or paying taxes.

In industrial economies, many of these indirectly mediated tasks have been separated into distinct professions. They can then be performed by laborers who have acquired highly specialized skills, often skills that have little to do with the directly productive labor they support. The relatively recent arrival of such words as "executive," "management," "marketing," and "service" in the economic vocabulary reflects this change.[19] The vagueness of these terms reflects the difficulty of pinning down the exact content of much indirectly mediated labor. What follows is a selection of the most important tasks.

Some conventional economists come close to idolizing the labor of investment decisions: what factories, pipelines, roads, and trucks should be built and where they should be located; what "human resources" should be developed and deployed in corporations, schools, and universities. This labor can be divided by scale: the planners who direct national "industrial policy" and organize giant projects such as electrical and telecommunications grids; financial investors who allocate new resources for investments across industries and countries; and the many senior and middle managers who organize investments for particular corporations, agencies, or departments. The arrangement of these specialists is socially inconsistent and not always economically efficient. The most important tasks are performed by highly skilled but modestly rewarded government employees, the mid-scale of finance by extravagantly rewarded generalists who usually double-up as irresponsible speculators, while the lowest scale of investment labor is usually combined with other, scarcely related, management responsibilities.

Once the investments have been made, the authority of management is more concerned with men than with machines. Managers must respond to the vagaries caused by nature's disorders. Industrial production systems are largely self-contained and follow largely preset rules of operation; humans must always be scheduled, motivated, disciplined, and joined into communities. Human freedom and weakness ensure that there is always work to be done, although much actual management labor should probably be classified as instrumentally neutral (see below).

The development of management as a profession is one response to the need for more authority in complex industrial economies (see chapter 1). The development of regulatory labor is another. Efficient centralized production is possible only if men can count on consistency in the products they use and can trust the strangers who have produced them. The labor of regulation involves establishing and enforcing the standards that ensure both consistency and trust. Regulation now extends to almost all aspects of productive economic activity—steel alloy strength, road drainage, taste variation in tea. It also extends to almost all aspects of professional caring labor—schools, hospitals, welfare systems, hairdressers, and so on.

Regulatory labor requires detailed knowledge of highly technical matters, high moral standards, fine judgments, a balance of pragmatism and idealism, and a thorough consideration of many aspects of the good—real and apparent, immediate and eventual, of producer and consumer. All of these factors suggest that regulatory labor is best supported by a strong and almost transcendental authority. That many regulators work for governments or for quasi-governmental organizations is not surprising. Overall, regulatory labor, with its dedication to excellence in labor and production, has received too little social esteem in industrial societies.

On the floor of a modern factory, most labor is support labor—men who watch for problems and then solve them. The precise border between operating and supporting is not always clear, but the conceptual difference is enormous. The supporting laborer is not a bad machine. He is a valuable man, offering distinctly human intelligence and skill. Support labor also includes accountants, bookkeepers, information technology professionals, technical specialists and researchers, quality control workers, and managers' secretaries.

The labor of distribution is so old that some of the earliest extant written documents are merchants' notes. Even in a largely self-sufficient agricultural economy some stuff was traded, but most was produced on the family farm or in the home. In industrial economies, almost all production is centralized, so trade—the labors of gathering, transporting, dividing, and allocating stuff—is a crucial economic activity. The automotive industry requires tens of thousands of different parts to be gathered from hundreds of locations, and then the cars must be divided out, via thousands of dealers, to their hundreds of thousands of consumers. In addition, industrial economies rely on humans to organize and operate the modes of transport—the networks of roads, rail, ships, and air transport and the "lines" of pipe, cable, and bandwidth.

Economists should remember that money is only a flexible tool, not a fixed standard of value. It is an important tool for the social organization of trade and industrial production, and it is also used as an indicator of social status. As might be expected, as the industrial economy has developed the labors of the money economy have become more complex, professional, and diverse. The few preindustrial traders and merchants have given way to an army of new specialists: insurers who exchange a contingent promise for current cash; bankers who gather, disburse, and guard the money needed to fund investment projects; multicurrency traders; experts in financial obligations of various sorts; and a collection of analysts and journalists to keep all the financiers in the know. However, many money laborers do nothing very useful (see below).

As preindustrial philosophers often observed, money seems to have a corrupting effect on many who labor with it. Perhaps this corruption springs from the alienation of laboring with something that is itself useless; perhaps it is the relative ease with which money can be multiplied; perhaps it is the power of holding something that others desperately want; perhaps it is the especially extravagant consumption rewards that come from dishonesty with money. The reason can be debated, but the implication is clear. Monetary labors need close supervision if they are not to become socially destructive. Industrial economies have generally risen to the challenge, although the battle between greed and regulation is never definitively won.

Finally, training labor deserves its own category. Preindustrial craft apprentices were trained informally by their masters, but many types of labor in industrial societies involve complex and detailed skills that are best learned through formal instruction. Training labor resembles the transcendental labor of education, but the two differ in content and aims. Education aims at providing knowledge and understanding in order to open up the human spirit to the transcendental good, while training, at its highest, encourages a dedication to efficiency. Its aims are usually much more modest—the inculcation of particular skills, taught without any interest in cultural contexts or deeper meanings.

There are many types of indirectly mediated labor, but all have a few common themes. To start with, this labor is generally quite specialized. Each laborer knows about only a few things, but he knows them very well. The labor done by a single preindustrial grain merchant is now divided into many professions—appraisers, market estimators, lenders, trading specialists, quality control experts, buyers. Each has its own carefully defined and developed expertise. The deployment of so many experts greatly increases the efficiency of production while the willingness of producers and consumers to rely on the expertise and goodwill of many specialists is an example of the deep trust that runs through industrial economies.

Indirect productive labor often makes significant intellectual demands. While preindustrial laborers could rely on tradition and work inefficiently, industrial specialists are expected to use technical knowledge, conceptual understanding, and honed intuition to "think through" complex situations as efficiently as possible. The labor of an investor or regulator can be just as intellectually demanding as that of a scholar or doctor, although not as spiritually elevating. At a more modest level, the intellectual demands of support labor in a factory make it more appealing than directly productive farm and factory labor, which involve more routine tasks. The intellectual demands sometimes seem to be greater than the socioeconomic system can meet. Many people with positions of authority in investment, regulatory, and management labor hardly seem up to the job.

Finally, indirectly mediated labor is often disproportionately effective. The objectively small accomplishments of the detailed labor of the many specialists both support and are quickly multiplied by the great productivity of the industrial system. Of course, this effectiveness also creates responsibilities. The effects of small failures and apparently trivial errors are also multiplied.

Economically Pointless Labor

Throughout this book, I have emphasized that economic activity is, or should be, oriented to the good. Men are good, labor is good, and consumption is good. Economies should be organized to support these various goods. The good is never easy to achieve, since men are also morally weak. The weaknesses in preindustrial economies were mostly caused by the economic problem, the threat and reality of absolute poverty. In contrast, industrial economies suffer from evils of abundance. I have already mentioned consumerism, the craving for harmfully large amounts of stuff. In the domain of labor, the tremendous efficiency of production has created a related evil—instrumentally neutral labor. This refers to the useless labors that engage many men and women in industrial economies.

Destructive labor is also economically pointless, or worse, but it is by no means an industrial creation.

Instrumentally Neutral Labor

An example is probably the best way to approach instrumentally neutral labor. Most men employed in financial markets play zero-sum games—each dollar or euro that is won by one financial laborer is simply lost by another. There is a flurry of activity that might suggest that something valuable or informative is happening, but actually these professionals are receiving generous rewards in exchange for gambling. Most of the financial industry could disappear without having any effect on any economic good.[20] By extension, the labor of those who provide these sophisticated gamblers with the tools of their trade—computers, legal advice, travel arrangements, and office supplies—must also be effectively useless.

The title of "instrumental neutrality" refers to the two key aspects of this sort of labor: it is instrumental in that it purposely deals with things (in this case financial securities), and it is neutral in that it promotes no good other than giving the laborer something to do.[21] Instrumentally neutral labor often has clear sociological meaning (finance professionals, for example, are usually very well rewarded); it can be very demanding of time and effort; and it can stimulate what looks like genuine economic activity (for example, the production of computers and paper). Economists should look through these attributes. The crucial issue is the good, which is absent. Indeed, the varieties of instrumentally neutral labor are just elaborations of the economic pointlessness of an endless moving back and forth of piles of sand.

When machines "spin their wheels," little damage is done. It is different for men. Instrumentally neutral labor is evil because it thwarts men in their most basic orientation, which is toward the good. Pointless activity, no matter how exciting and well rewarded, is an insult to human dignity.

Some types of labor provide a little good, but a good that is dwarfed by the human "opportunity cost," the good that the laborer could possibly do. The additional two blades on the latest razor add a tiny bit to the good of comfort, but the required efforts of research, development, and marketing are so vastly disproportionate to the good—so many of the skills of the laborers involved are effectively squandered—that the labor should be considered instrumentally neutral.

Instrumental neutrality cannot be judged simply by appearances or subjective judgment. Some neutral laborers, including most of those supporting finance professionals and some of the professionals themselves, believe that their tasks have a good purpose. They are deceived, more or less willfully. On the other hand, the detailed bureaucracy of regulation may often feel futile to those involved, but some of it is vital for the functioning of the beneficial but complex economic and social systems of the industrial economy. Careful analysis is required to disentangle the long and interlocking chains of cause and effect.

Several families of instrumentally neutral labor can be identified. The least controversial is discarded labor. The purest example of this is the pointless tasks forced upon prisoners in order to induce despair. Discarded labor also includes the production of crops for the government to buy and destroy and the writing of reports that will never be read and that teach the writer nothing. There are also overmanned factories in which each person has something to do, but some of everyone's and all of some people's labor is actually discarded.

Some activities are largely pointless. Finance has already been mentioned. Law may have a larger and more useful core than finance, but much of the legal labor in modern societies is either a poor substitute for trust or an effort to create unnecessary conflict and confusion. A good part of marketing and advertising labor is also pointless. A principal goal, after all, is to persuade people to consume something that they would not otherwise desire. Some management consulting is valuable, but many types are pointless.

All of these activities involve much hustle and bustle, employing a small army of supporting laborers.

Technological innovation has done wonderful things, but much contemporary labor of innovation is instrumentally neutral because it aims only at trivial improvements. The additional razor blades, the even lighter and sleeker mobile telephone, totally clear beer—the advantages do not justify the substantial labor involved. Indeed, industrial economies are marked by a culture of pointless innovation—extensive research and testing, new production lines, and a whole marketing industry of exaggeration and indoctrination.

The combination of innovation and satiety has created instrumentally neutral labors of supersatiety. Electronic toys provide a clear example. After the novelty wears off, video games provide children with no more good (fun, learning, or wonder) than do ball games. If the simple ball satisfies these needs ("sates"), then the complex video games are supersating. All of the additional labor involved—specialized electronics, game design, console manufacture, advertising, additional electricity to run the games, therapy for addled-brained gamers—is instrumentally neutral. Many aspects of industrial prosperity create supersated labor. Each case for the good of comfort can be argued, but surely some houses are too big, some wardrobes too extensive, some vacations too luxurious, and some gifts too ostentatious for the good of those who enjoy them. The labor that goes into these excesses is instrumentally neutral.

Finally, superfluous regulation produces a great deal of instrumentally neutral labor in industrial societies. Regulations that strive for perfect safety, perfect social relations, and perfect justice are doomed to fail, but their drafting, enforcement, and revision require a great deal of labor. Some paperwork is vital, but some is pointless.

Where does all the instrumentally neutral labor in industrial societies come from? There are economic explanations. The emphasis on trivial improvements that helped create consumption satiety now encourages labors of supersatiety. The need to find jobs for laborers whose tasks have been taken over by machines encourages the creation of jobs that do not get in the machines' way. The spread of higher education, made possible by the efficiency of industrial production, encourages the creation of skilled and challenging jobs, whether or not they do anything good. The observation of the great benefits from specialization in caring labor encourages the creation of even more specialized jobs, even if they are not useful.

These explanations do not fully satisfy. Economic trends are not unstoppable, and economic rules are not unchangeable. There must be a social choice to continue on the paths that have led to efficiency, even when the paths no longer lead to any good destination, but only to supersatiety and instrumentally neutral labor. Economic ignorance may be part of the explanation of this social choice, but some strands of the modern worldview must also play a part. Apparently, men would rather search for social position and something to do than make more valuable use of their ability to labor.

However it is explained, instrumentally neutral labor is one of the worst features of the modern industrial economy. It is not even clearly better than the dehumanizing factory labor that it has largely replaced or the desperate toil of preindustrial peasants. The industrial economy functions well enough to support more children, more prayer, and more beauty. The men and women who spent their days trading stocks and bonds or making shaving ever so slightly easier could be engaged in much more valuable unmediated caring or transcendental labors.

Destructive Labor

Instrumentally neutral labor is bad and largely new. Economically destructive labor is worse and as old as mankind. It is evil and it is not likely to go away.

Destructive violence, the socially approved use of deadly force, is probably the most common sort of destructive labor. It is not always easy to distinguish the economically destructive labor of armies of conquest and annihilation and the transcendental governing labor of protection. In practice, armies and police forces often move from one to the other type of labor with remarkable ease. The labor of destructive violence is highly esteemed socially, although perhaps somewhat less so after the terrible wars of the twentieth century. Even when war is feared, soldiers are almost universally admired for their willingness to face death in their labor, whether it is protective or destructive. Subjectively, the labor of destructive violence also seems to offer significant psychological and even spiritual satisfaction.

The advent of the industrial economy has not made this labor much more specialized or professional, but it has made it more indirect. When fighting was done primarily with rocks or swords, soldiers had close contact with their adversaries. Guns made the victims almost invisible. In the most sophisticated contemporary warfare—for example, when the actual killing is done by robot drones—the human touch is as distant as in a fully automated factory. Industry also magnifies the passive side of this labor—far more men are killed in modern than in premodern wars.

While destructive violence is the most dangerous type of destructive labor, three other types can be identified.

Vandalism refers to individualistic and socially castigated destructive labor. In one sense, the vandal and the destructive soldier are doing the same thing—both destroy for the sake of destruction. Socially, their labor is quite different—the vandal's violence is aimed at his own society, while the soldier acts against a common enemy. In addition, vandals must always find their own consumption rewards, while soldiers are generally allocated rewards by the polity they serve.

Nonviolent illegal labor is less obviously damaging than vandalism, but often just as socially destructive. Theft of all sorts, from the simplest burglary to the most sophisticated swindle, is probably the most common variety of this type of labor. There is also the more or less honest trade in illegal goods, from smuggling to the distribution of proscribed drugs. In general, the more complex the economic regulations, the greater the opportunities for illegal labor.

There is sometimes a gap between law and morality, so some destructive labor is quite legal but still evil. The labors of pornography provide a clear example. In most industrial societies, it is perfectly legal to desecrate bodies and destroy souls in many sorts of "erotic" labor, ranging from prostitution to publishing. The labors involved in the "pornography" of violence and greed also belong in this category.

The writing of this chapter caused me more difficulty than almost anything else in this book. I worried about almost everything—the types of labor I was forgetting; where in the list this or that job belonged, jobs that did not fit neatly into any single category (journalist, hairdresser, dog-walker); the fairness of my examples; the order of the hierarchy. My troubles were greater than the importance the issues merited. This hierarchy is less central to the schema of human economics than many other features: the definition of the field as centered on labor and consumption, the division of goods into external and internal, the hierarchies of the goods and lists of the evils. The difficulty sprung from the novelty of this list—it involved more new and challenging concepts than anything else in this book.

Novelty in itself is of little value, in ideas just as in music or fashion. The key question is whether the new ideas are also good ones. Of course, I believe that my ideas are good—why else develop them? In any case, I hope that this morally charged typology, however imperfect in its details, offers several significant improvements over what is currently on offer from economists and other social scientists: the priority given to labors of being and care; the respectful treatment given to women's labor; the integration of reproduction into labor economics; the praise of indirect productive labor, especially of regulation; and the concept of instrumentally neutral labor.

It may be a lot to digest. Fortunately, the ground covered in the next two chapters, which are dedicated to consumption, is more familiar.

16

Consumption in the World

Consumption is easier to approach than labor. There is much less to study, since there are no consumption counterparts to the labors of care, instrumental neutrality, and destruction. Also, conventional economists have spawned fewer confused ideas about consumption, largely because their refusal to grapple with moral weakness creates only serious distortions in the study of consumption, while it almost totally invalidates large parts of the study of labor. Most profoundly, there is something simpler about consumption. As I will explain at the end of this chapter, consumption starts with men's animalistic needs and never fully departs from that earthy base. In contrast, labor involves some of men's most godlike qualities—caring, making, and sharing.

Still, consumption and labor have a close and nearly symmetrical physical and metaphysical relationship. Both provide signs of social status and individual, psychological meaning; both are necessary for life; both have much more than necessity about them; both can be divided in morally and practically meaningful ways. These similarities make this chapter a largely symmetrical partner to chapter 14, which dealt with the sociology and psychology of labor. The discussions of economic sociology in the two chapters are roughly analogous, but the counterpart to the discussion of the psychology of labor here is a discussion of the philosophy of consumption.

This substitution springs from one way in which consumption is more challenging than labor. The goods of labor are relatively easy to identify—labor is good to the extent that it serves the external economic goods and that it respects its internal good, the dignity of the laborer. The psychology of labor is mysterious, since it is so intimately tied up with the mysterious temptations of evil. For consumption, it is the other way around. The psychology is relatively straightforward—a mix of need and desire tinted with easily identifiable moral weakness. The moral philosophy, however, is challenging. Where does consumption, which is so resolutely worldly, fit into men's search for the good, the search of creatures who are a puzzling mix of worldly and transcendental?

Consumption in the Context of Sociology

Consumption is intensely individualistic—my house, my food, my holiday. It is also intensely social—we share and compare what we consume, and we use consumption as a marker of social divisions. This polarity of the personal and social in consumption is an unchanging part of the human condition.[1] However, the industrial economy has changed consumption in two significant ways—by enhancing the importance of conspicuous consumption and by creating mass consumption.

Community and Caste in Consumption

Like labor, consumption patterns provide sociological markers. The consumption implications of biological differences are particularly clear. Women and men wear sexually specific clothes and use sexually specific beauty products (that would be "skin care" for men). Children and adults wear different clothes and often eat different foods. In consumption, as in many other social domains, these distinctions have been threatened by the androgynous and age-egalitarian strands of the modern worldview. Still, many old consumption distinctions remain, and some new ones have been developed—boys' and girls' toys remain distinct, and men and women tend to buy different types of cars.

Even more than for labor, shared consumption is rarely important enough to define significant communities on its own. A shared taste for soup might support a fan club, and shared troubles with a particular model of car might support a complaint club, but such groupings have much less personal and social resonance than the communities held together primarily by kinship, religion, nationality, perceived ethnicity, or even shared labor. Common consumption practices are frequently found in these more fundamental communities, but the uniforms and typical dishes serve as markers or signs—not as a source—of community. Urban gangs and employees at banks may wear specified items of clothing, but showing up in the right outfit is not enough to allow a would-be tough or teller to join up.

The role of consumption is probably most important in the smallest communities, those of households and extended families. Shared meals—common food, supplemented in industrial societies by identical crockery and cutlery—provide a physical representation of, or a tangible counterpart to, the unity of the eaters. Similarly, a house or apartment usually requires or reflects some sort of a community among its residents. In modern societies, these communities have been weakened by the antifamily strand of the modern worldview, which has been aided by the declining practical need for domestic productive labor. Meals are increasingly eaten apart, and houses are increasingly either not shared at all or shared with near strangers. The loving domestic care of the housewife has increasingly been replaced by the frantic balancing of careers.

Consumption goods can also signify wider communities. Distinctive architecture, home decorations, clothing styles, and food demarcate many types of unity—of professions, castes, or residence. Again, many of these distinctions have been eroded in industrial economies. Suit-wearing or pierced-eyebrow strangers can still easily recognize their fellows from a distance, but everyone, rich and poor, wears jeans these days. At best, and it is a moderate best, global trade has spawned vast but shallow international consumption communities. Everyone, from Anchorage to Abidjan, now wears jeans.

Of all consumption communities, those of caste have probably held up best against the homogenizing forces of modernity. Marketing professionals identify a wide range of "consumption demographics" for almost all types of stuff, from basic food to the perceived luxuries of holidays. Caste members feel it is appropriate, and sometimes even obligatory, to wear certain identifying types of clothes (jeans of a particular cut or color), eat certain types of foods, and live in certain types of housing. These consumption-caste correlations follow incomes in a rough way—the relatively rich generally buy more expensive things than the relatively poor—but the precise relations of social caste and consumption patterns are more subtle than money can measure.

The social meaning of caste based consumption is both changing and consistent. It changes because it can only be defined in relation to the shifting configurations of economy and society. This relativity makes precise consumption-caste comparisons over time and distance impossible. Only after a series of fairly arbitrary adjustments—for differences in caste definitions, caste relations, and available stuff—can the social meaning of the consumption of a member of the "upper middle class" or the "senior office worker caste" in Britain be compared with that of his father or that of someone in roughly the same economic position in the United States or France.

The meaning is consistent in that sociologists and economists can identify some common patterns. For example, the consumption patterns of the "nouveaux riche" are much the same, whether they have acquired their social privilege from conquest, a sudden accumulation of wealth, or a shift in political balance. The newly risen copy the consumption habits of the privileged whom they are displacing, but the imitation is mixed with a sweeping away of perceived decay. The displaced privileged see the new consumption habits as crass and "in poor taste." Other examples of consumption consistency include the elite fascination with the consumption of high art, the tricky relations between popular and elite taste, and the desire to live in neighborhoods segregated by caste.[2]

Conspicuous Consumption

Conspicuous consumption is another socioeconomic pattern, one that is significant enough in industrial economies to deserve its own heading. The phrase was introduced by Thorstein Veblen to describe the use of consumption stuff solely to demonstrate caste membership.[3] Ostentatious consumption was practiced to some extent in preindustrial economies,[4] but it has flourished in all industrial economies. The ever increasing abundance of consumption items offers a fertile economic ground for the practice. And the increased centrality of economic concerns has created a widespread, although largely erroneous, trust in consumption items as a sign of caste membership. In addition, the failure of consumption items actually to define caste and the rapid modern shifts in both economic and social relations create caste anxiety; many people are either uneasy about maintaining their caste position or think they should be able to move up the social scale.

Like all consumption-caste indicators, conspicuous consumption is relative. It is impossible to understand what my car says about my social status without first understanding the current status language of cars. Conspicuous consumption's reliance on social context helps explain why satiety has not slowed down consumption in industrial economies. The process works as follows. A few already sated members of my caste acquire some superfluous item, perhaps a sleek sports car. They are motivated to this conspicuous consumption by some variety of caste anxiety. Their conspicuous consumption induces caste anxiety in me; I am afraid that I will fall behind if I don't acquire my own Porsche. It's not that I am greedy or wasteful; I just want to have enough stuff to show that my social position has remained the same relative to theirs. Of course, it is a shame that the "enough" stuff is more than I can make good personal use of, but status symbols do not need to be useful.

Men are often unconscious of such sociological motivations. They believe, or half-believe, that their interest in particular items of conspicuous consumption is personal rather than social. I may argue that driving the sports car offers a much-needed release from the intellectual tension of my job, that it will improve my response time, and that the car is a good investment. Such reasons may sometimes be more than mere rationalizations, but the desire for conspicuous consumption provides a more persuasive explanation for the sale of sports cars—and more generally for the continuing desire for more stuff in sated industrial economies—than does any collection of individual needs and desires.

As a socioeconomic practice, conspicuous consumption is not all bad. It provides a social dimension and some social meaning for the many comforts made available by modern industry. It is *mostly* bad, though. It is futile—stuff is consumed without creating any personal good. It is almost unstoppable—the capacity to produce is the only limit, and that capacity is very high in industrial economies. It leads to bad labor—society creates instrumentally neutral jobs to produce and promote largely useless stuff, and people take pointless jobs so they can relieve their caste anxiety by acquiring this largely useless stuff. It strips stuff of social meaning—in our growth-oriented industrial economies, more and better is always coming along, so today's tokens of exclusive caste membership will lose most of their social value tomorrow. It is also socially destabilizing—the desire to keep up or catch up (Veblen's "emulation") creates an unattractive consumption hustle, as both climbers and defenders strive for more.

Mass Consumption

In preindustrial economies, there was a great deal of similar consumption—food made from the same varieties of crops or livestock and prepared according to the same recipes; houses made from the same designs and materials; clothing made in the same styles from the same fabrics. The advent of industry and advertising has so intensified this similarity that it deserves a new name: "mass consumption."[5]

In comparison to the preindustrial pattern, mass consumption is vastly larger in scale. Many more varieties of stuff are consumed in much higher quantities—millions or billions of the same models of telephones, cigarettes, and soap. Mass consumption stuff is also much closer to being identical. Producers make every effort to use chemically identical materials and mechanically identical processes in order to ensure exactly the same consumption experience. The industrial techniques of mass production (the efficient use of the capital described in chapter 1) ensure that those efforts are quite successful. Mass consumption is now the standard in rich countries for most types of stuff, from packaged foods and electric power to coffins and air travel.

Consumers have quite reasonably abandoned consumption standards set in the house or village for the sake of mass consumption. Consumers benefit from mass production's enormous economies of scale—factory techniques make products that are more consistent and less expensive than any home or village producer can manage. Industrial enterprises also have greater resources to invest in improving the quality of products and the efficiency of production. These investments pay off frequently enough that the objective superiority of factory-made over handcrafted alternatives increases over time. Only members of elite castes can now afford to cherish the variety and scarcity of small-scale craft production. This preference is an example of conspicuous consumption at its most twisted—desiring an inferior product because it is scarcer and more expensive. Still, even the elite are extensive mass consumers. Many preindustrial aristocrats employed personal coach-makers, but no one today would think of hiring a personal jet-maker.

The principal disadvantage of mass consumption, as of so many aspects of the modern industrial economy, is that it is alienating. The meaningful tie between consumption and labor is lost. Socially, it is hard to use any particular item as a token of membership for a small group when the big group—the whole middle class, the nation, or the world—has access to exactly the same item. The romantic antimoderns are also right to identify something soul-deadening in the uniformity of mass consumption.[6] The elite purchasers of home-made stuff have only a partial escape. They may be able to escape some of the drab uniformity of mass consumption, but the labor-consumption tie between a prosperous Londoner shopping in a local Moroccan craft boutique and the Moroccan craftsman is still quite distant.

Mass consumption's potential for alienation has been recognized from the beginning by both antimoderns and industrial producers, although the producers' concerns were more commercial that existential—how to persuade potential customers that an industrial product would fit into their lives. The main anti-alienation tool was advertising, or "marketing" as practitioners now called it. The basic approach has not changed—producers create a brand or product qualities that might give consumers some sort of meaning, something to "hang onto."[7] The meaning of brands varies. They can be symbols of products' genuine attributes. They can also be almost entirely mythical, as in the Coke feeling. Or they can be based on the magnification of the importance of differences that are small enough not to interfere with production efficiency, such as the differences in car models built from the same manufacturing platform. The existence of shallow brand communities suggests that advertising does help to reduce consumer alienation. Widespread consumer indifference in the face of the cornucopia of industrial consumption goods suggests that the effect is modest.

In some cases, the fight against alienation is fought in a quite different way—by using the massing effect of mass consumption to create economic unity. Within any country, every house, from hovel to mansion, has identical electrical sockets. When there were national telephone companies, they spread a few virtually identical models of telephones across the nation to rich and poor alike. A fast-food restaurant such as McDonald's strips food of almost all sociological significance. The nineteenth-century socialist dream of the universal brotherhood of man is now realized in the class-oblivious crowds eating bland food in ugly restaurants. It is a unifying experience, but also an alienating one.

The Moral Philosophy of Consumption

Most people rarely worry about what constitutes a good job. They may become philosophical at a few times during their labor lives—at the beginning of a career, when a first child is born, and perhaps during a midlife crisis. For the rest, however, compulsion, striving for excellence, and social expectations are usually enough to keep them going without much thought. In contrast, consumers in sated industrial economies often feel troubled by philosophical questions about consumption—what is the right stuff to consume and what is the right attitude with which to approach consumption? The doubts come in both directions. On one side, perhaps I do not have enough or am not concerned enough with what I buy and use. On the other, perhaps I have too much stuff and am too materialistic. Or perhaps it is not so much me as my society that is materialistic.

One Unworthy Philosophy about Consumption

The word "materialistic" is less than two centuries old, but both excessive attention to consumption and complaints about that attention are as old as philosophy, perhaps as old as mankind.[8] Wise men of various creeds and cultures have long castigated their unenlightened contemporaries, and it seems—to judge by the spread, frequency, and vehemence of the attacks—that the people have generally ignored them.

Conventional economists are exceptional. They are philosophers who endorse exactly what almost all sages have condemned. Indeed, economists have long worn the badge of materialism with pride. Bentham, who thought all pleasure was physical, and Marx, who invented dialectical materialism, were perhaps the most vehement advocates of the this-world creed, but there have been almost no vociferous dissenters in the profession. The new school of happiness economists (see chapter 1) is a partial exception. Its members are utilitarians who have been mugged by reality—past a fairly modest level, people with higher incomes do not score higher on happiness surveys. The remaining professionals posit an "economic man" who is an unreconstructed utilitarian of a reasonably strict school (see chapter 2). For him, consumption provides utility, and more consumption is better than less consumption because it provide more utility, if only marginally more. That is the way the equations of the neoclassical model work. For nations, the highest economic good is unthinkingly assumed to be economic growth, which consists largely in the production and consumption of more stuff.[9]

To be fair to the profession, as long as the economic problem persisted, this reductive view of reality did not necessarily lead to a serious error about the consumption good. When additional consumption actually prevents death, then that addition supports life, the highest economic good. Poverty-ending consumption fails to serve the good only when it is associated with some evil greater than the good of life—perhaps cannibalism or apostasy. Such possibilities rarely arose in eighteenth- or nineteenth-century Europe, but absolute poverty was still widespread. More was truly better, at least if the additional stuff went mostly to the absolutely poor. Unfortunately, the economists lose credit by failing to emphasize that condition; they even sometimes argue against feeding the poor.[10]

Even when the economic problem has been solved, the materialist assumption does not always lead to bad economic advice. Men always want more from the world. That worldly more is not as great a good as life, but it is a good that should be pursued unless the search interferes with the pursuit of other, higher goods. Until satiety arrives and as long as noneconomic goods are not disturbed, more consumption is better than less. Unfortunately for the conventional economists, satiety has arrived for many types of stuff, and more consumption in a prosperous economy may threaten many other important goods, perhaps including the good of appropriate consumption. Conventional materialism's consistent refrain of "more is better, more is better" may still sometimes be right, but there is no way of knowing when without broadening the philosophical enquiry.

Some modern critics of materialism, including antimodern economists, argue that modern men are more materialistic than their premodern ancestors. They sometimes cite as evidence the social and academic respectability awarded to conventional economists and their reductive advice, but their case is primarily based on the observation that there is so much more stuff to be materialistic about. They point out that the abundance of industrial prosperity has allowed a new form of this moral weakness to develop: consumerism. The case for extraordinary modern materialism is reasonably strong, but it would be stronger if complaints about a bad attitude toward stuff had not been so consistent in all periods and places, even (or perhaps especially) including monasteries.

Whether or not modern men are more materialistic than their ancestors, they face the eternal human disappointment with stuff. No matter how much there is, how fine it is, how much more I have than my neighbors, stuff does not bring meaning to life. Traditionally, sages used the discovery of stuff-disappointment as a teaching moment, an opportunity to entice men to look for higher goods. Modern society is short of such sages and critical of many higher goods, both novelties that are far more significant than the increased supply of stuff. The lack of alternatives to consumption and the abundance of stuff may make disenchanted modern consumers more inclined than their preindustrial ancestors to turn to more consumption in the vain hope that the elusive meaning will finally arrive. In that sense, the modern economy could be more materialistic. The lack of acceptable higher goods also means that consumption disappointment is more likely to lead consumers to nothing, to the distinctly modern disease of social alienation.

Four Worthy Philosophies About Consumption

For professional purposes, conventional economists are crude materialists, but they are almost alone in intellectual and spiritual history. Even premodern materialist philosophers were not of the crude school; they did not usually think that more stuff is better than less. Epicurus, who first argued that everything was made of material atoms, took a quite "spiritual" approach to consumption.[11] The many traditions of unconventional thinking—unconventional only from the materialist perspective of conventional economics—have come up with several approaches to the good of consumption.

To start with, consumption might basically be a good thing. Leisure is necessary for the pursuit of noble transcendental goods—or so argued many premodern philosophers and practical men—and wealth is necessary for leisure. Freedom from toil generally came along with an abundance of stuff, at least by the standards of the time. So ample consumption was a sign of nobility, a nobility that could be used to pursue glory, wisdom, or some other great good. In addition, some extravagance in consumption was part of the representative responsibility that came with aristocracy. Finery and refinement were signs of a transcendental grandeur. The availability of stuff might also be a sign of divine favor. It would be churlish to reject such a gift.

Alternatively or additionally, consumption might be good as long as it is pursued in moderation. In this Aristotelian view, the claims about the good of consumption are all true, but there is a danger of excess. Too much desire for ostentation is bad for the character; it distracts men from their higher callings and overly stimulates their sensuous desires. Excess can lead to avarice and a general meanness of spirit. Socially, it can be disruptive. The sight of extravagance might trouble the poor, as would the taxes levied on them to make such excess possible. A Christian could add that too much consumption threatens social solidarity by making it hard for rich and poor to see each other as neighbors who are equal in the eyes of God.

Epicurus not only endorsed moderation in consumption, but also demanded indifference. The traditional Epicurean and Stoic view was that consumption is not bad in any reasonable quantity, but only as long as the consumer is able to avoid feeling passionately about what is consumed. For these philosophers, the dislike of passion was more important than the particular object of non-desire, but more passion-friendly philosophers also felt that it is appropriate to approach stuff with indifference, because stuff contributes so little to the good. If you are made greatly happy by the prospect of gaining vast amounts of stuff, then you are expecting too much from that stuff. If you are greatly upset by losing all your stuff, then you were too attached to it.

The last alternative is that stuff could be generally bad. It cannot help but lead men away from the best part of their nature. Luxuries inevitably corrupt the character, whereas want toughens and ennobles it. The fight against greed is lost before it begins if the fighter has soft pillows, no fear of hunger, and a realistic possibility of owning a nicer horse. The love of money is the root of all evil, as Saint Paul says (1 Timothy 6:10). It may also be the root of some non-evil, but why get started when the risks are so high? The best way to avoid the love of money is to disdain the stuff that money can buy.

The proponents of these various approaches disagree on how much evil stuff can actually cause, but they agree that the goods that stuff can offer directly are of moderate value. That fundamental judgment is in accord with the discussion of the economic good in chapter 10. Once absolute poverty is out of the question, the approach to consumption need not be a crucial moral issue. Still, consumption is an important economic activity. It should be done right.

None of the proposals is quite right. The first is too extreme for humans, creatures who are prone to moral weakness. The last is too extreme for creatures who are given the whole world to cultivate. The second, the ideal of moderation, is too detached from the abundant generosity and hospitality that is enjoined on Christians. Stoic indifference is even more detached. It is also unrealistic; humans are too much in the world to be able simply to ignore its charms.

Neither Animals Nor Angels

As always in my discussions of philosophy, I rely on the Christian worldview—plausible, well-tested, and deeply respectful of both men's transcendental calling and their worldly responsibilities. That worldview teaches that consumption is central to the nature of animals, and that men are, among other things, animals. Men and beasts share a physiologically identical need for food and warmth. Human nature, however, so completely transforms the animal needs that this commonality can easily be forgotten. Animal nutrition takes place with almost no sign of any sort of thought. It changes only in response to ecological shifts or human intervention. In contrast, men's diet is learned, taught, and considered. It changes over the generations along with men's tastes and technological competence. Animals never try to improve on what their instincts lead them to find (although they can sometimes be taught), while humans take delight in the refinement of taste and are willing to offer additional labor for the sake of added gustatory pleasure.

In addition, where animals follow instincts in their consumption, men create structures—rules, patterns, divisions, and organized judgments—to make sense of reality. Men transform the animal need for nutrition into carefully organized meals and diets. They transform the animal need for adequate warmth into wardrobes and fashion, structures rich in social and transcendental meaning about sexual differentiation, social position, modesty and indecency, the beautiful and the plain. Men's need for shelter is almost instinctive and animalistic, but their houses are built to exemplify distinctly human categories—clean/dirty, private/public, child/adult, formal/informal.[12]

For all of this elaboration, human consumption cannot ever depart completely from the animalistic and the physical. On the contrary, most consumption is firmly rooted in the physical world. Each of the four traditional types of consumption stuff—food, clothing, shelter, and heat—provides something absolutely necessary for bodily survival. Rich and poor share this physicality. In both preindustrial and industrial economies, wealthy men mostly have better food, more clothing, and larger, more comfortable houses than do poor men. The rich may also be able to take advantage of the physical aid of servants. Nor has physicality disappeared with the coming of industry. Industrial prosperity has added much more physical stuff: electric lighting, air conditioning, kitchen appliances, trains, cars, computers, telephones. Some of this stuff serves animalistic needs and desires less than did the traditional foursome, but the stuff itself cannot be made without elements gathered from the physical world.

The ultimate physicality of consumption stuff helps explain why consumption is good, why the good of consumption is modest, and why consumption can be dangerous. Consumption is good because it is part of human nature to receive the world's gifts. In consumption, men not only receive these gifts, but they humanize them by transforming and elaborating the things of the world into things with human meaning. The good of consumption is modest because men's greatest goods are not physical but transcendental. Changes in consumption can have only a limited influence on how men strive after these great goods. Planes, phones, and e-mail do not fundamentally alter the trials and triumphs of romance, study, and worship.

Consumption can be dangerous because the things of this world, transformed and humanized, can easily become an inadequate substitute for the true Good. Enhanced physical consumption can be offered as a poor substitute for a higher way. That substitution can be seen in consumerism. It can also be seen in modern medicine, in which curative labor is too often exchanged for a consumption approach that leaves sick people feeling more like broken machines than like suffering but loved members of a family; in modern entertainment, in which the pursuit of beauty is too often exchanged for consumption that aims at cruder satisfactions; and (according to Catholic teaching) in the consumption of contraceptive devices, in which purely physical concerns take the place of the true and higher meaning of sexual activity.[13]

The consistently physical base of consumption also makes it clear that men are not angels, purely spiritual creatures.[14] While we do not live on bread alone, we need bread to live. Economists should not forget the relatively modest position of the economic good, but neither should they forget that consumption, no matter how physical, is indeed good for men. Any effort to "overcome" the pleasures and virtues of consumption is deeply misguided. Rather, consumption should be accepted as a basic and good element of the human condition.

Appropriate Consumption

The internal good of consumption is appropriateness (see chapter 10). The discussion of animals and angels provides a guide to what sort of consumption is actually appropriate. Consumption should accord with men's worldly nature and desires, but it should also respect men's transcendental calling. Because men have animalistic needs, the appropriateness of consumption is partly objective, consisting in the stuff consumed. Because men have desires, understanding, and judgment, appropriateness is partly subjective, consisting in the way men approach consumption. Because men are morally weak, the desire for consumption stuff can be disordered.

The Christian worldview has led me to this evaluation of the consumption good, but the Christian spiritual tradition, which should come to my aid in its further development, lets me down. Until very recently, almost all Christian saints and philosophers have taken a too negative view of consumption—too little attention paid to the gospel enthusiasm for wedding feasts and expensive ointment, too much emphasis on the gospel condemnations of "riches."[15] Perhaps the human economics introduced in this book can lead to a fuller understanding of how the good consumer can both welcome the gifts of the world with gratitude and enthusiasm and avoid gloating and greedily grasping for more.

That fuller understanding of appropriate consumption will encompass an appropriate attitude to poverty. Poverty is highly praised in the Christian tradition, but only monks and other holy men are expected to forswear all of the material things of this world. For the rest, poverty is expected to be symbolic, giving up on the cares of the world. The symbolic sense is too easy, as it ignores consumption completely. The literal sense is both too hard, as there is always more stuff to give up on until absolute poverty leads to death, and too narrow in its application, as everyone, not merely monks, should be able to live a life of spiritually admirable consumption poverty.

The teaching of Jesus is the natural Christian starting point. He warns that it is difficult for the rich to enter heaven (Mark 10:23). Clearly, too much consumption does present a significant moral challenge. Jesus clearly has in mind a contrast between the riches of "treasure" in heaven, which are to be coveted, and the riches of the overly desired consumption goods of this world, which are to be shunned. Perhaps he is also warning especially against the dangers of a privileged economic position. Perhaps he is calling for a willingness to do without more-than-basic stuff, a willingness that is impossible as long as a man clings to his riches.

That social-psychological analysis suggests that the too rich man is best defined by a covetous attitude and exaggerated enthusiasm for actual or potential consumption goods, while the admirably poor man is best defined by a humble acceptance of what he has and a lack of worry about what he lacks. In the search for admirable poverty, the relatively poor man in any society starts with the advantage of having less to detach himself from. It is not a huge advantage, though, since relative poverty provides only modest protection against the moral weakness of riches, the exaggerated enthusiasm for stuff. The advent of industrial prosperity does not change the moral challenge substantially for either the relatively rich or the relatively poor. There is much more more-than-basic stuff around, but that easy abundance is just as likely to sharpen the desires of a man who is stuck in the rich attitude as to dull those of a man who embraces the poor man's approach.

It is not easy to translate the advice to avoid rich-thinking and practice poor-thinking into either personal decisions or social policies. To want more than a fair share of consumption goods or to value them more than is right is to think rich, but it is not obvious what share is fair and what value is right. Perhaps the best approach is to call on another Christian virtue, generosity. The willingness to give and to give up consumption stuff is a sign of taking an appropriate distance from the strife and selfishness of "the world." From that perspective, the monastic vows of poverty can be an inspiration. It is not required of monks or any other men to do without any particular piece of stuff, even the most trivial industrial gadget. What is asked of monks, and what other men should ask of themselves, is to be generous with what they have, to be ready, even eager, to forgo all the stuff of the world for the sake of heavenly treasure.[16]

The world is generous to us humans. It offers us sufficient elements to ward off absolute poverty. More than that, it offers enough to allow us to consume as much as is good for us, as long as we use our humanizing skills well. This potential bounty of creation implies that appropriate consumption need not be frugal. Indeed, too much frugality suggests a spurning of both the world's gifts and our abilities. There is nothing about the "good life" of plenty—feasts and fine clothing, comforts and luxuries—that cannot be reconciled with our search for the highest good. When approached correctly, with a spirit of poverty and generosity, all consumption, even the most luxurious, can signify and strengthen the human community in all of its many aspects.

17

A Typology of Consumption

Labor goes out from the laborer into the world. Its divisions have more to do with the destination than with the source. Consumption comes in from the world to the consumer, so the varieties of consumption—necessity, comfort and luxury—have much more to do with the consumer and his society than with the world. The same gold can be formed into the luxuries of jewelry and the necessities—or are they comforts?—of dental fillings. The actions and attitudes of men make the difference.

This chapter describes those differences. Most of it is quite conventional, at least by the standards of this book. The three-fold division of consumption stuff can be traced back at least two centuries and is still used by some economists, although not by neoclassical purists.[1] My understanding of the three terms is only modestly unorthodox, and my evaluation is hardly shocking—necessities are very good, comforts can be good but should be treated with caution, and luxuries can be good but should be treated with extreme caution. Yet at the end of the chapter, I make perhaps the most unconventional practical suggestion in this book: a call for an economy based on sustainable poverty.

What Is Truly Necessary?

Consumption necessities refer to all the consumption stuff that is required to defend the highest economic good—life—and to ward off the internal economic evil of absolute poverty. Necessities are part of the good of appropriate consumption and of every other internal economic good: labor for the sake of necessities is dignified; production should be efficient enough to produce necessities for all; every just allocation arrangement provides necessities for all; respect for the environment should leave no men without necessities.

The universal provision of consumption necessities should be the first goal of economic policy, just as the obtaining of necessities is the first step in any individual's economic life. But just what are these vital necessities? The problems involved in providing a list were glossed over in earlier discussions of life and absolute poverty, and for a good reason. The boundaries of the basic economic stuff of life are not easily determined. The good of life has clearly been denied when a man cannot avoid starving or freezing to death, but there is no obvious reason to stop with stuff that was recognized as necessary in 1700. The good of life is equally denied by death brought about from the lack of clean water, antibiotics, central heat, cars without airbags, and open-heart surgery.

More subtly, but equally crucially, life can be lost if a suicidal person is deprived of emotional and spiritual support. Consumption does not directly keep the potential suicide alive. However, comforters must be fed and housed and have the time available to give solace. Even more subtly, life relies on men's fertility and the world's fecundity. If parents hold back on having children for fear that they cannot provide them with the necessary stuff, then the good of life is in some way tarnished.

There might be yet more. Life is the greatest economic good, but economists cannot forget that life should be lived in a dignified way, a way which supports the other external economic goods—in health and in enjoyment of freedom, community, and beauty, not to mention some comfort. Perhaps some of the consumption stuff required to support these goods should also be considered necessities. Indeed, many moralists would now consider universal primary education, part of the economic good of freedom, to be a basic human good.[2] If so, it is necessary for an economy to produce enough stuff for teachers to live on and enough time for pupils to study.

The almost certain inclusion of clean water and antibiotics and the possible inclusion of education on the list of necessities indicate one quality of this list—it will change over time. When Plato sketched out the necessities of life in the most basic sort of community, he included clothing, shoes, bread, and wine, but it would never have occurred to him to worry about water purity, let alone about wonder drugs, or universal education.[3] A thinker from a tribe of hunter-gatherers would presumably have drawn up an even more modest list than Plato's. There is something unsatisfactory about making changes on a list of human necessities—are not men always the same?—but it cannot be avoided. Human knowledge is always limited; much has been learned about how well the world can be humanized since the first fields were cultivated.

Controversy is another quality of the list of necessities. The closer the study, the less likely is unanimity on just how much should be on it. For example, food will surely be included, but how much and of what sorts? I have already said that men were so poorly nourished in preindustrial economies that absolute poverty, by modern standards, was ubiquitous. Modern standards do not, however, provide a clear minimum acceptable level of nutrition. Should it be enough to avoid minimal brain damage, enough to have a ruddy glow of health, or perhaps enough to take care of the dietary needs of the gluten-intolerant? Good arguments can be made for almost any stopping point.

The possible addition of education hints at yet another quality of the list—it will involve sociology as well as pure stuff. It is not sufficient merely to produce enough consumption stuff for teachers and students to labor at education; the stuff must actually be available to them, and availability depends on socioeconomic arrangements. The social questions are particularly convoluted for the necessities needed to support potential lives. It is hard to determine whether enough stuff is potentially available for children whom parents might want to welcome into the world, especially when the motivations for not wanting children are not primarily economic.

Along with sociology, the list must take ambient technology into account. In a simple preindustrial economy, good transport was more of a luxury than a necessity, since most communities were almost self-sufficient. In the globally integrated industrial economy, access to transport may well be a necessity—it brings necessary stuff, including life-saving relief in case of natural disaster. If freedom and knowledge are considered necessary goods, then some sort of telecommunications would certainly be on the list. Even if the list includes only the direct supports of physical life, the life-support that comes from being connected to the world makes the phones or an Internet connection a near-necessity.

A long list of necessities is a sign of a prosperous economy, but the list should not be too long. Some claims for necessary status must be rejected. Men need decent housing, but decency does not require a bedroom for every child. Televisions are ubiquitous in industrial economies, but humans do not need them. The universal allocation of such non-necessities within rich countries may serve the internal economic good of allocation justice, but it cannot be defended on the grounds of human necessity.

Finally, the list should be realistic. Stuff can only really be considered necessary if it is, or might easily be, readily available to all. Current knowledge and production potential are the only possible starting points for discussion. Of course, realism should always be tempered with idealism. If there is one lesson from the economic history of the last three centuries, it is that men tend to underestimate their ability to serve the economic good. It once seemed unrealistic to promise that no one need die of hunger, but famines are now the responsibility of bad public policy, not the hostile forces of nature.[4] It once seemed unrealistic to consider vaccinations a human necessity, but smallpox has been all but eliminated from the entire world. To hope that the list of necessities will lengthen over the next few generations is both idealistic and realistic.

Comforts

The economic good of comfort was defined, discussed, and rather slighted in chapter 9. The good of a more convenient and comfortable life was described as the lowest of the economic goods, trailing far behind life, health, freedom, beauty, and community. To the extent that consumption non-necessities serve only this modest good, their moral value is accordingly modest. However, comforts as a type of consumption stuff are not quite the same as comfort as an economic good. Consumption comforts include all the stuff that is neither basic enough to be considered a necessity nor special enough to be considered a luxury. Understood in this way, as occupying the consumption middle ground, comforts serve comfort, but they also serve higher goods.

My equivocal use of the word "comfort"—to describe both a minor good and stuff that can serve more important goods—may be a bit confusing, but it follows both everyday and traditional professional usage. It also reflects the ambiguous relations of humans with any stuff that is not absolutely necessary. Such stuff seems to be superfluous, seductive, and truly valuable all at once. Even if the list of necessities is long, it will not include many valuable comforts. At the elite end of society, much stuff is required to store and transmit knowledge and to make things beautiful. At the more popular end, much stuff is helpful in the fortification of communities, and comfort is a real, if modest, economic good.

In preindustrial economies, comforts were scarce and largely available only to the aristocratic caste. The moral value of comforts for the few should have been balanced against the economic problem of absolute poverty for the many. On that balance, the consumption of more than a modest quantity of comforts was callous; it was more important to wrestle with the economic problem. Of course, this sort of egalitarian evaluation is anachronistic—before the industrial economy came along, the comforts and luxuries of the aristocracy were considered almost incommensurate with the worldly misery of the poor. Thinking and economic practices changed with the advent of the modern worldview and the industrial economy, but the first economists were caught between eras. They neither accepted the good that was traditionally assigned to the aristocratic lifestyle nor anticipated the fecundity of the industrial economy, so they castigated comforts and conveniences as vain fripperies.

Industrial fecundity has shifted the moral balance. Men can easily provide themselves with all necessities, however long the list. The prevalence of both instrumentally neutral labor and supersated consumption in rich societies shows how much potential production there is—in many categories, industrial economies not only produce more stuff than men need, but more than they can actually use, and they create this surplus while keeping a large number of workers "spinning their wheels." When so much consumption is possible, comforts need not be condemned. Indeed, the abundance of comforts in industrial economies has some beautiful aspects—it makes it easier for men to pursue all the economic goods; it reflects the abundance of nature; it shows men taking good advantage of their world-taming abilities; it offers great amounts of stuff that can be given away in hospitality and generosity; it provides remarkable amounts of the good of comfort, a modest good but a good nonetheless.

Of course, there are caveats. Men can easily provide themselves with all necessities, but in practice they only do so in part of the world. The global wealth gap and the persistence of absolute poverty are scandalous, and to the extent that dedication to the production of comforts detracts from narrowing the gap and eliminating absolute poverty, that dedication to lesser goods is also scandalous. Then there is the balance between the pursuit of consumption comforts and the pursuit of other objectives, social or personal. Some comforts help the search for the transcendental, but some may distract men from that search. In modern societies, there may well be too many trivial comforts and too much effort dedicated to the development of more, and often more trivial, comforts. Satiety also carries its own moral risks. Poverty is not as simple a matter as not having (see chapter 16), but it is hard to maintain a spirit of poverty in the midst of a culture of satiety and supersatiety.

To draw a line between a pleasing abundance of comforts and a depraved excess is also hard. Consider heating. When Benjamin Franklin popularized stoves that heated whole rooms rather than just the few feet directly in front of an open hearth, he mocked the traditional lack of interest in this quite physical comfort: "I suppose our Ancestors never thought of warming Rooms to sit in."[5] He sounded revolutionary then, but minimalist now; it is hard to argue that it is excessive to demand more comfortable houses than "our Ancestors" inhabited. However, perhaps we have gone too far. In our homes, both temperature and humidity are controlled room by room, hour by hour, with air conditioning widely considered a necessity in warm climates. Some experts worry that children growing up in such climatic perfection are not sufficiently robust. Perhaps our descendants will say, "It is no wonder that our Ancestors had no Fortitude of Soul, since they had none of Body."

Can Everyone Be Comfortable?

Almost everyone in prosperous industrial economies already consumes enough comforts to be considered comfortable. Indeed, full consumption satiety is in sight. In other words, not only can men fully solve the economic problem, but they can look forward to consuming everything that it is possible to consume. Such a prediction may seem extreme, or even ludicrous, since fairly significant consumption developments—the Internet, e-mail, inexpensive videos for the home—are less than a decade old and technologists are still buzzing with ideas.

If history is any guide, their innovative effort will certainly bear fruit, but there are limits to how much the human consumption experience can be improved. Men have many ways to deal with the world, but not an infinite number of ways. Indeed, it is possible to list quite quickly the needs and desires that stuff can satisfy—nutrition, intoxication, physical comfort, garments, decoration, travel, communications, information, energy in its various forms, entertainment. Others may want to add a few categories, but no one would suggest that there are hundreds more.

Before the advent of industry, men's ability to satisfy their worldly desires was underestimated. The last two centuries have been marked by a steady stream of innovations in almost every category. Men can fly, send sounds and images around the world, draw vast amounts of energy out of the earth, store incredible amounts of information in tiny spaces, and transmit that information at stunning speeds. Men can do all these things with remarkably little effort.

Now, though, for each category on the list, satiety is in sight. The basic four types of stuff—food, shelter, clothing, and fuel—are satisfied or super-satisfied. As for the others, there is still some room for improvements, but less all the time. More advanced mobile telephones will presumably do more remarkable things, but the goal of communications—the ability to talk to anyone at any place at any time—has basically been achieved. The same is true for information. Libraries will eventually go online, but that is no more than a refinement. I can already find everything that has been or is being thought anywhere in the world right from my own computer. Again, transport could get still faster and more efficient, but the whole world is already within reach. Even labor has become comfortable. Workplaces are safe and pleasant; physical strains are minimized; the workday is as comfortable as the many days off. Everyone may not yet be comfortable, but as far as comforts are concerned, the human reach and grasp now look to be fairly well balanced.

And yet, people in industrial economies often seem uncomfortable and restless about the stuff they have, as if there were much more to accomplish. Some of their discontent reflects genuine gaps—the newest comforts that are not yet available to all; the forthcoming next generation of this or that technology which will move consumption a little closer to satiety; the few residents who manage (through a combination of incompetence, belligerence, and isolation) to escape the fullness of industrial prosperity. Most of the discontent, however, seems to be centered on something less objective.

There are several subjective reasons for feeling stuff-troubled. The caste anxiety of conspicuous consumption certainly plays a role. Rather than bask in the comforts they have, men crave what their neighbors have, either some ever-so-slightly greater comforts or some simply useless tokens of higher social caste. The overvaluation of the economic good, especially the good of comfort, also contributes. Men expect too much meaning from comforts and are too prone to think that the problem is in the comforts rather than the expectations. Perhaps even more basic is a discontent with their physical limits. Humans can never be fully comfortable in a life that tends towards decay and ends in death, in experiences that are no better than their limited senses can absorb, in accomplishments that only imperfectly reflect the transcendental aspects of their nature. In some basic way, no economy can ever be prosperous or well organized enough to make men comfortable.

Luxuries

In premodern times, before consumption comforts became widespread, luxuries were almost exclusively considered part of the aristocratic lifestyle. Part of the responsibility and pleasure of being an aristocrat was the cultivation of luxuries of all sorts. There were simple collections, from the bronze pots and crude ornaments described by Homer to the almost incredibly ornate trinkets of the Renaissance. Some types of stuff—the finest wines, the most elegant works of art—were considered so sophisticated that only the nobility could be trained to appreciate them. There was also the noble refinement of everyday stuff. The poor would sleep on straw; the rich on feather mattresses. Of course, many types of finesse were not embodied in stuff, but whenever stuff was called for, it was to be luxurious. The finesse of skilled riding was accompanied by carefully bred horses, finely tooled saddles, and elegantly designed barns.

All these luxuries served as the consumption signs and symbols of nobility—excellent in their rareness, beauty, extravagance, and effort required for production. In preindustrial economies, these four premodern attributes came together without any conscious social effort. If something was beautiful or opulent, it was likely also to be sufficiently scarce and expensive to be reserved for the privileged few.

The advent of the industrial economy and the modern worldview has challenged everything about the preindustrial economy of consumption luxuries. To start with, the easy identification of luxury and aristocracy has been made much more difficult by the virtual abandonment of the premodern notion of aristocracy. There are still elite castes, but they have lost almost all of their transcendental glow. The social category of a distinct leisure class has been eroded on both sides—the elite are expected to hold down regular jobs, and regular people have plenty of time for leisure activities. In consumption, the idea of special things for special people now seems almost nonsensical. It makes no sense to specify some types of stuff as so refined that they should only be owned by those with sufficient refinement to appreciate the best. Luxuries just look like particularly extravagant comforts.

Industrial efficiency makes rareness scarce. Everyone has comfortable mattresses, and even the cheapest cars are wonders of engineering. Most art is mass produced, and copies of individual masterpieces are almost as fine as the originals. Miners have to control the supply of so-called precious stones, lest consumers realize that they could easily become common stones. Luxuries are scarce usually because men have decided to make them so, either by deciding not to produce very many, as in top-of-the-line cars or "collectible" coins and knick-knacks, or by the construction of completely artificial limits to acquisition, as in self-declared exclusive country clubs. When there is genuine scarcity, as in beachfront property, luxury status is almost assured. Inefficient production, as in handicrafts, is almost enough to guarantee luxury status by itself. Old things are scarce because they are not made any more, so even the ugliest and most useless antiques can become luxuries.

Industrial efficiency should make beauty common. Artists can work in media that are susceptible to mass consumption—the printed page, cinema, photography. Buildings are so easily built that everyone can have access to beautiful ones—beautiful houses for themselves, beautiful public buildings for their communities. The many manufactured comforts should be beautiful, because beauty can easily be integrated into industrial design and production. Unfortunately, the modern tendency to uglification has limited the spread of this aspect of luxury, so much so that even the elite have lost much of their taste for the exceptionally beautiful. The rich still commission exclusive art, but the art is more loved for its exclusiveness than for its beauty.

The extravagance of luxury is still possible, but it is harder to identify in an economy of consumer satiety. There may be some difference between the convenience and efficiency of consumption comforts and the opulence and ease of true luxuries, but as comforts become more comfortable they increasingly encroach on the traditional domain of luxuries. The gap between first class and economy on an airplane is pretty small next to the gap between sitting in a fine carriage and walking on a muddy road.

As for the sense that luxury embodies a tremendous effort—the thousands of hours of labor that produced the aristocratic family's embroidered linens or the hundreds of servants that were required to keep an aristocrat's wardrobe in pristine condition—it has largely been swept away by the superiority of mass-produced over handmade stuff. That practical logic is only reinforced by the egalitarianism of modernity. Members of the elite would not feel right wearing clothes that looked dramatically different from those worn by members of other classes. They must content themselves with paying more for a wardrobe that only experts can identify as luxurious.

The social leveling and industrial efficiency of the modern worldview has destroyed most of the old sort of luxury, but a new sort has taken some of its place. The technique is to identify stuff that would otherwise have nothing special about it as luxurious—luggage, scarves, perfume.[6] The goal is not so much exclusiveness or even quality as aura. Anyone who is willing to pay the price can buy the luxury perfume at the counter, but each buyer should still feel special. These bourgeois luxuries have no aristocratic connotations. Their scarcity is either artificial or imaginary, and their quality is often doubtful, but they are still cherished. Humans seem to crave some sort of distinction in stuff, if only a perceived one. These bourgeois luxuries are much more amply available than the old aristocratic luxuries. Unlike traditional luxuries, which were in short supply because there were not enough men available to make them, bourgeois luxuries can be produced in any desired quantity. Indeed, a whole "luxury goods" industry has developed to make them available to a large—but not too large—number of people.

Are Luxuries Good?

Luxuries have received a great deal of criticism. In premodern societies, ascetics took a dim view of the good of any consumption beyond the barest necessities, and Christians took a dim view of greed and pride, which they thought were too easily associated with the possession of luxuries. Moderns, including economists, have objected to many attributes of the old luxury economy: the claimed transcendental aura; the impracticality of the stuff; the wastefulness of putting so much effort into the production of stuff that benefits so few men; the anti-egalitarian symbolism of exclusive luxuries.

In premodern times, luxuries also received a great deal of praise, as embodying some of the finest accomplishments of men. It is hard to know what common men thought of luxuries, since aristocrats both enjoyed all the luxuries and wrote all the books. Still, there seems to have been tacit approval from the poor. Servants rarely rose up against their masters or went on strike for the sake of a more egalitarian distribution. In contrast, modern thinkers rarely praise luxuries. Only a few economists are happy to endorse them, and then only as long as all have a chance to obtain them, either through hard work (for expensive goods) or through public display (for scarce ones).[7] The popular judgment is mixed. The modern heirs of the common man, denizens of the great "middle class," show little yearning for lost aristocratic luxuries, but they have enthusiastically endorsed bourgeois luxuries as meaningful social tokens.

The modern dislocation of the traditional meanings of luxury consumption makes it hard to offer a judgment on the consumption of luxuries, since it is hard to know what one is praising or criticizing. Perhaps it is best to leave the old aristocratic connotations of luxury aside. They now belong to historians and sociologists, perhaps to philosophers, but not to economists.

My judgment on the new bourgeois "luxury goods" is mixed. The emphasis on scarcity is a bit absurd in the midst of the industrial economy's abundance, but absurdity is not in itself a sign of men's moral weakness. Rather than either praise or condemn the re-creation of luxuries on moral grounds, I think it is more valuable to draw a social lesson from this unexpected and spontaneous development: socioeconomic hierarchies seem to be a much more durable part of the human condition than either nobility or the economic problem. Unless men stop believing that there should be consumption markers for the elite, they will continue to find ways, no matter how devious, to define some stuff as luxurious.

Bourgeois luxuries are not especially beautiful. That lack is a shame, although not surprising in the midst of modernity's ugliness. But perhaps there is no longer any need to link beauty with luxury. The modern worldview has destroyed the traditional understanding of aristocracy, but it has opened up nobility of the human condition to members of all castes. The appreciation of beauty and refinement, once an aristocratic privilege, can now be everyone's transcendental delight. Unfortunately, it will take more than exhortations from economists to dislodge modernity's distrust of the beautiful, a distrust that has little to do with antiluxury sentiments, indeed little to do with any aspect of economics.

While I am engaging in economists' exhortations, here is one on the moral risks of bourgeois luxuries. The disappearance of aristocratic nobility has only increased the danger that luxuries will encourage greed and pride. The old elite often did not live up to its responsibility for refinement and cultural representation, but the new elite does not even have a standard to live up to. Cultural critics often concentrate on the particularly garish excesses of the nouveaux riche, but all elite consumption verges on unjustified extravagance. A call to poverty seems particularly applicable when only bourgeois luxuries are to be abandoned.

Living with Necessities—Sustainable Poverty

This book is drawing to a close. Up to this point, I have strictly avoided anything like radical proposals for economic reform. In the next, final chapter, I will argue that such proposals are not necessary. Modern society as a whole could do with significant changes, but its economic aspect, the industrial economy, is already in pretty good shape and addressing many of its most significant problems. That kind of judgment is just as applicable to the consumption side of the economy. Satiety among the rich, absolute poverty in retreat among the poor—it is beyond the economic dreams of the most enthusiastic utopian socialist.

Still, it is not acceptable simply to ignore the antimoderns' telling criticisms of the industrial economy, especially of the spiritually empty splendor of industrial consumption. Too much of the industrial-consumption lifestyle is depressing and distasteful—the frivolity of so many products, the relentless advertising, the ugly expanse of nearly identical shopping centers, the nonsensical "new and improved." It makes preindustrial consumption—its emphasis on necessities, simplicity, and wholeness—sound appealing.

Suggesting a reversal of history is pointless. Even if men could lose their industrial competence, a return to the old ways of nearly ubiquitous absolute poverty and squalor would be a step backwards. Still, it might just be possible to combine some of the virtues of traditional consumption patterns with two strands of the modern worldview: the universalist idea that everyone should have all consumption necessities and the worldly optimism that confidently sets men's ingenuity to the task of providing them. The result would be a consumption economy of sustainable poverty.

In this highly hypothetical future economic organization, consumption would not extend far past necessities. The list of necessities could be long and modern; it could include e-mail and airplanes, surgery and hybrid crops. The goal is not to make men poor in the preindustrial style, but to cultivate a new spirit of industrial poverty. Everyone would have all necessary consumption goods, but no one would have a great deal more. Some people could have a bit more than they need and a few could even be rich, by some modest standard, but the division of the small, overall surplus is a secondary issue. The key features would be the universal minimum level of consumption and a typical level not far above the minimum.

The economy of sustainable poverty would have no room for economic growth, at least growth understood as the consumption of ever more comforts. Men would have to be reasonably happy with the consumption goods that were already available. In other words, the desire to get a little more from the world, which was described as basic to human nature in chapter 5, would have to be curtailed or channeled in some other direction. Environmental excellence might be one direction for that worldly effort. Another might be the support of a larger population, since the list of consumption necessities would include the pronatalist potential to keep alive all the children whom parents might feel it appropriate to raise.

Relative to the currently dominant model of ever increasing industrial production, this thought-experiment economy has some appeal. The central benefit would be that, perhaps, the temptation to overvalue consumption would be reduced by the lack of consumption goods. It is even possible that the lack of virtually universal excess would be accompanied by a culture of generous solidarity. When less for the relatively poor would bring the threat of absolute poverty, the relatively rich might feel more inclined to help out than when, as is generally the case in industrial societies, less merely means fewer comforts. There is also the advantage of steering people away from instrumentally neutral labors. A social decision not to focus on the production and acquisition of more consumption goods could leave more space for higher interests.

History teaches no lessons on the possibility or impossibility of a future consumption economy of sustainable poverty. It only teaches that nothing much like it has ever existed. The closest approximation was probably the former Communist countries, but their near-poverty was unintentional and inextricably linked with a morally objectionable political ideology. The question of whether the early leaders of the industrial economy could or should have directed society toward sustainable poverty rather than toward satiety and supersatiety is a moot counterfactual. Speculation is pointless.[8]

Could such a consumption economy succeed? From here, there are no serious technical obstacles. The world's rich would have to give up on stuff, the world's poor would have to make more stuff, and labor would have to be rebalanced extensively. Such changes are significant, but the economic accomplishments of the last two centuries required far greater changes. Most of the world's poor are already on the path to greater production. For the rich, it is easier to produce less than to produce more. A move towards sustainable poverty would be more like a slight change of course than a totally new direction.

As is most often the case when it comes to men's desires, the biggest threats to this proposed way of life are moral. Men may be too weak to be content with less than they might have. The utopian socialists worried correctly that the desire for more consumption would doom their experimental communities.[9] The challenge would be no less now. Indeed, it is greater, since the "ever more" consumption economy is more firmly established and plays a larger social role than it did in the mid-nineteenth century. If sustainable poverty is ever to come, it will have to wait for some of the strands of modernity that support "ever more" to wither and for some new strands to develop.

The best way to get more meaning from consumption is to consume less. For the moment, such a reversal is only a pipe dream. But all that is necessary to get started in this new direction is a social choice. After all, the economy is largely under human control.

18

What Should We Talk about Now?

The first two responses to my announcement of a forthcoming book on economics were usually something like, "So what do you think of the economy?" and "So what are you going to recommend?" My reply to both questions was disappointing: "This book is about all economies—past, present, and future—not just this one. Particular judgments and detailed recommendations would not really fit in." While true, that answer was a bit disingenuous. The contemporary industrial economy was certainly the main example I had in mind while writing, so it seems appropriate to gather my thoughts on that economy together as a sort of conclusion.

The Goods of the Industrial Economy

The best way to provide a judgment of the industrial economy is to make two lists, one for the economy's goods and another for its evils, and then to compare them. I start with the economic goods, which are remarkable by any historical standard.

By far the most important industrial good, worth the first ten places on a list of the top twenty, is the solution of the economic problem. For the first time in human history, men no longer have to suffer from absolute poverty. For the first time in human history, the first two great economic goods, life and health, can be offered to all, including to all children that parents wish to have. That potential has been fully realized in much of the world. Between 60 percent and 80 percent of all people alive today—in total, many more people than were alive at any single time up to a few decades ago—can expect to enjoy sufficient food, clothing, heat, and shelter throughout their lives, as well as basic medical care (the exact proportion depends on how "sufficient" and "basic" are defined). Most of these people have much more stuff than is necessary for survival, and relatively few are in danger of working themselves to death to get what they have.

This accomplishment is real. It is not an apparently free lunch that actually has to be paid for by someone else. Unlike the riches of premodern aristocrats, the modern multitude has not gained its affluence at the expense of some other group of poor people, either at home or abroad. Rather, they have made their own prosperity through hard work and cooperative action. This recipe for industrial prosperity can be followed by any society, no matter how poor its starting position. All that is required is correctly oriented dedication and effort. Better yet, the effort involved is now relatively modest. The path from poverty to prosperity has been well marked out, and the technology and techniques necessary for prosperity are readily available.

Some pessimists argue that while the prosperity lunch is free for now, future generations will have to pay because of our damage to the natural world. The pessimists forget that our descendants will receive from us not one but two legacies. They will inherit damages that need to be rectified, but alongside the degradation they will also receive the technical and cultural tools that should make that rectification relatively easy. Other pessimists worry that a shortage of given capital (raw materials) will eventually bring back absolute poverty. Economists can counter with the observation that for two centuries increased production has been accompanied by a steadily increasing abundance of resources. Not only has more always been found, but the effort involved in making the raw stuff useful for men has generally diminished. There is no obvious reason for that pattern to change.

To be sure, a great swath of the world's population—estimates range from 500 million to 1.5 billion people—still suffers from the economic problem. Even if the lowest estimate of those living in or close to absolute poverty is right, the number is certainly too high.

The absolutely poor are one side of the evil of the global wealth gap, to be discussed below. Still, the destitution cannot be blamed on the industrial economy, since the destitution exists only where industrial techniques are absent. As the sway of industry increases, the proportion of the world's population living in absolute poverty declines. That proportion has been falling for decades.[1]

The solution of the economic problem takes up the top ten places on the list of modern industrial goods; there are many candidates for the next ten. Almost all the other economic goods have been well served by the industrial economy. Here are my suggestions for the rest of the list, in roughly descending importance:

1) Time. Industrial productivity has reduced immensely the amount of time needed for the labor of survival. The result is years free for schooling and retirement, weeks of holidays, and a long stream of weekends. Whether the abundant leisure has been used wisely is a social, not an economic, question. The economic contribution can hardly be doubted.

2) Learning. Books, newspapers, magazines, journals, telephone, radio, television, Internet—industry provides not only the time but also the tools for the spread and deepening of knowledge. Again, society may not make full use of these tools, but the economy has done its part.

3) Communication. Rapid transport, organized post, telephones, unbelievably cheap telephones, e-mail—neighborhoods and families are no longer bound by distance, friendships can be kept alive across cities and oceans, traditions can be maintained despite physical absence.

4) The welfare state. Industrial societies have put the principle of the universal destination of economic goods into partial practice. Basic and advanced goods are offered to all who are poor, weak, ill, mad, or old, indeed to all who are in need. For all of the welfare state's problems, overall it represents a noble use of industrial abundance. The practice is only partial because the virtue is bounded by political borders.

5) Globalization. Prosperity has brought the world closer. It has added numerous new organizations that cross all sorts of political boundaries: commercial corporations; networks to gather and disseminate news and culture; infrastructures for travel and tourism;

and global supervisory organizations for everything from the protection of human rights to the uses of the sea.

6) Social revaluation of productive labor. The motives for the modern appreciation of the common man are not solely economic, but the industrial economy, which requires respect for the dignity of most types of labor, is a principal beneficiary. Skills are appreciated; "hands" have become human resources.

7) Can-do solutions. Economic problems can be solved in a way that most important human troubles (the meaning of life, say, or the difficulty of marriage) cannot. The industrial economy is extremely good at solving its problems, everything from contagious disease to the inadequate dissemination of fast Internet connections.

8) Creature comforts. Whatever your desires may be, if economic activity can possibly satisfy them, the industrial society probably does. Servants have all but disappeared, but they are hardly missed. Even the relatively poor enjoy comforts beyond any preindustrial dream of avarice.

9) Cities. It is not an accident that the Bible describes life with God as taking place in a (heavenly) city. Cities are where men can best develop friendship and culture, create interesting labor, build magnificent buildings, and support fine institutions. The industrial economy has allowed most people to live in cities. In rich societies, the cities have little of the squalor that marred pre-industrial urban life.

10) Glass, steel, and plastic. Industry may not have made the world more beautiful, but it has provided the tools. These new or vastly improved materials let men do many more wonderful things with the landscape.

This list is not meant to be exhaustive, but it should give a taste of the many good things that have come with industrialization. Of course, as yet relatively few people—only 20–30 percent of the world's population—enjoy all of these industrial goods. Many people who are not in absolute poverty still live in squalid cities, lack quite simple creature comforts, and so forth. I will criticize that lack of universality in a moment, but it should be kept in perspective. This is definitely a glass that is half-full rather than half-empty, because the most important economic good, the elimination of absolute poverty, is also by far the most widespread. In addition, the glass of secondary goods keeps filling up. For almost any measure of industrial abundance—clean water, years of schooling, steel production, energy produced—the rate of growth is much faster than the growth in the world's population.

The Evils of the Industrial Economy

The list of major evils in the industrial economy is much shorter, only three items long.

The first is the overvaluation of the economic good. Men in industrial societies generally pay too much attention to economic activity, expect too much from it, and sacrifice the pursuit of too many other goods for the sake of modest economic gains. This overvaluation can be seen in education, which has been increasingly turned away from a search for wisdom and knowledge to training for economic service; in politics, which is too oriented to the increase of wealth; in social hierarchies, which are increasingly influenced by crude economic accomplishments; in employment, in the too high expectations of meaning from labor; in consumption, in the spiritually empty cornucopia that entices men to consumerism.

Alienation comes next. Assembly lines were alienating for the factory worker (they still are, but relatively few men still have to work on them). The more recent development of instrumentally neutral labor, the spread of paid pointless tasks, is probably more soul-destroying. So is the corresponding retreat, in both practice and social esteem, of the valuable unpaid labors of love and care. Unions used to provide a modest counterforce to labor alienation, but they are declining, and less formal workplace communities are increasingly ephemeral. Consumption does not escape the alienating force of industry. Mass consumption and the advertising that surrounds it can create weak communities, but the identification with product and the brand tends to sap the more valuable meaning that comes from the shared consumption traditions and patterns of families and peoples.

Finally, the global wealth gap is indeed bad. There are too many very poor people. The very rich people dedicate too much time and effort to trying to get richer, too little to trying to help those for whom more wealth would be much more valuable. The wealth gap is narrowing, at least by the counts that matter (stuff rather than cash income), but its persistence shows just how weak the modern commitment to economic universality really is. The prevalence of the welfare state shows that men can care about some neighbors, but the concern drops off sharply across all borders. There are, of course, no easy cures to the wealth gap, but the resistance to immigration from poor to rich countries—probably the technique that is easiest to enact and most likely to succeed—shows just how little dismay the rich really feel in the face of this huge economic difference.

The Economy and the Rest

Economic comparisons should be undertaken with extreme caution. Little of the economic good is susceptible to numerical analysis, and few of those goods are commensurate. Such comparisons are only valid when the two sides are so vastly unbalanced that the one is bigger or better than the other by almost any standard. That is the case for the evaluation of the industrial economy. The list of goods is both longer and weightier than the list of evils. The goods represent fundamental improvements in the human condition in the world, while the evils sound more like problems that could be addressed, at least in part, by the can-do spirit. For all of its shadows, the industrial economy is a good thing.

If my praise is right, then antimodern thinkers who harshly criticize the industrial economy must be largely wrong. Their idea is that the modern economy is killing the good life. That perception is skewed—it exaggerates both the evil and the ultimate importance of modern economic changes. Still, it is based on something true—not so much about the industrial economy as about the modern experiment of which the economy is an integral part. The modern worldview has been developed and implemented for the last two centuries in Europe and North America. Outside of the economy, it is hardly a catalogue of successes. Enlightenment thinkers called for a religion within the limits of reason alone. The result: the decline of all religion, replaced by widespread alienation. They called for governments based on the consent of the people. The result: some of the worst tyrannies men have ever created, which have now been replaced by democracies that increasingly inspire apathy and mistrust. They called for a philosophy based only on experience. The result: an ugly mixture of crippling doubt and distasteful solipsism. Then came the post-Enlightenment thinkers. They called for human relations based on feelings rather than on responsibility or duty. The result: widespread irresponsible sexual behavior, broken families, and social fragmentation. They called for self-knowledge through emotional autobiography. The result: self-indulgence. They called for a new self-expressive sort of art. The result: a dark and ugly vision in high culture and a popular culture of the crudest sensationalism.

In comparison to that list, the dangers of the modern economy look quite moderate. Even when it comes to economic evils, their noneconomic cousins are generally more evil. Consider alienation. Without a doubt, the modern economy is alienating. No one seems to care much about these soul-deadening patterns and trends. Worse, when attention is paid, for example in motivational campaigns by employers, the supposed cure often seems only to aggravate the disease.

Still, economic alienation is among the least significant aspects of modern alienation. In men's search for meaning, labor and consumption can generally provide a relatively small portion of the solution. Meaninglessness in these activities can create only a relatively small amount of despair. For most people, the big answers have come from religion, royalty, society, the community, and the family—the transcendental truths and greater causes that somehow validate the struggles of life and the mystery of suffering and death. In every one of these domains, the modern experiment has sucked out meaning as thoroughly as an effective vacuum cleaner sucks dust out of a rug. The problems of economic alienation pale in comparison. Economic alienation is probably felt more keenly because it is one of the few domains (romantic love is another) in which secular society expects any meaning to be found. The unrealistically high expectations deserve the blame, not the failure to meet them.

The industrial economy stands out as a rare success in the modern experiment. It is not alone; modern medicine and science are also on this list. But those who wish for a major reconstruction of the modern world, for a truly postmodern experiment, will want to spare, not demolish, the modern economy.

Can the goods of the modern economy be maintained in a postmodern culture? I argued in chapter 4 that the modern economy could not have been generated without the modern worldview. Perhaps it also cannot survive that view's demise. Some of the most radical antimoderns certainly accept the correlation. They say that they are willing to give up low infant mortality because that is the price which has to be paid for a revival of faith.

That seems extreme. History, economic and otherwise, is too marked by men's freedom for it to possibly know in advance the contours, economic and otherwise, of a postmodern society. And the argument for backward economic movement is implausible since the modern experience has changed the "givens" of the situation. The coming of industry might have been bad—it certainly brought many evils in its early decades—but the industrial economy is now mostly good and its maintenance is easy. It will take little effort to keep it going—the social structures are in place, the technologies are mastered, and our collective memory has been imbued with the goods and corresponding responsibilities of industrial prosperity. Indeed, it would almost certainly be even harder to abolish this socioeconomic configuration than to fit it in, suitably altered, with whatever comes next.

What Is to Be Done?

The industrial economy does not need tremendous improvements. Unlike the academic discipline of conventional economics, which is something of a disaster area, the actual economy works quite well. Of course, adjustment to circumstances is constantly needed. Reforms are always needed for something—central banking, environmental protection, pension funding, and so forth. However, the necessary reforms in such matters do not require anything like a major economic reconfiguration. Indeed, the economic good is so well served that my first advice to would-be economic reformers is to turn to one of the many more deeply troubled aspects of modern society.

Still, improvements can be made.

At the personal level, each of the three listed evils can be addressed, however imperfectly. The remedy for overvaluation of economic concerns is a conversion of heart. Rather than wanting as much professional success and consumption stuff as my neighbor, I should make a conscious effort to want less than he has, or even to enter into my own private economy of sustainable poverty. In an economy of satiety, where enough is almost guaranteed, moral virtue lies in recognizing and being grateful for prosperity. The remedy for economic alienation is two-fold—to expect less meaning from the economic life and to look for that economic meaning where it is most likely to be found, in the willing gift of labor to the world and in the grateful and generous acceptance of the world's gifts in consumption. As for the wealth gap, the rich can narrow it by trying less hard to get richer or even to stay rich. Why not go into a line of work that is less lucrative and less productive, but more loving?

At the level of public policy, the biggest problem is the denigration of simple caring labors in favor of paid work of all sorts. Women should be rewarded for taking up maternal and other caring responsibilities. Equally, it would be good to roll back some of the professionalism that now dominates care of the weak. If that line of reform does not appeal, then there are many other worthy economic causes—in favor of the protection of the environment, helping the poor, and restraining the rich; against the antifamily orientation of many economic programs of the welfare state, the excessively elevated social position of finance, and the centrality of economic growth in public policy. These are issues for rich societies. I am not familiar enough with the economic challenges of relatively poor societies to give any suggestions, but I am sure similar lists could easily be drawn up.

Thanks to the globalization of the industrial economy, there are also global issues. Some, such as those dealing with trade, law, and environment, are basically technical questions. Different local rules can be made more uniform or techniques can be created to resolve conflicts among them. Many answers are defensible, especially once the conventional ideal of "free markets" is abandoned.

The challenge of the global wealth gap is more significant. I have already suggested that immigration could be part of the solution. The ease of moving countries in the industrial economy—immigrants no longer need to cut their ties with their homeland—raises significant social issues, but from a purely economic perspective, the poor should be considered the best judges of whether immigration is a good idea. If there is a problem with newcomers taking unfair advantage of the welfare state (whether that actually happens is a disputed question), then it is better to change the welfare state than to close the borders. Economic shifts in the other direction—foreign aid and foreign investment—also help, although human moral weakness can sharply reduce the good of such transfers, especially if the overwhelming goal of reducing the wealth gap is forgotten. In the business of cross-border economic transfers, less emphasis should be put on profit and targets and more on charity and service.

This book started with a complaint about the selfish and narrow perspective of conventional economics in the face of the tremendous accomplishments of the industrial economy. I have tried to create an economic model that lives up to the reality of both economic and human nature, without ignoring the economic implications of human weakness. It is fitting to end on almost exactly the opposite note—with a chapter largely dedicated to appreciation and with a call for charity and service. Those virtues offer solutions for most human problems, perhaps for all of them. With charity and service, men can accomplish great things, turn darkness into light, sorrow into joy. They are certainly applicable to economics, which should, after all, be something of a joyful science.

Bibliography

Aarts, L. J. M., R. V. Burkhauser, et al., eds. *Curing the Dutch Disease: An International Perspective on Disability Policy Reform.* Aldershot, UK: Avebury, 1996.

Abernathy, G. L., ed. *The Idea of Equality: An Anthology.* Richmond, VA: John Knox Press, 1959.

Alford O. P., H., C. Clark, et al., eds. *Rediscovering Abundance: Interdisciplinary Essays on Wealth, Income and Their Distribution in the Catholic Social Tradition.* Notre Dame, IN: University of Notre Dame Press, 2006.

Anonymous (1956). "Seeds and Seedlings: The Doctrine of Perfectibility." *Theosophy* 44: 516–18 (available at http://www.wisdomworld.org/setting/perfectibility.html).

Anthony, P. D. *The Ideology of Work.* London: Tavistock Publications, 1977.

Aquinas, T. *Summa Theologica.* Westminster, MD: Christian Classics, 1981.

Arendt, H. *The Human Condition.* Chicago: University of Chicago Press, 1988.

Aristotle. *Complete Works.* Princeton, NJ: Princeton University Press, 1984.

Aron, R. (1969). *Les désillusions du progrès: Essai sur la dialectique de la modernité.* Paris: Calmann-Lévy, 1969.

Ayres, C. E. *The Problem of Economic Order.* New York: Farrar and Rinehart, 1938.

Bandow, D. and D. L. Schindler, eds. *Wealth, Poverty, and Human Destiny.* Wilmington, DE: ISI Books, 2003.

Barnhill, D. L. and R. S. Gottlieb. *Deep Ecology and World Religions: New Essays on Sacred Ground.* Albany, NY: State University of New York Press, 2001.

Baron-Cohen, S. *The Essential Difference: Men, Women and the Extreme Male Brain.* London: Allen Lane, 2003.

Baudrillard, J. *The Consumer Society: Myths and Structures.* London: SAGE Publications, 1998.

Baumol, W. and A. Blinder. *Economics, Principles and Policy.* Orlando: Harcourt Brace, 1998.

Beabout, G. R. and E. J. Echeverria. "The Culture of Consumerism: A Catholic and Personalist Critique." *Journal of Markets and Morality* 5(2), 2002.

Beals, R. L., H. Hoijer, et al. *An Introduction to Anthropology (Fifth Edition).* New York: Macmillan, 1977.

Beardwell, I., L. Holden, et al. *Human Resources Management: A Contemporary Approach (Fourth Edition)*. Harlow, UK: FT Prentice Hall, 2004.

Beckerman, W. "The Measurement of Poverty." In *Aspects of Poverty in Early Modern Europe*, edited by T. Riis. Firenze: European University Institute, 1981.

Belloc, H. *An Essay on the Restoration of Property*. London: The Distributist League, 1936.

Belshaw, C. *Environmental Philosophy*. Chesham, UK: Acumen, 2002.

Benedict, S. *The Rule of St. Benedict (in English)*. Collegeville, MN: The Liturgical Press, 1982.

Berg, M. *The Machinery Question and the Making of Political Economy 1815–1848*. Cambridge: Cambridge University Press, 1980.

Berry, W. *Home Economics*. San Francisco: North Point Press, 1987.

———. *The Art of the Commonplace*. Washington, DC: Counterpoint, 2002.

Bignell, J. *Media Semiotics: An Introduction*. Manchester: Manchester University Press, 2002.

Black, J., ed. *A Dictionary of Economics*. Oxford: Oxford University Press, 1997.

Blake, W. *Poems and Prophecies*. London: Everyman, 1991.

Blaug, M. *Economic Theory in Retrospect (Fifth Edition)*. Cambridge: Cambridge University Press, 1996.

Blaug, M. "Misunderstanding Classical Economics: The Sraffian Interpretation of the Surplus Approach." In *Competing Economic Theories: Essays in Memory of Giovanni Caravale*, edited by S. Nistico and D. Tosato. London: Routledge, 2002.

Blomberg, C. *Neither Poverty Nor Riches: A Biblical Theology of Material Possessions*. Leicester: Apollos, 1999.

Boileau, D. A., ed. *Principles of Catholic Social Teaching*. Milwaukee: Marquette University Press, 1998.

Boylan, T. A. and P. F. O'Gorman. *Beyond Rhetoric and Realism in Economics: Towards A Reformulation of Economic Methodology*. London: Routledge, 1995.

Brennan, G. and P. Pettit. *The Economy of Esteem: An Essay of Civil and Political Society*. Oxford: Oxford University Press, 2004.

Brocas, I. and J. D. Carillo, eds. *The Psychology of Economic Decisions*. Oxford: Oxford University Press, 2003.

Bryson, L., C. Faust, et al., eds. *Aspects of Human Equality: Fifteenth Symposium of the Conference on Science, Philosophy and Religion*. New York: Harper and Brothers, 1956.

Buchli, V., ed. *The Material Culture Reader*. Oxford: Berg, 2002.

Burke, E. *Reflections on the Revolution in France*. Indianapolis: Bobbs-Merrill, 1955.

Burleigh, M. *Death and Deliverance: "Euthanasia" in Germany c. 1900–1945*. Cambridge: Cambridge University Press, 1994.

Callinicos, A. *An Anti-Capitalist Manifesto*. Cambridge: Polity, 2003.

Calvez, J.-Y. and J. Perrin. *Eglise et Société Economique.* Paris: Editions Montaigne, 1958.
Campbell, J. *Joy in Work, German Work.* Princeton, NJ: Princeton University Press, 1989.
Camus, A. *L'étranger.* Paris: Gallimard, 1942.
Casey, M. *Truthful Living: Saint Benedict's Teaching on Humility.* Chippenham, UK: Gracewing, 2001.
Carlyle, T. "Occasional Discourse on the Negro Question." *Fraser's Magazine for Town and Country* XL (February 1849): 531 (available at http://cepa.newschool.edu/het/texts/carlyle/carlodnq.html).
Cartwright, N. *The Dappled World, A Study of the Boundaries of Science.* Cambridge: Cambridge University Press, 1999.
Catholic University of America. *The New Catholic Encyclopedia, Second Edition.* Detroit: Gale, 2003.
Catechism of the Catholic Church (Revised Edition). [CCC] London: Geoffrey Chapman, 1999.
Centro di studi filosofici di Gallarate. *Enciclopedia filosofica (seconda edizione).* Firenze: G. C. Sansoni, 1967.
Chabot, J.-L. *La Doctrine Sociale de l'Eglise.* Paris: Que-sais-je, 1992.
Charles, R. S. J. *Christian Social Witness and Teaching: The Catholic Tradition from Genesis to Centesimus Annus.* Leominster UK: Gracewing, 1998.
Chenaux, P. *Une Europe Vaticane?: Entre le Plan Marshall et les Traités de Rome.* Paris: Editions Ciaco, 1990.
Chenu, M.-D. *The Theology of Work: An Exploration.* Dublin: Gill and Son, 1963.
———. "Arbeit". *Handbuch Theologischer Grundbegriffe.* H. Fries. München, Kösel. 1: 75–86, 1962.
Chesterton, G. K. *The Outline of Sanity.* Dublin: Carraig Books, 1974.
Clark, E. *The Want Makers.* London: Hodder and Stoughton, 1988.
Coase, R. H. *The Firm, the Market, and the Law.* Chicago: University of Chicago Press, 1988.
Cole, G. D. H. *Socialist Thought: The Forerunners 1789–1850.* London: Macmillan, 1953.
———. *The Second International 1889–1914 (in two parts).* London: Macmillan, 1956.
Collard, D. *Altruism and Economy: A Study in Non-Selfish Economics.* Oxford: Martin Robertson, 1978.
Colman, A. M., ed. *Companion Encyclopedia of Psychology.* London: Routledge, 1994.
Commons, J. R. "Institutional Economics." *American Economic Review* 21: 648–57, 1931.
Connolly, H. *Sin.* London: Continuum, 2002.
Conrad, J. W. *An Introduction to the Theory of Interest.* Berkeley, CA: University of California Press, 1959.
Copleston, F. *A History of Philosophy: Volume IX Maine de Biran to Sartre.* London: Search Press, 1974.

Craig, E., ed. *Routledge Encyclopedia of Philosophy*. London: Routledge, 1998.
Crocker, D. A. and T. Linden, eds. *Ethics of Consumption: The Good Life, Justice, and Global Stewardship*. Lanham, MD: Rowman and Littlefield, 1998.
Crowley, J. E. "The Sensibility of Comfort." *American Historical Review* 104(3), 1999 (available at http://www.historycooperative.org/journals/ahr/104.3/ah000749.html).
Crump, T. *The Phenomenon of Money*. London: Routledge & Kegan Paul, 1981.
Davidson, C. *A Woman's Work is Never Done: A History of Housework in the British Isles 1650–1950*. London: Chatto & Windus, 1982.
Dawson, D. *The Origins of Western Warfare: Militarism and Morality and the Ancient World*. Boulder: Westview Press, 1996.
Day, D. *The Long Loneliness*. New York: Harper and Row, 1952.
de Geus, M. *The End of Over-Consumption: Towards a Lifestyle of Moderation and Self-Restraint*. Utrecht, Netherlands: International Books, 2003.
de Grazia, S. *Of Time Work and Leisure*. New York: The Twentieth Century Fund, 1962.
de Lubac, H. *Le Drame de l'humanisme athée*. Paris: Cerf, 2000.
de Sales, F. *Introduction à la vie dévote*. Paris: Editions du Seuil, 1962.
Descartes, R. *Discours de la méthode*. Paris: Flammarion, 1966.
Desroche, H. *Coopération et développment: Mouvements coopératifs du développement*. Paris: Editions ouvrières, 1964.
Diel, P. *Symbolism in Greek Mythology: Human Desire and Its Transformations*. Boulder: Shambhala, 1980.
Dixon, P. *Making the Difference: Women and Men in the Workplace*. London: Heinemann, 1993.
Dorr, D. (1992). *Option for the Poor: A Hundred Years of Vatican Social Teaching* (Revised Edition). Dublin: Gill and Macmillan.
Douglas, M. and. I., Baron. *The World of Goods, Towards an Anthropology of Consumption*. London: Allen Lane, 1978.
Dowrick, S. and S. Grundberg, eds. *Why Children?* London: The Women's Press Group, 1980.
Drenth, P. J. D., J. A. Sergeant, et al., Eds. *European Perspectives in Psychology (Volume 3, Work and Organizational)*. Chichester, UK: John Wiley & Sons, 1990.
Drucker, P. *The Concept of the Corporation*. New York: John Day, 1946.
———. *Management*. London: Heinemann Professional Publishing, 1974.
Dugger, W. M. *Underground Economics: A Decade of Institutional Dissent*. Armonk, NY: M. E. Sharpe, 1992.
Dumazedier, J. *Vers une civilisation du loisir?* Paris: Editions du seuil, 1962.
Dumont, L. *Homo hierarchicus: Le système des castes et ses implications*. Paris: Gallimard, 1979.
Dupré, L. *Passage to Modernity: An Essay in the Hermeneutics of Nature and Culture*. New Haven, CT: Yale University Press, 1993.
Eatwell, J., M. Milgate, et al., eds. *New Palgrave: A Dictionary of Economics*. Basingstoke, UK: Macmillan, 2001.

Einzig, P. *Primitive Money: In its Ethnological, Historical and Economic Aspects.* Oxford: Pergamon Press, 1966.

Ekelund, R. B. and R. F. Hebert. *A History of Economic Theory and Method.* New York: McGraw-Hill, 1975.

Eliade, M., ed. *The Encyclopedia of Religion.* New York: Macmillan, 1987.

Elliot, R. and A. Gare, Eds. *Environmental Philosophy: A Collection of Readings.* Milton Keynes, UK: The Open University Press, 1983.

Elvin, M. *The Pattern of the Chinese Past: A Social and Economic Interpretation.* Stanford, CA: Stanford University Press, 1973.

Ferber, M. A. and J. A. Nelson, eds. *Feminist Economics Today: Beyond Economic Man.* Chicago: University of Chicago Press, 2003.

Ferguson, N. *The Cash Nexus: Money and Power in the Modern World, 1700–2000.* London: Penguin, 2001.

Fields, G. S. *Distribution and Development: A New Look at the Developing World.* New York: Russell Sage Foundation, 2001.

Finley, M. I. "Aristotle and Economic Analysis." *Aristotle (384–322 BC).* M. Blaug. Aldershot, UK: Edward Elgar, 1970.

———. *The Ancient Economy.* Berkeley, CA: University of California Press, 1985.

———. *Ancient Slavery and Modern Ideology.* London: Chatto and Windus, 1980.

Fogarty, M. P. *Christian Democracy in Western Europe: 1820–1953.* London: Routledge & Kegan Paul, 1957.

Fogel, R. W. *The Fourth Great Awakening and the Future of Egalitarianism.* Chicago: University of Chicago Press, 2000.

Folbre, N. *The Invisible Heart: Economics and Family Values.* New York: New Press, 2001.

Fonseca, E. G. d. *Beliefs in Action: Economic Philosophy and Social Change.* Cambridge: Cambridge University Press, 1991.

Furubotn, E. G. and R. Richter. *Institutions and Economic Theory: The Contribution of the New Institutional Economics.* Ann Arbor, MI: University of Michigan Press, 2000.

Foster, J. "Class." *The New Palgrave: A Dictionary of Economics.* J. Eatwell, M. Milgate and P. Newman. London: Macmillan, 1987. 1: 432–34.

Fox-Genovese, E. *The Origins of Physiocracy: Economic Reform and Social Order in Eighteenth Century France.* Ithaca, NY: Cornell University Press, 1976.

Friedman, M. and R. Friedman. *Capitalism and Freedom.* Chicago: University of Chicago Press, 1962.

———. *Free to Choose: A Personal Statement.* Harmondsworth, UK: Penguin, 1980.

Fullbrook, E., ed. *The Crisis in Economics: The Post-Autistic Economics Movement: The First 600 Days.* London: Routledge, 2003.

Furubotn, E. G. and R. Richter. *Institutions and Economic Theory: The Contribution of the New Institutional Economics.* Ann Arbor, MI: University of Michigan Press, 2000.

Gadamer, H.-G. *Truth and Method (Second, Revised Edition)*. London: Sheed & Ward, 1989.
Galbraith, J. K. *The Affluent Society (updated edition)*. London: Penguin, 1998.
Gaudium et Spes. London: Catholic Truth Society, 1966.
Gay, P. *The Enlightenment—An Interpretation: The Science of Freedom*. New York: W. W. Norton, 1996.
Geertz, C. *The Interpretation of Cultures*. London: Hutchinson, 1973.
Gerhart, B. and S. L. Rynes. *Compensation: Theory, Evidence and Strategic Implications*. Thousand Oaks, CA: Sage Publications, 2003.
Ghatak, S. *Introduction to Development Economics (Fourth Edition)*. London: Routledge, 2003.
Giddens, A. *The Constitution of Society: Outline of the Theory of Structuration*. Cambridge: Polity Press, 1984.
Gilson, É. *La société de masse et sa culture*. Paris: Librarie philosophique J. Vrin, 1967.
Gould, H. A. *The Hindu Caste System: The Sacralization of a Social Order*. Delhi: Chanakya Publications, 1987.
Grelle, B. and D. A. Krueger, Eds. *Christianity and Capitalism: Perspectives on Religion, Liberalism and the Economy*. Chicago: Center for the Scientific Study of Religion, 1986.
Grint, K. (1998). *The Sociology of Work: An Introduction (Second Edition)*. Cambridge: Polity Press, 1998.
Grossbard-Shechtman, S. and C. Clague, eds. *The Expansion of Economics: Towards a More Inclusive Social Science*. Armonk, NY: M. E. Sharpe, 2002.
Gruchy, A. G. *The Reconstruction of Economics*. New York: Greenwood, 1987.
Habermas, Jürgen. *Between Facts and Norms, Contributions to a Discourse Theory of Law and Democracy*. Cambridge: Polity Press, 1992, translation 1996.
Halévy, E. *La formation du radicalisme philosophique*. Paris: Germer Baillière, 1904.
Hall, R. H. *Dimensions of Work*. Beverly Hills, CA: Sage Publications, 1986.
Handy, C. *Beyond Certainty: The Changing Worlds of Organizations*. London: Hutchinson, 1995.
Hardman, O. *The Ideals of Ascetism: An Essay in the Comparative Study of Religion*. London: SPCK, 1924.
Hausman, D. M. *The Inexact and Separate Science of Economics*. Cambridge: Cambridge University Press, 1992.
Hawkins, M. *Social Darwinism in European and American Thought, 1860–1945: Nature as model and Bature as threat*. Cambridge: Cambridge University Press, 1997.
Hayek, F. A. *The Road to Serfdom*. London: Routledge, 1976.
Hegel, G. W. F. *Hegel's Logic (from the Encyclopaedia of the Philosophic Sciences)*. Oxford: Oxford University Press, 1975.
Hegel, G. W. F. *The Philosophy of History*. New York: Willey, 1944 (available at http://www.class.uidaho.edu/mickelsen/texts/Hegel%20-%20Philosophy%20o f%20History.html).

Herr, T. *Catholic Social Teaching: A Textbook of Christian insights.* London: New City, 1991.

Hill, S. and C. Lederer. *The Infinite Asset: Managing Brands to Build New Value.* Boston: Harvard Business School Press, 2001.

Himmelstrand, U., ed. *Interfaces in Economic and Social Analysis.* London: Routledge, 1992.

Hirschleifer. "The Expanding Domain of Economics." *American Economic Review* 75(6): 53–68, 1985.

Hobbes, T. *Leviathan.* London: Penguin, 1968.

Hobgood, M. E. *Catholic Social Teaching and Economic Theory: Paradigms in Conflict.* Philadelphia: Temple University Press, 1991.

Hocart, A. M. *Kings and Councillors.* Chicago: University of Chicago Press, 1970.

Hofstadter, R. *Social Darwinism in American Thought 1860–1915.* Philadelphia: University of Pennsylvania Press. 1945.

Hogan S. J., W. T. *Steel in the 21st Century.* New York: Lexington Books, 1994.

Holland, J. *Modern Catholic Social Teaching: The Popes Confront the Industrial Age 1740–1958.* New York: Paulist Press, 2003.

Hollenbach S. J., D. *The Common Good and Christian Ethics.* Cambridge: Cambridge University Press, 2002.

Hornblower, S. and A. Spawforth, Eds. *The Oxford Classical Dictionary (Third Edition).* Oxford: Oxford University Press, 1999.

Howard, M. *War in European History.* Oxford: Oxford University Press, 1976.

Huber, J. and G. Spitze. *Sex Stratification: Children, Housework, and Jobs.* New York: Academic Press, 1983.

Hudson, S. D. *Human Character and Morality: Reflections from the History of Ideas.* Boston: Routledge & Kegan Paul, 1986.

Hunnicutt, B. K. *Work Without End: Abandoning Shorter Hours for the Right to Work.* Philadelphia: Temple University Press, 1988.

Hutchison, T. W. *Knowledge and Ignorance in Economics.* Oxford: Basil Blackwell, 1977.

Hvid, H. and P. Hasle, Eds. *Human Development and Working Life: Work for Welfare.* Aldershot, UK: Ashgate, 2003.

Illanes, J. L. *On the Theology of Work: Aspects of the Teaching of the Founder of Opus Dei.* Dublin: Four Courts Press, 1982.

Jacquard, A. *J'accuse l'économie triomphante.* Paris: Calmann-Lévy, 1995.

John Paul II. *Laborem exercens.* London: Catholic Truth Society, 1981.

———. *Salvifici Doloris.* London: Catholic Truth Society, 1984.

———. "Sollicitudo Rei Socialis." *Catholic Social Thought: The Documentary Heritage.* D. J. O'Brien and T. A. Shannon. Maryknoll: NY, Orbis, 1987.

———. *Mulieris Dignitatem (On the Dignity of Women).* Homebush: NSW Australia, 1988.

———. "Centesimus Annus." *Catholic Social Thought: The Documentary Heritage.* D. J. O'Brien and T. A. Shannon. Maryknoll, NY: Orbis Books, 1991.

———. *Veritatis Splendor.* London: Catholic Truth Society, 1993.

———. *The Gospel of Life (Evangelium Vitae)*. Sherbrooke, QC: Médiaspaul, 1995.

———. *The Theology of the Body: Human Love in the Divine Plan*. Boston: Pauline Books and Media, 1997.

———. *Novo Millennio Ineuente*. London: Catholic Truth Society, 2002.

———. "Homily for the Beatification of Mother Theresa of Calcutta." (Available at vatican.va/holy_father/john_paul_ii/homilies/2003).

Johnson, D. G. "Population, Food, and Knowledge." *American Economic Review* 90(1): 1–15, 2002.

Jones, J. D. *Poverty and the Human Condition: A Philosophical Inquiry*. Lewiston, NY: The Edward Mellen Press, 1990.

Joyce, P., ed. *Class*. Oxford: Oxford University Press, 1995.

Jungk, R. *Tomorrow is Already Here*. London: Rupert Hart-Davis, 1954.

Kanigel, R. *The One Best Way: Frederick Winslow Taylor and the Enigma of Efficiency*. New York: Viking, 1997.

Keynes, J. M. "Economic Possibilities for our Grandchildren." *Essays in Persuasion*. London: Macmillan, 1931.

Kimura, D. *Sex and Cognition*. Cambridge, MA: MIT Press, 1999.

Kincaid, H. *Philosophical Foundations of the Social Sciences: Analyzing Controversies in Social Research*. Cambridge: Cambridge University Press, 1996.

Kinsella, N. *Unprofitable Servants: Conferences on Humility*. Dublin: M. H. Gill and Son Ltd., 1960.

Klamer, A., ed. *The Value of Culture: On the relationship between economics and arts*. Amsterdam: Amsterdam University Press, 1996.

Kolm, S.-C. "The Impossibility of Utilitarianism." *The Good and the Economical: Ethical Choices in Economics and Management*. P. Koslowski and Y. Shionoya. Berlin: Springer: 85–115, 1993.

Lacroix, J. *Personne et amour*. Paris: Editions du Seuil, 1955.

Laidlaw, J. *Riches and Renunciation: Religion, Economy and Society among the Jains*. Oxford: Oxford University Press, 1995.

Lambert, M. D. *Franciscan Poverty: The Doctrine of the Absolute Poverty of Christ and the Apostles in the Franciscan Order 1210–1323*. London: SPCK, 1961.

Larrabee, E., ed. *Mass Leisure*. Glencoe, IL: The Free Press, 1958.

Lasch, C. *The Culture of Narcissism: American Life in an Age of Diminishing Expectations*. New York: W. W. Norton, 1978.

Lawson, T. *Reorienting Economics*. London, Routledge, 2003.

Layard, R. *Happiness: Lessons from a New Science*. London: Penguin, 2005.

Leo XIII. "*Rerum Novarum*: The Condition of Labor." In *Catholic Social Thought: The Documentary Heritage*. D. J. O'Brien and T. A. Shannon. Maryknoll: NY, Orbis Books.

Lewis, I. M. *Social Anthropology in Perspective: The Relevance of Social Anthropology*. Cambridge: Cambridge University Press, 1985.

Lewis, P., ed. *Transforming Economics: Perspective on the critical realist project*. London: Routledge, 2004.

Lévi-Strauss, C. *Le cru et le cuit*. Paris: Plon, 1964.
Lichtheim, G. *Marxism: An Historical and Critical Study*. London: Routledge and Kegan Paul, 1961.
Lichtheim, G. *The Origins of Socialism*. London: Weidenfeld and Nicolson, 1969.
Linhart, R. *Lénine, les paysans, Taylor: Essai d'analyse matérialiste historique de la naissance du système productif soviétique*. Paris: Editions du Seuil, 1976.
Livi-Bacchi, M. *A Concise History of World Population*. Oxford: Blackwell, 2001.
Long, D. S. *Divine Economy: Theology and the Market*. London: Routledge, 2000.
Lubar, S. and W. D. Kingerly, Eds. *History from Things: Essays on Material Culture*. Washington, DC: Smithsonian Institution Press, 1993.
Lukacs, G. *History and Class Consciousness: Studies in Marxist Dialectics*. Cambridge, MA: MIT Press, 1971.
Lunt, P. K. and S. M. Livingstone. *Mass Consumption and Personal Identity: Everyday Economic Experience*. Buckingham, UK: Open University Press, 1992.
Lutz, M. A. and K. Lux. *Humanistic Economics: The New Challenge*. New York: The Bootstrap Press, 1988.
MacIntrye, A. *Whose Justice? Which Rationality?* London: Duckworth, 1988.
———. *After Virtue: a Study in Moral Theory (Second Edition)*. London: Duckworth, 1985.
Madanu, F. *Understanding of the Poor in Job: In the Context of Biblical Wisdom Literature*. Hyderabad, India: St. John's Regional Seminary, 1997.
Maddison, A. *Monitoring the World Economy*. Paris: OECD, 1995.
Magnusson, L. *Mercantilism: The Shaping of an Economic Language*. London, Routledge, 1994.
Malthus, T. *An Essay on the Principles of Population*. Harmondsworth, Middlesex UK: Penguin, 1970.
Manent, P. *La Cité de l'homme*. Paris: Flammarion, 1997.
Manuel, F. E. and F. P. Manuel. *Utopian Thought in the Western World*. Oxford: Basil Blackwell, 1979.
Mark, M. and C. S. Pearson. *The Hero and the Outlaw: Building Extraordinary Brands Through the Power of Archetypes*. New York: McGraw-Hill, 2001.
Martin, M. and L. C. McIntyre, Eds. *Readings in the Philosophy of Social Science*. Cambridge, MA: MIT Press, 1994.
Marwick, A., C. Emsley, et al. *Total War and Historical Change: Europe 1914–1955*. Buckingham, UK: Open University Press, 2001.
Marx, K. *Capital*. New York, Vintage, 1976.
Marx, K. and F. Engels. *The Marx-Engels Reader (Second Edition)*. New York: W. W. Norton, 1978.
Maslow, A. H. *Motivation and Personality (Third Edition)*. New York: Harper and Row, 1987.
Mason, R. (1998). *The Economics of Conspicuous Consumption: Theory and Thought since 1700*. Cheltenham, UK: Edward Elgar, 1998.

Mathias, P. and S. Pollard, Eds. *The Cambridge Economic History of Europe, Volume VIII*. Cambridge: Cambridge University Press, 1989.

Mayo, H. B. *Introduction to Marxist Theory*. New York: Oxford University Press, 1960.

McEvedy, C. and R. Jones. *Atlas of World Population History*. Harmondsworth, UK: Penguin, 1978.

McInerny, D. J. *Difficult Good: A Thomistic Approach to Moral Conflict and Human Happiness*. New York: Fordham University Press, 2006.

McNeill, W. H. *The Pursuit of Power: Technology, Armed Force, and Society since AD 1000*. Oxford: Blackwell, 1983.

Meek, R. L. *The Economics of Physiocracy: Essays and Translations*. London: George Allen & Unwin, Ltd., 1962.

Meikle, J. L. *Twentieth Century Limited*. Philadelphia: Temple University Press, 1979.

Melchior, A. "Global Inequality: Perceptions, Facts and Unresolved Issues." *World Economics* 2(3): 87–108, 2001.

Melton, G., ed. *The Individual, the Family, and Social Good: Personal Fulfillment in Times of Change*. Lincoln: University of Nebraska Press, 1995.

Melville, H. *Moby Dick or The Whale*. Evanston, IL: Northwestern University Press, 2001.

Merton, R. K. *Social Theory and Social Structure (Revised and enlarged edition)*. Glencoe, IL: The Free Press, 1957.

Mill, J. S. "Utilitarianism." *The Six Great Humanistic Essays of John Stuart Mill*. A. Levi. New York: Washington Square Press, 1963.

———. *Principles of Political Economy*. Toronto: University of Toronto Press, 1965.

———. *Essays on Some Unsettled Questions of Political Economy*. London: Longmans, Green, Reader & Dyer, 1875.

Miller, D. *Material Culture and Mass Consumption*. Oxford: Basil Blackwell, 1987.

Mirowski, P. *More Heat than Light*. Cambridge: Cambridge University Press, 1989.

Mirowski, P., ed. *Natural Images in Economic Thought: "Markets read in tooth and claw"*. Cambridge: Cambridge University Press, 1994.

Misner, P. *Social Catholicism in Europe: From the Onset of Industrialisation to the First World War*. London: Datron, Longman and Todd, 1991.

Mitchell, B. R. *International Historical Statistics: Europe 1750–2000 (Fifth Edition)*. London: Palgrave Macmillan, 2003a.

———. *International Historical Statistics: Africa, Asia & Oceania 1750–2000 (Fourth Edition)*. London: Palgrave Macmillan, 2003b.

Moe, K. S., ed. *Women, family and Work: Writings on the Economics of Gender*. Oxford: Blackwell, 2003.

Mokyr, J., ed. *The Oxford Encyclopedia of Economic History*. Oxford: Oxford University Press, 2003.

Mollat, M. and P. Wolff. *The Popular Revolutions of the Late Middle Ages*. London: George Allen & Unwin, 1973.

Montes, L. "*Das Adam Smith Problem*: Its origins, the stages of the current debate, and one implication for our understanding of sympathy." *Journal of the History of Economic Thought* 25(1): 63–90, 2003.

Morse, J. R. *Love and Economics: Why the Laissez-faire family doesn't work.* Dallas: Spence Publishers, 2001.

Moser, P. K. and J. D. Trout, Eds. *Contemporary Materialism: A Reader.* London: Routledge, 1995.

Mullainathan, S. and R. H. Thaler. "Behavioral Economics." *NBER Working Paper* (7948), 2000.

Mumford, L. *Technics and Civilization.* London: George Routledge & Sons, Ltd., 1934.

Nava, M. and others. *Buy This Book: Studies in Advertising and Consumption.* London: Routledge, 1997.

Negri, A. *Travail et technique dans la pensée d'Auguste Comte.* Paris: L'Harmattan, 2003.

Nelson, J. A. *Feminism, Objectivity and Economics.* London: Routledge, 1996.

———. *Economics for Humans.* Chicago: University of Chicago Press, 2006.

Nicholson, J. *Men & Women: How Different are They?* Oxford: Oxford University Press, 1993.

Nisbet, R. *History of the Idea of Progress.* London: Heinemann, 1980.

North, D. C. and R. P. Thomas. *The Rise of the Western World: A New Economic History.* Cambridge: Cambridge University Press, 1973.

North, D. C. (1990). *Institutions, Institutional Change and Economic Performance.* Cambridge: Cambridge University Press, 1990.

Novak, M. *Morality, Capitalism and Democracy.* London: The IEA Health and Welfare Unit, 1990.

———. "Eight arguments about the Morality of the Marketplace." *God and the Marketplace, Essays on the Morality of Wealth Creation.* J. Davies. London: IEA Health and Welfare Unit: 8–30, 1993.

———. *The Catholic Ethic and the Spirit of Capitalism.* New York: Free Press, 1993.

O'Boyle, E. J. *Personalist Economics: Moral Convictions, Economic Realities, and Social Action.* Boston: Kluwer Academic, 1998.

O'Brien, D. J. and T. A. Shannon. *Catholic Social Thought: The Documentary Heritage.* Maryknoll, NY: Orbis Books, 1992.

Offer, A. *The Challenge of Affluence, Self-Control and Well-Being in the United States and Britain since 1950.* Oxford: Oxford University Press, 2006.

Olson, M., ed. *A Not-So-Dismal Science.* Oxford: Oxford University Press, 2000.

Ortner, S. B. and H. Whitehead, Eds. *Sexual Meanings: The Cultural Construction of Gender and Sexuality.* Cambridge: Cambridge University Press, 1981.

Parker, S. *Leisure and Work.* London: George Allen & Unwin, 1983.

Parry, J. and M. Bloch. *Money and the Morality of Exchange.* Cambridge: Cambridge University Press, 1989.

Passmore, J. *Man's Responsibility for Nature: Ecological Problems and Western Traditions.* London: Duckworth, 1974.

Paul VI. "*Populorum Progressio*, On the Development of Peoples." In *Catholic Social Thought: The Documentary Heritage*. D. J. O'Brien and T. A. Shannon. Maryknoll, NY: Orbis, 1967.

Phelps, E. S., ed. *Altruism, Morality and Economic Theory*. New York: Russell Sage Foundation, 1975.

Piderit, J. J. *The Ethical Foundations of Economics*. Washington DC: Georgetown University Press, 1993.

Pieper, J. *Leisure the Basis of Culture*. London: Collins, 1952.

Plato. *The Collected Dialogues of Plato*. Princeton, NJ: Princeton University Press, 1961.

Polanyi, K. *The Great Transformation: The Political and Economic Origins of Our Time*. Boston: Beacon Press, 2001.

Polsky, A. J. *The Rise of the Therapeutic State*. Princeton, NJ: Princeton University Press, 1991.

Pontifical Council for Justice and Peace. "Work as the Key to the Social Question: The Great Social and Economic Transformations and the Subjective Dimension of Work." Vatican City: Libreria Editrice Vaticana, 2002.

Pontifical Council for Justice and Peace. *Compendium of the Social Doctrine of the Church*. London: Burns & Oates, 2004.

Preece, R. *Animals and Nature: Cultural Myths, Cultural Realities*. Vancouver, BC: UBC Press, 1999.

Preston, R. H. *Religion and the Ambiguities of Capitalism*. London: SCM, 1991.

Price, C. *Time, Discounting and Value*. Oxford: Blackwell, 1993.

Proctor, R. N. *Racial Hygiene: Medicine under the Nazis*. Cambridge: Harvard University Press, 1988.

Puth, R. C. *American Economic History, Second Edition*. New York: Holt, Rinehart and Winston, 1988.

Quigley, D. *The Interpretation of Caste*. London: Clarendon Press, 1993.

Rawls, J. *A Theory of Justice (Revised Edition)*. Oxford: Oxford University Press, 1999.

Reisman, D. *The Institutional Economy: Demand and Supply*. Cheltenham: Edward Elgar, 2002.

Régamey, P. R. *La Pauvreté et l'homme d'aujourd'hui*. Paris: Aubier, 1963.

Ricoeur, P. *Histoire et vérité*. Paris: Editions du Seuil, 1955.

Rimlinger, G. *Welfare Policy and Industrialization in Europe, America and Russia*. New York: John Wiley & Son, 1971.

Riordan S. J., P. *A Politics of the Common Good*. Dublin: Institute of Public Administration, 1996.

Ritzer, G. *Enchanting a Disenchanted World: Revolutionizing the Means of Consumption*. Thousand Oaks, CA: Pine Forge Press, 1999.

Rosen, M. *On Voluntary Servitude: False Consciousness and the Theory of Ideology*. Cambridge: Polity Press, 1996.

Rosenberg, A. *Philosophy of Social Science (Second Edition)*. Boulder: Westview Press, 1995.

Rosman, A. and P. Rubel. *Feasting with Mine Enemy: Rank and Exchange Among Northwest Coast Societies*. New York: Columbia University Press, 1971.

Rosman, A. and P. Rubel. *The Tapestry of Culture: An Introduction to Cultural Anthropology (Fifth Edition)*. New York: McGraw-Hill, 1981.

Ross, J. A. *International Encyclopedia of Population*. New York: Macmillan, 1982.

Rothschild, E. *Economic Sentiments: Adam Smith, Condorcet and the Enlightenment*. Cambridge, MA: Harvard University Press, 2001.

Rowland, T. "The Authority of Experts and the Ethos of Modern Institutions." *Communio*. 28: 745–70, 2001.

Rösener, W. *Peasants in the Middle Ages*. Cambridge: Polity Press, 1992.

Ruskin, J. *Seven Lamps of Architecture*. New York: Dover, 1989.

———.*Unto This Last. Four Essays on the First Principles of Political Economy*. Hendon: Nelson, 2000.

Saad-Filho, A., ed. *Anti-Capitalism: A Marxist Introduction*. London: Pluto Press, 2003.

Sahlins, M. *Stone Age Economics*. New York: Aldine de Gruyter, 1972.

Salaman, G., ed. *Labor: Processes and Control*. Milton Keynes, UK: Open University Press, 1985.

Saler, B. *Conceptualizing Religion: Immanent Anthropologists, Transcendent Natives and Unbounded Categories*. New York: Berghahn Books, 2000.

Scarre, G. *Utilitarianism*. London: Routledge, 1996.

Schenk, R. "On Human Work." *Nova et Vetera* 2(1): 129–45, 2004.

Scherer, F. M. *Industry Structure, Strategy, and Public Policy*. New York: HarperCollins College Publishers, 1996.

Schervish, P. G., ed. *Wealth in Western Thought: The Case For and Against Riches*. Westport, CT: Praeger, 1994.

Schindler, D. C. "The Redemption of Eros: Philosophical Reflections on Benedict XVI's First Encyclical." *Communio* 33(3): 388–99, 2006.

Schmitz, K. L. *At the Center of the Human Drama, The Philosophical Anthropology of Karol Wojtyla/Pope John Paul II*. Washington, DC: Catholic University of America Press, 1993.

Schor, J. B. *The Overworked American: The Unexpected Decline of Leisure*. New York: Basic Books, 1991.

Schumacher, E. F. *Small is Beautiful: A Study of Economics as if People Mattered*. London: Blond & Briggs, 1973.

Scott, J. W., ed. *Feminism and History*. Oxford: Oxford University Press, 1996.

Searle, J. R. *The Construction of Social Reality*. London: Allen Lane, 1995.

Segalman, R. and A. Basu. *Poverty in America: The Welfare Dilemma*. Westport, CT: Greenwood Press, 1981.

Seligson, M. A. and Passé-Smith, Eds. *Development and Underdevelopment: The Political Economy of Global Inequality (Third Edition)*. Boulder: Lynne Rienner, 2003.

Sen, A. and B. Williams, eds. *Utilitarianism and Beyond*. Cambridge: Cambridge University Press, 1982.

Sen, A. and J. Drèze, eds. *The Political Economy of Hunger*. Oxford: Oxford University Press, 1990.
Shanks, M. "Human Goods in Ethical Business." *The Good and the Economical: Ethical Choices in Economics and Management*. P. Koslowski and Y. Shionoya. Berlin: Springer: 180–210, 1993.
Short, W. J. *Poverty and Joy: The Franciscan Tradition*. London: Darton, Longman & Todd, 1999.
Silk, L. *Contemporary Economics: Principles and Issues*. New York: McGraw-Hill, 1970.
Silver, M. L. *Under Construction: Work and Alienation in the Building Trades*. Albany: State University of New York Press, 1986.
Simon, Y. R. *Work, Society, and Culture*. New York: Fordham University Press, 1971.
Simon, H. A. *Economics, Bounded Rationality and the Cognitive Revolution*. Aldershot UK: Edward Elgar, 1992.
Simon, H. A. *Administrative Behavior: A Study of Decision-Making Processes in Administrative Organizations (Fourth Edition)*. New York: The Free Press, 1997.
Simon, J. *The State of Humanity*. Oxford: Blackwell, 1999.
Smelser, N. J. and R. Swedberg, eds. *The Handbook of Economic Sociology*. Princeton, NJ: Princeton University Press, 1994
Smith, A. *An Inquiry into the Nature and Causes of the Wealth of Nations*. Indianapolis: Bobbs-Merrill, 1961.
Snooks, G. D. *Economics Without Time: A Science Blind to Forces of Historical Change*. Houndmills, Basingstoke: Macmillan, 1993.
———. "Great Waves of Economic Change: The Industrial Revolution in Historical Perspective, 1000 to 2000." *Was the Industrial Revolution Necessary?* G. D. Snooks. London: Routledge: 43–79, 1994.
Spengler, J. J. "Economic Thought of Islam: Ibn Khaldun." *St. Thomas Aquinas (1225–1274)*. M. Blaug. Aldershot, UK: Edward Elgar, 1964.
Spiegel, H. W. *The Growth of Economic Thought (revised and expanded edition)*. Durham: Duke University Press, 1983.
Statistical Abstract of the United States: 2002. Washington, DC: U.S. Department of Commerce, 2002.
Steckel, R. H. and R. Floud, eds. (1997). *Health and Welfare during Industrialization*. Chicago: University of Chicago Press, 1997.
Strasser, S. *Satisfaction Guaranteed: The Making of the American Mass Market*. New York: Pantheon, 1989.
Studenski, P. *The Income of Nations*. New York: New York University Press, 1958.
Sullivan, R. J. "Trends in Agricultural Labor Force." *The State of Humanity*. J. Simon. Oxford: Blackwell, 1999.
Swados, H. *On the Line*. London: Peter Davies, 1958.
Taylor, P. W. *Respect for Nature: A Theory of Environmental Ethics*. Princeton, NJ: Princeton University Press, 1986.

Taylor, C. *Sources of the Self.* Cambridge, MA: Harvard University Press, 1989.

———. *A Catholic Modernity? Charles Taylor's Marianist Award Lecture.* New York: Oxford University Press, 1999.

———. "What's Wrong with Negative Liberty." *Contemporary Political Philosophy, An Anthology.* R. E. Goodin and P. Pettit. Oxford: Blackwell, 1997.

Thurow, L. "Psychic Income: Useful or Useless." *American Economic Review* 68(2): 143–45, 1978.

Tilgher, A. *Homo Faber: Storia del concetto di lavoro nella civilita occidentale: Analisi filosofica di concetti affini.* Rome: Libreria di Scienze e Lettere, 1929.

Tilly, C. *Coercion, Capital, and European States, AD 990–1990.* Oxford: Basil Blackwell, 1990.

Tims, M. *Mary Wollstonecraft: A Social Pioneer.* London: Millington Books, 1976.

Tobias, M., ed. *Deep Ecology.* San Marcos, CA: Avant Books, 1988.

Tomaney, J. "A New Paradigm of Work Organization and Technology?" *Post-Fordism: A Reader.* A. Amin. Oxford: Blackwell, 1994.

Townsend, P., ed. *The Concept of Poverty: Working Papers on Methods of Investigation of the Poor in Different Countries.* London: Heinemann, 1970.

Towse, R., ed. *Cultural Economics: The Arts, the Heritage and the Media Industries.* Cheltenham, UK: Edward Elgar, 1997.

Tregarthen, T. *Economics.* New York: Worth Publishers, 1996.

United Nations Development Program. *Human Development 1998.* New York: Oxford University Press, 1998.

Valdés, B. *Economic Growth: Theory, Empirics and Policy.* Cheltenham, UK: Edward Elgar, 1999.

van Creveld, M. *Technology and War: From 2000 B.C. to the Present.* London: Brassey's, 1991.

Veblen, T. *The Theory of the Leisure Class.* New York: Dover, 1994.

Verga, G. *The House by the Medlar Tree [I Malavoglia].* London: Wedenfeld & Nicolson, 1950.

Vialatoux, J. *Signification humaine du travail.* Paris: Les Editions Ouvrières, 1962.

Volf, M. *Work in the Spirit: Toward a Theology of Work.* Oxford: Oxford University Press, 1991.

von Balthasar, H. U. *The Glory of The Lord, a Theological Aesthetics: Vol. 1, Seeing the Form.* Edinburgh: T&T Clark, 1982.

———. *Theo-Drama: Theological Dramatic Theory, Volume II, The Dramatis Personae: Man in God.* San Francisco: Ignatius Press, 1990.

———. *Unless You Become Like This Child.* San Francisco: Ignatius Press, 1991.

———. *Leben aus dem Tod: Betrachtungen zum Ostermysterium.* Einsiedeln, Germany: Johannes Verlag, 1997.

von Mises, L. *Human Action: A Treatise on Economics.* London: William Hodge and Company, 1949.

Vromen, J. J. *Economic Evolution: An Enquiry into the Foundations of New Institutional Economics.* London: Routledge, 1995.

Warr, P., ed. *Psychology at Work (Fifth edition)*. London: Penguin, 2002.
Weber, M. *The Protestant Ethic and the Spirit of Capitalism*. London: Unwin, 1985.
———. *Economy and Society*. Berkeley, CA: University of California Press, 1978.
White, I. S. "The functions of advertising in our culture." *Marketing: Critical Perspectives on Business and Management*. M. J. Baker. London: Routledge. 5: 363–72, 1959.
Wiles, P. J. D. *The Political Economy of Communism*. Oxford: Basil Blackwell, 1962.
Williams, R. H. *Dream Worlds: Mass Consumption in Late Nineteenth-Century France*. Berkeley, CA: University of California Press, 1982.
Winter, J. M., ed. *War and Economic Development*. Cambridge: Cambridge University Press, 1975.
Wolf, A. *Does Education Matter? Myths about Education and Economic Growth*. London: Penguin, 2002.
World Health Organisation. *The World Health Report 2002—Reducing Risks, Promoting Healthy Life*. Geneva: World Health Organisation, 2002 (available at http://www.who.int/whr/2002/en/).
Zamagni, S., ed. *The Economics of Altruism*. Aldershot UK: Edward Elgar, 1995.

Notes

Chapter 1

1. This claim of a clear historical divide in economic organization is closely related to the development of a distinctive modern worldview, discussed in chapter 4. One of the many intellectual curiosities of the history of economics is how little attention economists pay to economic history. With the exception of Marx and some of his followers, they mostly ignore discussions of the "spirit" of industry. Economic historians also often gloss over the significant qualitative differences between pre-industrial and industrial economies. Discussions in terms of consistent economic growth rates, as in Maddison, *Monitoring the World Economy,* are much more misleading than helpful.
2. The phrase is from Keynes, "Economic Possibilities for our Grandchildren." The lifestyle is described as the "age of pestilence and famines . . . characterized by high and fluctuating mortality rates with expectation of life at birth varying between 20 and 40 years. Most of the already-developed countries were in this state from prehistoric times to the eighteenth century." From the article by Regina McNamara, citing a model by Adbel R. Omran, in Ross, *International Encyclopedia of Population,* 2 (461).
3. "What is the basic task that economists expect the market to carry out? The answer most frequently given is that the market resolves THE fundamental problem of the economy: the fact that all decisions are constrained by the scarcity of available resources." Baumol and Blinder, *Economics, Principles and Policy,* 49. This definition fits poorly with the alternative definition of economics as a study of preferences and choices, since many choices are among goods in ample supply.
4. See Layard, *Happiness: Lessons from a New Science* and Offer, *The Challenge of Affluence,* both influenced by the remarkably mundane vision of happiness offered by Daniel Kahneman, for example, in his essay in Brocas and Carillo, *The Psychology of Economic Decisions.*
5. Some evidence, with references, in Sullivan, "Trends in Agricultural Labor Force."

6. See Scherer, *Industry Structure, Strategy, and Public Policy*, for U.S. statistics (27). The pattern is similar in all industrial economies.

7. Hogan, *Steel in the 21st Century* has some data, but he is too conservative. More generally, see the articles in Mokyr, *The Oxford Encyclopedia of Economic History*. A single statistic—in Wyoming, some seven hundred miners are able to operate a mine that provides enough coal to generate electricity for six million people.

8. This claim needs to be qualified. See Sahlins, *Stone Age Economics* for a discussion of the leisure of the poverty of hunter-gatherers, which was eventually replaced almost everywhere by the harder work and less poverty of agriculture.

9. Some commentators—de Grazia, *Of Time, Work and Leisure*; Hunnicutt, *Work Without End*; and Schor, *The Overworked American*—argue that the increase in leisure time has stopped or reversed. For a more objective interpretation, see Fogel, *The Fourth Great Awakening and the Future of Egalitarianism*; and Aarts, Burkhauser, et al., *Curing the Dutch Disease*.

10. This estimate, which is very rough, was made by dividing the employment categories provided in table 591 of the *Statistical Abstract of the United States: 2002*.

11. On Titans, see Hornblower and Spawforth, *The Oxford Classical Dictionary*; and Diel, *Symbolism in Greek Mythology*: "Titanic banalization entails the dispersion of energy over a multitude of worrying material desires . . . which tend to consolidate around an obsessive ambition to improve the world. . . . [T]he human intellect in titanic revolt shows little concern for truth, for the secretly lawful meaning, for the spirit of life" (119). Cicero, writing in what might be considered a proto-industrial civilization, explains: "We [men] alone have the power of controlling the most violent of nature's offspring, the sea and the winds, thanks to the service of navigation. . . . [W]e confine the rivers and strengthen or divert their courses. . . . [B]y means of our hands we try to create as it were a second Nature within the world of Nature." From *De Natura Deorum* 2 (60, 153), cited in Passmore, *Man's Responsibility for Nature*, 18. Titanism has become a central strand in the modern worldview, although it is fundamentally incompatible with such other strands as the democratic polity or the elevation of individual feeling. Jungk, *Tomorrow Is Already Here*: "Their efforts do not aspire to the mastery of continents, still less to that of the entire globe, but . . . to win power over the sum total of things . . . [t]o occupy God's place, to repeat his deeds, to recreate and organize a man-made cosmos according to man-made laws of reason, foresight and efficiency. . . . [W]ith the rise of the applied sciences and technology, the pillars of democracy, Christianity and personal ethics . . . have begun to totter" (17–18). For a theological-anthropological analysis, see von Balthasar, *Theo-Drama*, Vol. 2 (420–26).

12. The noneconomic nature of science and technology is recognized in conventional neoclassical theory by treating "technology" as an exogenous variable, i.e. by ignoring it.

13. Puth, *American Economic History* provides a short and clear summary of the factors contributing to U.S. economic development.
14. The administrative nature of modern government is discussed in Habermas, *Between Facts and Norms*.
15. "What is society, whatever its form may be? The product of men's reciprocal action.... Assume a particular state of development in the productive faculties of man and you will get a particular form of commerce and consumption. Assume particular stages of development in production, commerce and consumption and you will have a corresponding social constitution, a corresponding organisation of the family, or orders or of classes, in a word, a corresponding civil society.... Hence it necessarily follows that the social history of men is never anything but the history of their individual development, whether they are conscious of it or not. Their material relations are the basis of all their relations." From an 1846 letter of Marx, in Marx and Engels, *The Marx-Engels Reader* (136–37).
16. See Ricoeur, *Histoire et vérité* and Manent, *La Cité de l'homme*.

Chapter 2

1. Many economists deny that they make any claims about human nature, taking refuge in the idea that economics is really a science—"economics, like all other sciences..." as Silk, *Contemporary Economics* (11), explains. There has been some retreat, although the scientific label has not yet been fully abandoned. See, for example, Tregarthen, *Economics* (13). For a more intellectually rigorous critique of conventional economic anthropology, see Rowland, "The Authority of Experts and the Ethos of Modern Institutions."
2. The origin and anthropological weakness of the neoclassical definition of "economic man" is well discussed in chapter 3 of Fonseca, *Beliefs in Action*.
3. See Mirowski, *More Heat than Light*.
4. See Mirowksi, *Natural Images in Economic Thought*; Hawkins, *Social Darwinism in European and American Thought*; and Hofstadter, *Social Darwinism in American Thought*. Social Darwinism has a complex relationship with economics, since Darwin himself was strongly influenced by the pseudoscientific economic analysis of Malthus.
5. See Taylor, "What's Wrong with Negative Liberty"; and John Paul II, *Veritatis Splendor*.
6. On the history of economics, I have used Blaug, *Economic Theory in Retrospect*; and Spiegel, *The Growth of Economic Thought*. On utilitarianism, see Kolm, "The Impossibility of Utilitarianism"; Mill, "Utilitarianism"; Scarre, *Utilitarianism*; and Sen and Williams, *Utilitarianism and Beyond*. On the time preference in the theory, see Conrad, *An Introduction to the Theory of Interest*; and Price, *Time, Discounting and Value*. I am aware of the various debates among believers, particularly between

rule and act utilitarianism, but all forms of the felicific or hedonic calculus suffer from the fundamental errors listed here. MacIntyre, *After Virtue* provides a cutting philosophical explanation of the meaninglessness of the concept of "utility" as a guide to action. For a more theological critique of the whole notion of consequentialist ethics, see John Paul II, *Veritatis Splendor* (chap. 2).

7. The notion that virtue is found in the mean, that is between two extremes, is developed in Aristotle, *Nicomachean Ethics*, 2.6. The idea that the mean is not appropriate to theological virtues is developed in Aquinas, *Summa* Ia 2.64.4.

8. The earlier description was "idleness." See Polanyi, *The Great Transformation*.

9. As Manuel and Manuel, *Utopian Thought in the Western World* (482) point out, Turgot, identified as the first exponent of the modern idea of historical progress, thought ordinary workers would be bound to a subsistence level of wages. Ricardo's pessimism is disputed—see the discussions in chapter 4 of Berg, *The Machinery Question and the Making of Political Economy 1815–1848*; and Blaug, "Misunderstanding Classical Economics"—but he undeniably emphasized the "law" of diminishing returns and the conflicts between the different factors of production. Marx accepted Ricardo's belief in the inevitability of declines in wages and saw no hope for the capitalist system. As late as 1871, the most that John Stuart Mill can say of "the great mechanical inventions of Watt, Arkwright, and their contemporaries" was that they temporarily allowed production "to keep up with, or even surpass, the actual increase of population," (Mill, *Principles of Political Economy*, book 1, chapter 13, section 3). See Fonseca, *Beliefs in Action* (38). On the socialist response to nineteenth-century despair, see chapter 19 of Spiegel, *The Growth of Economic Thought*.

10. Valdés, *Economic Growth* provides the first basic principle of economic growth—"In the long-run, per capita output growth grows at a positive rate which shows no tendency to diminish" (10).

11. This perspective inspired the original appellation, by Thomas Carlyle. "[T]he Social Science—not a 'gay science,' but a rueful—which finds the secret of this universe in 'supply-and-demand,' and reduces the duty of human governors to that of letting men alone, is also wonderful. Not a 'gay science,' I should say, like some we have heard of; no, a dreary, desolate, and indeed quite abject and distressing one; what we might call, by way of eminence, the dismal science." Carlyle, "Occasional Discourse on the Negro Question" (530–31).

Chapter 3

1. See the relevant chapters in Spiegel, *The Growth of Economic Thought*. Chapters 5 and 6 of Mirowski, *More Heat than Light* provide both a history of critical responses to the neoclassical model and a damning critique of its assumptions. His

view has been shared by some practitioners. For example, Sir Henry Phelps Brown, President of the Royal Economic Society, said, "In no other field of empirical inquiry has so massive and sophisticated a statistical machinery been used with such indifferent results." Cited in Hutchison *Knowledge and Ignorance in Economics* (71). About half of Blaug, *Economic Theory in Retrospect* is dedicated to the description of the history of neoclassical economics, but the author then effectively (although perhaps not quite fully consciously) dismisses marginalist efforts: "I contend that perfect competition is a grossly misleading concept . . ." (594). Quite recently, there is Nelson, *Economics for Humans*. An extensive series of books dedicated to "Economics as Social Theory" from Routledge, a leading academic publisher, suggests the range of discontent and, overall, the lack of very helpful alternative visions. See, as an example of the latter, the critical realism described in Lawson, *Reorienting Economics*; and Lewis, *Transforming Economics*.

2. For the old institutionalists, Veblen, *The Theory of the Leisure Class* is the foundational text. Veblen's influence can be seen in Commons, "Institutional Economics"; Ayres, *The Problem of Economic Order*; and Gruchy, *The Reconstruction of Economics*. More recent books that might be classed as institutional include Reisman, *The Institutional Economy*; Dugger, *Underground Economics*; and Olson, *A Not-So-Dismal Science*, the last offering a somewhat broader analysis. For new institutionalism, see Coase, *The Firm, the Market, and the Law*; Furubotn and Richter, *Institutions and Economic Theory*; North and Thomas, *The Rise of the Western World*; and North, *Institutions, Institutional Change and Economic Performance*. Vromen, *Economic Evolution* compares the old and new schools. He points out the influence of Darwinian "natural selection" and functionalist explanations—both unacceptable intellectual constructions in human economics—on both schools.

3. Lutz and Lux, *Humanistic Economics*.

4. Maslow, *Motivation and Personality*.

5. Simon, *Economics, Bounded Rationality and the Cognitive Revolution*; and Simon, *Administrative Behavior*.

6. Phelps *Altruism, Morality and Economic Theory*; Collard *Altruism and Economy*; and Zamagni, *The Economics of Altruism*. For a philosophical critique of the concept of altruism, see Schindler, "The Redemption of Eros" (388–99).

7. See Moe, *Women, Family and Work*; Ferber and Nelson, *Feminist Economics Today*; Folbre, *The Invisible Heart*; and Nelson, *Feminism, Objectivity and Economics* for introductions.

8. Himmelstrand, *Interfaces in Economic and Social Analysis* provides good examples of various types of social scientists trying to work through economic issues. Grossbard-Shechtman and Clague, *The Expansion of Economics* offers some examples of economists trying to learn from social scientists. For economic sociology, see Smelser and Swedberg, *The Handbook of Economic Sociology*.

On economic psychology, see Colman, *Companion Encyclopedia of Psychology*; Warr, *Psychology at Work*; and Drenth, Sergeant, et al., *European Perspectives in Psychology*. On behavioral economics, see Mullainathan and Thaler, "Behavioral Economics." Douglas and Baron, *The World of Goods* is an effort to combine economics with anthropology, but it assumes that anthropological insights must be integrated with the neoclassical economic model. Some of the essays in Geertz, *The Interpretation of Cultures* provide much less dogmatic, and more enlightening, anthropological-economic analysis. On money, see Crump, *The Phenomenon of Money*; Einzig, *Primitive Money*; Parry and Bloch, *Money and the Morality of Exchange*; and Finley, *Ancient Slavery and Modern Ideology*.

9. See Fullbrook, *The Crisis in Economics* for a description.

10. "Utopian socialism" is a term used to describe many thinkers. I follow Marx and refer to Saint-Simon and other planners of idealistic communities. On the socialist response to nineteenth-century despair, see chapter 19 of Spiegel, *The Growth of Economic Thought*. On utopian optimism, both premodern and modern, see Nisbet, *History of the Idea of Progress*; and the more profound analysis in Manuel and Manuel, *Utopian Thought in the Western World*, especially chapters 19 and 24–28. The utopian socialists were much too optimistic about human moral potential, but they were remarkably accurate in their understanding of human economic potential. The Marquis de Condorçet, writing before the French Revolution, predicted that "not only will the same amount of ground support more people, but everyone will have less work to do, will produce more, and satisfy his wants more fully" (cited in Spiegel, 270). Fourier understood that working hours would decrease and that men would match the labor to their nature. I have also looked at Cole, *Socialist Thought* and Halévy, *La formation du radicalisme philosophique*.

11. Marx's economic theory is so reductive that he can be considered a one-idea crackpot, but he was also the most sociologically and historically aware economist of the nineteenth century. Unlike almost all of his peers, he took account of the dynamism of the new industrial economy, the close relations between social and economic organizations (even if he was profoundly wrong on the ontological order of priority), and the ideological content of money. My understanding of Marx and Marxian economics has been helped by the discussion in Blaug, *Economic Theory in Retrospect*; and Mayo, *Introduction to Marxist Theory*. My understanding of Marxism (the "ism" refers to a social as well as narrowly economic interpretations) has been helped by Cole, *The Second International*; Lukacs, *History and Class Consciousness*; Lichtheim, *The Origins of Socialism*; and Lichtheim, *Marxism*.

12. For post-Marxist thinking, see, for example, Jacquard *J'accuse l'économie triomphante*; Callinicos, *An Anti-Capitalist Manifesto*; and Saad-Filho, *Anti-Capitalism*. On cooperativism see *Coopération et développment*.

13. The New Austrian School of economics is best read in the literate works of its

early leaders, especially Mises, *Human Action* and Hayek, *The Road to Serfdom*. Although many economists think of themselves as heirs to this tradition, libertarian economists probably have the best claim. There are many differences within this school, but all share the optimistic, liberal anthropological premise that men should be seen primarily as individuals whose actions are so rational that they do not need any sort of social regulation. Such websites as Libertyhaven.com, libertariannation.org, and Americasfuture.net provide ample examples where this thinking can lead, to paranoia about the intentions and economic role of government.

14. William Wordsworth poetically complained that the modern emphasis on "getting and spending" causes men to "lay waste our powers" (from "The World Is Too Much with Us"). William Blake"s vision of the close connection between modern philosophy and science and the creation of industry is obscure but powerful. "I turn my eyes to the Schools & Universities of Europe / And there behold the Loom of Locke, whose Woof rages dire, / Wash'd by the Water-wheels of Newton: black the cloth in heavy wreathes folds over every Nation: cruel Works / of many Wheels I view, wheel without wheel, with cogs tyrannic / Moving by compulsion each other, not as those in Eden, which, / Wheel within Wheel, in freedom revolve in harmony & peace." Jerusalem I.15.13–20, in Blake, *Poems and Prophecies*. Carlyle provided a scarcely less poetic complaint—"The huge demon of Mechanism smokes and thunders, panting at his great task, in all sections of English land; changing his shape like a very Proteus; and infallibly at every change of shape, oversetting whole multitudes of workmen..." cited in Berg *The Machinery Question* (12). Berg summarizes the critical view, "The cultural critics blamed the machine for bringing to England"s new industrial towns a bleak, quantitative, utilitarian society" (ibid). See also chapter 6 of Ekelund and Hebert, *A History of Economic Theory and Method*.

15. In many ways, John Ruskin is the ancestor of agrarian thinking, through the intermediary of the "arts and crafts" movement. See, Ruskin, *Unto This Last*. G. K. Chesterton's distributist economics—more or less explained in Chesterton, *The Outline of Sanity* and Belloc, *An Essay on the Restoration of Property*—is usually cited as a founding influence. Schumacher, *Small Is Beautiful*; Berry, *Home Economics*; and Berry, *The Art of the Commonplace* are more modern, and more idiosyncratic, examples of criticism of the industrial economy. The delightful Day, *The Long Loneliness* provides a Christian expression. Mumford, *Technics and Civilization* provides a simple but accurate critique of this type of thinking. "Romanticism as an alternative to the machine is dead: indeed it never was alive" (287).

16. The philosophy of ecology is discussed in Passmore, *Man's Responsibility for Nature*; Elliot and Gare, *Environmental Philosophy*; Taylor, *Respect for Nature*; and Belshaw, *Environmental Philosophy*. See also Preece, *Animals and Nature*.

Extreme positions are expressed in Tobias, *Deep Ecology* and criticized in the essay by Michael Zimmerman in Barnhill and Gottlieb, *Deep Ecology and World Religions*.

17. The puzzle is resolved by Rothschild, *Economic Sentiments*. From the beginning of modern economic thinking, tradition and authority were considered antithetical to sound economic practice. In the nineteenth century, the most socially conservative economic thinkers, for example, Frédéric le Play, were heavily involved in the promotion of economic novelty. See Piettre, *Pensée Economique et Théories Contemporaines*. That strong prejudice remains an unexpressed principle of almost all professional economists, whether left- or right-wing. Political conservatism can be traced back to an aside in Aristotle, *Politics* II.v.13-14 1269a. Burke, *Reflections on the Revolution in France* is considered the leading modern exponent —"[B]y preserving the method of nature in the conduct of the state, in what we improve we are never wholly new; in what we retain we are never wholly obsolete...."

18. Catholic social teaching starts with the Bible. Blomberg, *Neither Poverty nor Riches* goes over all the relevant biblical texts. The first two chapters of Régamey, *La Pauvreté et l'homme d'aujourd'hui* provide a briefer but more Catholic summary of the relevant texts. See also Madanu, *Understanding of the Poor in Job*, which also discusses non-Christian Indian society. A brief modern summary is found in *Gaudium et Spes*, section 64—"[T]he basic purpose of production is not mere increase of goods, nor gain, nor domination, but the service of man—of man in his entirety, with attention to his material needs and his intellectual, moral and spiritual demands in the proper order; the needs of any man, let us add, any group of men, any race or region. So economic enterprise must be carried out, according indeed to its own methods and laws, within the bounds of the moral order, so that God's plan for men is fulfilled." The main official texts can be found in O'Brien and Shannon, *Catholic Social Thought*. A summary is also in Pontifical Council for Justice and Peace, *Compendium of the Social Doctrine of the Church*. For analysis, see Piderit, *The Ethical Foundations of Economics*; O'Boyle, *Personalist Economics*; and, generally of less value, Boileau, *Principles of Catholic Social Teaching*; Calvez and Perrin, *Eglise et Société Economique*; Charles, *Christian Social Witness and Teaching*; Dorr, *Option for the Poor*; Grelle and Krueger, *Christianity and Capitalism*; Herr, *Catholic Social Teaching*; Holland, *Modern Catholic Social Teaching*; Long, *Divine Economy*; Misner, *Social Catholicism in Europe*; and Morse, *Love and Economics*. Chabot, *La Doctrine Sociale de l'Eglise* provides the best brief summary I have seen. I am less familiar with Protestant economic thinking, but see Preston, *Religion and the Ambiguities of Capitalism* and Volf, *Work in the Spirit*. Taylor, *A Catholic Modernity?* (19–25) provides a brief analysis of the changing Christian view of wealth.

19. John Paul II, *Laborem exercens*. It is discussed in Schenk, "On Human Work."

Chenu, "Arbeit" and his earlier but too optimistic *The Theology of Work* are also helpful.

20. See Fogarty, *Christian Democracy in Western Europe* and Chenaux, *Une Europe Vaticane?* In the last two decades, that Catholic heritage has been either forgotten or renounced.

21. The two sides of the debate are presented in Bandow and Schindler, *Wealth, Poverty, and Human Destiny*. Hobgood, *Catholic Social Teaching and Economic Theory* provides an extreme anti-"capitalist" perspective. The most articulate exponent of the "capitalist" view is probably Michael Novak. See, for example, his *Morality, Capitalism and Democracy*; "Eight Arguments About the Morality of the Marketplace"; and *The Catholic Ethic and the Spirit of Capitalism.* In my view, CST does not so much take a middle ground between the two extremes as attempt to introduce a new sort of analysis that avoids the anthropological errors which mar the whole idea of "capitalism," whether that idea is despised or endorsed.

22. In John Paul II, *Centesimus Annus.*

23. In *Centesimus Annus*, John Paul II almost gives an "economic system" a life of its own, almost independent of the culture that creates it: "Of itself, an economic system does not possess criteria for correctly distinguishing new and higher forms of satisfying human needs from artificial new needs which hinder the formation of a mature personality" (section 36).

24. For example, a system that "considers profit as the key motive for economic progress, competition as the supreme law of economics, and private ownership of the means of production as an absolute right that has no limits and carries no corresponding social obligations" might be "unfortunate," as Paul VI argues in *Populorum Progressio* section 26, but it is not much like the current system in industrial economies. The later discussion in John Paul II, *Centesimus Annus* makes the reverse error, of unquestioningly accepting profit as an "indication that . . . productive factors have been properly employed and corresponding human needs have been duly satisfied" (section 35).

25. In *Rerum Novarum*, found in O'Brien and Shannon, *Catholic Social Thought.*

26. See especially John Paul II *Centesimus Annus*, sections 30–42; the quote is from 32.

Chapter 4

1. The position of economic thought in the intellectual history of the time is discussed in chapters 12–17 of Macintyre, *Whose Justice? Which Rationality?* and chapter 3 of Manent, *La Cité de l'homme.* For an explanation of the premodern approach, see Finley, "Aristotle and Economic Analysis."

2. The first four chapters of Spiegel, *The Growth of Economic Thought* go over what is available. For example, for Plato, "the economic problem did not impress him as a particularly urgent one for the full-fledged citizens of the city-state" (21); of Aristotle, "Only a few of [his writings] refer specifically to economic matters, and if they do it is in connection with political or moral matters or with an examination of the general art of reasoning" (24); of Epicurus, "[he] proposes to resolve the economic problem by reducing the demand for goods rather than by increasing their supply" (38); of Roman education, "no thought was given to speculation about economics" (39); of original Christianity, "in the sayings of Jesus no weight is attached to economic considerations" (41); of medieval thinkers, "Man's material well-being in his earthly life seemed of little consequence in comparison with the great and overriding question of his salvation in the next world" (55). The first document that he cites as explicitly economic is the 1320 Treatise on Money by Nicholas Orseme, but he notes that the economic analysis serves the primarily political purpose of that document. In a great neighboring culture, "Economics, as such, did not occupy an important position in the medieval Islamic scheme of science, and the traditional character of Islamic society did not make for the improvement of this position" (from Spengler, "Economic Thought of Islam: Ibn Khaldun," 115). The dismissal of most labor in Aristotle is particularly brutal, "Hence those who are in a position which places them above toil have stewards who attend to their households while they occupy themselves with philosophy or with politics" (*Politics* I.7 1255 b 35).

3. For example, the "Leveling Kings" peasant rebellion in the 1630s in China involved the leveling of income through plunder, but contemporary observers were more struck by the social claims—"[The serfs would] slap them [the masters] across the cheeks and say: 'We are all of us equally men. What right had you to call us serfs? From now on it is going to be the other way around'" (cited in Elvin, *The Pattern of the Chinese Past*, 246). Finley, *The Ancient Economy* takes a strong view on popular revolts in the ancient world—"What is totally absent is anything we can recognise as a labour programme, anything to do with wages, conditions of employment, the competition of slaves" (81). Mollat and Wolff, *The Popular Revolutions of the Late Middle Ages* inadvertently shows how little resonance purely economic revolutionary claims had in the late Middle Ages in Europe.

4. For population increase, see Livi-Bacchi, *A Concise History of World Population* and McEvedy and Jones, *Atlas of World Population History*. Nutrition and population have not always moved in the same direction, but over the centuries of industrialization men have become both more numerous and better fed.

5. The view of modernity presented here is meant to be fairly conventional. I have been influenced by Taylor, *Sources of the Self*; MacIntyre, *After Virtue*; Dupré *Passage to Modernity*; and Manent, *La Cité de l'homme*, all of which are broadly

critical of modernity. From an economic perspective, the arguments in Dumont, *Homo hierarchicus* are helpful.

6. The interest in economics for its own sake developed slowly. Well into the nineteenth century, most exponents of modern enlightenment were more interested in throwing off spiritual than material shackles. Locke saw property and prosperity largely as protection against political tyranny. Montesquieu identified "commerce" as important, but not consumption goods. David Hume (see Hudson *Human Character and Morality*, 83) and Adam Smith were economic trailblazers. See Gay, *The Enlightenment—An Interpretation*. Even Comte, who identified the modern age as scientific, had little practical concern with the economic stuff that sceintific technology offered. See Copleston *A History of Philosophy*; de Lubac, *Le Drame de l'humanisme athée*; and Negri, *Travail et technique dans la pensée d'Auguste Comte*. Not until the end of the nineteenth century, with Mill or even Marshall, does the approach to economics sound normal to modern ears.

7. See Gadamer, *Truth and Method* for a thorough discussion of the ambiguities of putting the past in present terms, or trying to put the present in past terms.

8. This sort of axiomatic psychology is similar to that in Shanks, "Human Goods in Ethical Business." On economic methodology, see Boylan and O'Gorman, *Beyond Rhetoric and Realism in Economics*. On the philosophy of social science, see Rosenberg, *Philosophy of Social Science*; Martin and McIntyre, *Readings in the Philosophy of Social Science*; Giddens, *The Constitution of Society*; Searle, *The Construction of Social Reality*; Kincaid, *Philosophical Foundations of the Social Sciences*; and chapter 1 of Merton, *Social Theory and Social Structure*. Most scholars in this domain are limited by antitranscendental assumptions.

9. Modern scientists generally consider the use of "natures" to be outmoded. In *The Dappled World*, Cartwright persuasively argues that scientists—she includes economists in this group, although she is only interested in the neoclassical variety—do and should make use of them.

10. Actually, many modern philosophers are rather ashamed at life's mysteries and prefer to play rather tame word games. These analytic philosophers provide a thin intellectual gruel. It may be enough to nourish the modest ontological aspirations of conventional economics—see, for example, the tradition represented by Hausman, *The Inexact and Separate Science of Economics*—but my purposes require the richer fare of so-called Continental philosophy.

Chapter 5

1. The idea that human will is always directed to the good first appears in Plato, *Protagoros* 345D, and is a basic postulate of Aquinas (see *Summa* Ia II,8.1). John Paul II provides a more modern and subtle expression of the moral horizon of men's activity. See the summary in Schmitz, *At the Center of the Human Drama*. I

imply in the text that the will can be misdirected in two distinct senses, in its goal and in its means to reach that goal. Many philosophers would reject that split. What is important here is merely that the will is always morally charged and that it is often in some way defective.

2. The Romantic desire to go "back to nature" may appear to undermine the claim that the desire to humanize the world is universal, but the nature craved by Romantics is not really nonhuman. Rather, it is an idealized world in which men can shed their social vices and develop their spiritual gifts.

3. See Saler, *Conceptualizing Religion* and the essay "Religion as a Cultural System" in Geertz, *The Interpretation of Cultures*. Unfortunately, the modern discipline of anthropology has been strongly influenced by antitranscendental thinking.

4. It is easy enough to find expressions of human universality in all the great intellectual traditions, but it has been very difficult not to exclude both social inferiors and foreigners from the equality of dignity. For example, Aristotle was predominantly concerned with the equality of enfranchised members of advanced city-states. See Abernathy, *The Idea of Equality*; and Bryson, Faust, et al., *Aspects of Human Equality* for the history of these ideas.

5. The nature of sexual difference can be approached in various ways. Philosophy: von Balthasar *Theo-Drama* (365–82); theology: John Paul II, *Mulieris Dignitatem* and *The Theology of the Body*; cultural: Ortner and Whitehead, *Sexual Meanings*; biology: Kimura, *Sex and Cognition*, Baron-Cohen, *The Essential Difference* and Nicholson, *Men and Women*; history: Scott, *Feminism and History*; economics: Ferber and Nelson, *Feminist Economics Today* and Dixon, *Making the Difference*, although "feminist economics" suffers from many problems. A simple summary of the results from the various disciplines: the modern experiment in radical indifference to sex is a historical and cultural anomaly, based on a profound misunderstanding of biology, theology, and philosophy.

6. Mill, *Essays on Some Unsettled Questions of Political*, cited in Nelson *Economics for Humans* (19).

Chapter 7

1. The first and third quotes, from Alfred Marshall and Lionel Robbins, respectively, are taken from Lawson, *Reorienting Economics* (142). The second, by W. Stanley Jevons, is taken from http://ingrimayne.saintjoe.edu/econ/Introduction/Defintns.html. The fourth is from http://www.marxists.org/glossary/terms/e/c.htm#economics, a Marxist website. Alternatively, Gary Becker, who wishes to expand the domain of economic analysis, says, "The combined assumptions of maximizing behavior, market equilibrium, and stable preferences, used relentlessly and unflinchingly, form the heart of the economic approach." Cited in

Hirschleifer, "The Expanding Domain of Economics." More concretely, John Stuart Mill explained that the subject of "Political Economy as a branch of science" is "Wealth . . . the nature of Wealth, and the laws of its production and distribution. . . ." (cited in Lawson, 142).

2. For example, on labor—"The object of labor is, therefore, the objectification of man's species life: for he duplicates himself not only, as in consciousness, intellectually, but also actively, in reality. And therefore he contemplates himself in the world that he has created" (from the "Economic and Philosophic Manuscripts of 1844," Marx and Engels, *The Marx-Engels Reader*, 76). On consumption—"If it is clear that production offers consumption its external object, it is equally clear that consumption ideally posits the object of production as an internal image, as a need, as drive and as purpose" (from Marx and Engels, "Grundrisse," 229).

3. The standard *New Palgrave Dictionary of Economics* has no entry for "consumption," while Black, *A Dictionary of Economics* defines consumption in strictly monetary terms as "spending for survival and enjoyment," in contrast to spending for investment. The field of economic sociology does better, with two of thirty-one chapters of Smelser and Swedberg, *The Handbook of Economic Sociology* dedicated to consumption, although neither bothers to define the concept and both assume that only purchased goods are worthy of study. For an intelligent Marxist-style analysis, see Arendt, *The Human Condition*, section 13.

4. See Tilgher, *Homo Faber*; Vialatoux, *Signification humaine du travail*; the chapter "Travail et parole" in Ricoeur, *Histoire et vérité*; the chapter "La personne et le travail" in Lacroix, *Personne et amour*; Simon, *Work, Society, and Culture* (less insightful); Anthony, *The Ideology of Work* (left-wing); and, more generally Arendt, *The Human Condition*.

5. See the relevant chapters of Weber, *Economy and Society*; Merton, *Social Theory and Social Structure*; Campbell, *Joy in Work, German Work*; Salaman, *Labor*; and Hall, *Dimensions of Work*.

6. See, for example, the chapter on "Industrial (Occupational) and Organizational Psychology" by Wendy Hollway in Colman, *Companion Encyclopedia of Psychology*; Warr, *Psychology at Work*; and Drenth, Sergeant, et al., *European Perspectives in Psychology*.

7. A note on vocabulary: in this book I almost always use "caste" in preference to the more common "class" or the more ungainly and less familiar "social order" and "status group." "Caste" and "class" both come with unattractive intellectual baggage, of rigid heredity and Marxist economism, respectively. See Dumont, *Homo hierarchicus*; Quigley, *The Interpretation of Caste*; Rosman and Rubel, *The Tapestry of Culture*; and Beals, Hoijer et al., *An Introduction to Anthropology*. On caste and class see Gould, *The Hindu Caste System*. On the various words for social groupings, see Foster, "Class" and Joyce, *Class*. On the problems with using "class" in preindustrial societies, see chapter 2 of Finley, *The Ancient Economy*.

8. Marx argues that in capitalism the laborer is forced to alienate his "labor-power" through sale. See Marx, *Capital* 1.1.1.6.

9. For example, John Paul II, *Laborem exercens* is translated into English as *On human work*.

10. Arendt, *The Human Condition*.

11. See "Original Sin" by C. J. Peter and K. McMahon in Catholic University of America, *The New Catholic Encyclopedia*.

12. On leisure, see Pieper, *Leisure the Basis of Culture*, who is too schematic and too dismissive of the modern idea. De Grazia, *Of Time, Work and Leisure* follows the history of the idea in Europe—praised, criticized, and transformed. Also, see chapter 3 of Hunnicutt, *Work Without End*; Dumazedier, *Vers une civilisation du loisir?*; Larrabee, *Mass Leisure*; and Parker, *Leisure and Work*. Also, see the discussion in chapter 14 of this book.

13. Marxist economists follow Hegel in considering labor to be much more important than consumption, in fact to be the essential human act of self-expression. See chapter 1 of Grint, *The Sociology of Work*.

14. For a theological discussion of human love, see von Balthasar, *Unless You Become Like This Child*.

Chapter 8

1. The theoretical trap of assuming that more money is identical to more utility is explained in Mirowski, *More Heat than Light*.

2. See Cartwright, *The Dappled World* for a discussion of "ceteris paribus" clauses in laws.

3. Keynes is a distinguished but only partial exception. See his "Economic Possibilities for Our Grandchildren."

4. For example, Ibn Khaldun took it as common knowledge that, "Luxurious consumption and easy living serve . . . to soften both dynasty and population and to dissipate hardier qualities and virtues." Cited and discussed in Spengler, "Economic Thought of Islam: Ibn Khaldun" (136). Even early economists praised poverty rather than prosperity. See Rimlinger, *Welfare Policy and Industrialization in Europe, America and Russia* (14–17).

5. This idea is relatively recent, as it could not develop until economists both recognized the increasing power of the industrial economy and gained the ambition and the tools to measure everything. For the history, see Spiegel, *The Growth of Economic Thought*. For earlier notions of the national economic good, see Magnusson, *Mercantilism* on the mercantilists; and Meek, *The Economics of Physiocracy* and Fox-Genovese, *The Origins of Physiocracy* on the physiocrats.

6. The discussion in the article by Stanley Engerman in Steckel and Floud, *Health and Welfare during Industrialization* provides the necessary background. See

the annual editions of United Nations Development Program, *Human Development*.

7. The history and impracticality of worker control of factories is well discussed in Wiles, *The Political Economy of Communism*.

8. See Merton, *Social Theory and Social Structure*.

9 On the idea of the common good, see the chapter by Margaret Atkins, "Clarifying the Common Good" in Alford, Clark, et al., *Rediscovering Abundance*; Riordan, *A Politics of the Common Good*; and Hollenbach, *The Common Good and Christian Ethics*.

10. Friedman and Friedman, *Free to Choose* explain, "An important part of economic freedom is freedom to choose how to use our income," (89); "A free society releases the energies and abilities of people to pursue their own objectives" (181).

11. "It seems to me a very good thing, in theory as well as practice, that there should be a body of citizens primarily concerned in producing and consuming and not in exchanging." Chesterton *The Outline of Sanity* (136). "[I]nstead of searching for means to accelerate the drift out of agriculture, we should be searching for policies to reconstruct rural culture . . ." Schumacher, *Small is Beautiful* (104). Manuel and Manuel, *Utopian Thought in the Western World* discusses (439) the rural nature of utopian thinking after Rousseau, in contrast with the essentially urban utopias of Plato and More.

Chapter 9

1. See Aristotle, *Nicomachean Ethics* X; and Aquinas, *Summa* Ia II.66.1–3 for the classic texts. For a contemporary discussion, see McInerny, *Difficult Good*.

2. See *Catechism of the Catholic Church*, section 1750; and Cessario, *Introduction to Moral Theology* (166–91).

3. On the phrase "false consciousness," mostly used by Marxists, see Rosen, *On Voluntary Servitude*.

4. The increasing emphasis on the opposing direction of causality, that education is advantageous because it promotes personal or social prosperity, shows an upside-down moral hierarchy, as well as making almost no economic sense, as Wolf, *Does Education Matter?* points out.

5. That comment is based on the aesthetic philosophy of von Balthasar, *The Glory of The Lord*.

Chapter 10

1. This principle is strongly influenced by John Paul II, *Laborem exercens*.
2. See Sahlins, *Stone Age Economics*.

3. See Weber, *The Protestant Ethic and the Spirit of Capitalism*, with the necessary correctives in Manent, *La Cité de l'homme*.
4. See chapter 11 of Kanigel, *The One Best Way*; chapter 7 of Campbell, *Joy in Work, German Work*; and Linhart, *Lénine, les paysans, Taylor*. Lenin identified labor efficiency as a defining good of "late capitalism".
5. E.g. Rawls, *A Theory of Justice*.

Chapter 11

1. For the philosophy, see the relevant articles: "Male" by G. Morra in Centro di studi filosofici di Gallarate, *Enciclopedia filosofica*; and "Evil" by R. Jolivet and B. Whitney in Catholic University of America, *The New Catholic Encyclopedia*.
2. The key text, which introduced the phrase "structure of sin," is John Paul II, *Sollicitudo Rei Socialis* 36–37.
3. There is a wide range of opinion, from the black view of Machiavelli to the naïve optimism of theosophy (for the latter, see Anonymous, "Seeds and Seedlings: The Doctrine of Perfectibility"). Christians range from Calvinist darkness to Pelagian confidence. For the Catholic range, see Connolly, *Sin*. For a crosscultural view, see the article on "Sin and Guilt" in Eliade, *The Encyclopedia of Religion*.
4. Hobbes, *Leviathan*.
5. E.g. Coase, *The Firm, the Market, and the Law*.
6. "Greed is good" was popularized in the 1987 film *Wall Street*, but it is no more than a reworking of Bernard Mandeville's 1714 poem "The Fable of the Bees, or: Private vice, public benefits," an inspirational text for many early economists. The bleak view of Malthus, *An Essay on the Principles of Population* influenced all classical economists and is assumed in the neoclassical model. Darwin translated the social notion of Malthus into biology, and his laws of struggle and progress then made their way back into economics in the more "scientific" form of "social Darwinism." See Hofstadter, *Social Darwinism in American Thought*; Hawkins, *Social Darwinism in European and American Thought*; and Mirowski, *Natural Images in Economic Thought*.
7. The famous "invisible hand" is mentioned only briefly, in book 4, chapter 2 of Smith, *Wealth of Nations*. My description of the relationship between the apparent virtue of selfishness in this economic model and Smith's enthusiasm for "sympathy" in his discussion of moral sentiments—the "Adam Smith problem"—would not be accepted by all scholars. See Montes, "*Das Adam Smith Problem*" for details and MacIntrye, *Whose Justice? Which Rationality?* for background.

Chapter 12

1. See Weber *Economy and Society* and Gadamer, *Truth and Method* for the philosophical issues involved in retrospective judgments.
2. The idea is Hegelian, although the precise terminology is not his. For the philosophical idea, see Hegel, *Hegel's Logic* and for the application of the idea to (non-economic) history, see Hegel, *The Philosophy of History*.
3. "No one will ever confess to being greedy. Each person denies totally having such a baseness and vileness of the heart. One might explain that he is weighed down by the expenses of childcare, another that wisdom demands security: but no one ever has too much, there are always good reasons to have more. Even the most greedy people never confess that they are greedy, because in good conscience they do not think they are. No, greed is a prodigious fever, most invisible when it is strongest." De Sales, *Introduction à la vie dévote* III.14 (my translation).
4. The distinction between absolute and relative poverty is well understood by development economists. See chapter 4 of Fields, *Distribution and Development*; Beckerman, "The Measurement of Poverty"; chapters 2 and 4 of Jones, *Poverty and the Human Condition*; and chapter 1 of Segalman and Basu, *Poverty in America*.
5. Conventional economists discuss relative poverty in terms of income inequality. For theory and practice, see Seligson and Passé-Smith, *Development and Underdevelopment*; Townsend, *The Concept of Poverty*; and the Introduction to Ghatak, *Introduction to Development Economics*. The reliance on crude monetary measures such as the Gini coefficient is regrettable.
6. For Christ-like self-emptying, see Philippians 2:6–8. St. Francis of Assisi: "As pilgrims and strangers in this world, serving the Lord in poverty and humility . . . [the Franciscans should not be] ashamed, because the Lord made himself poor for us in this world. [T]he most high poverty makes you heirs and kings of the kingdom of heaven, making you poor in things but rich in virtues" (cited in Short, *Poverty and Joy,* 61). John Paul II provides a very succinct summary of the contemporary Catholic view: "[Mother Theresa desired] not just to be the least but to be the servant of the least . . . in touching the broken bodies of the poor she was touching the body of Christ . . . [She believed that] the greatest poverty is to be unwanted" (from the "Homily for the Beatification of Mother Theresa of Calcutta") The history of the Franciscan order demonstrates the difficulties of staying poor in a rich world (see Lambert, *Franciscan Poverty*). See also Régamey, *La pauvreté et l'homme d'aujourd'hui*; the essay on frugality by James Nash in Crocker and Linden, *Ethics of Consumption*; and, for an Indian perspective, chapter 1 of Laidlaw, *Riches and Renunciation*.
7. Antimodern moderns generally argue that the industrial economy must promote ugliness. See Ruskin, *Seven Lamps of Architecture* and Gilson, *La société de*

masse et sa culture. There has certainly been a historic correlation, but it may well be possible to change the relationship between industry and beauty for the better.

8. In philosophical terms, "The possessing class and the proletarian class represent one and the same human self-alienation" (from "The Holy Family," in Marx and Engels, *The Marx-Engels Reader*).

9. On advertising, see White, "The functions of advertising in our culture"; Bignell, *Media Semiotics*; Clark, *The Want Makers*; and Nava et al., *Buy This Book*.

10. "The proletariat will . . . centralize all instruments of production in the hands of the State, i.e., of the proletariat organized as the ruling class" (from "The Communist Manifesto," chapter 2, in Marx and Engels, *The Marx-Engels Reader*). In other words, the alienation inherent in bourgeois property relations will be eliminated by the creation of a new sort of "property," one which somehow belongs indiscriminately to the self-emancipating proletariat. For a broader sociological analysis, see Merton, *Social Theory and Social Structure*; Giddens, *The Constitution of Society*; Silver, *Under Construction*; and Grint, *The Sociology of Work*. More philosophically, there is Camus, *L'étranger* and his many other works. Aron, *Les désillusions du progrès* is skeptical.

11. On war and economics, see Winter, *War and Economic Development*; Ferguson, *The Cash Nexus*; Howard, *War in European History*; McNeill, *The Pursuit of Power*; Tilly, *Coercion, Capital, and European States*; van Creveld, *Technology and War*; and Marwick, Emsley, et al., *Total War and Historical Change*.

Chapter 13

1. The Christian meaning of suffering, including suffering in labor, is explored in John Paul II, *Salvifici Doloris*. The theology of labor is a theme in the spirituality of Opus Dei. See Illanes, *On the Theology of Work*.

2. "Consumerism" is used in this sense primarily by Catholic thinkers. The notion has been heavily criticized: "The exclusive pursuit of possessions thus becomes an obstacle to personal fulfillment and to man's true greatness. Both for nations and for individual men, avarice is the most evident form of underdevelopment" (Paul VI, *Populorum Progressio*, section 19). See also John Paul II, *Centesimus Annus*, sections 36 and 41; and Beabout and Echeverria, "The Culture of Consumerism: A Catholic and Personalist Critique" (ignoring the simplistic discussion of "capitalism" in the latter). More generally, see Galbraith, *The Affluent Society*; Ritzer, *Enchanting a Disenchanted World*; and Lasch, *The Culture of Narcissism*. More philosophically and hyperbolically, see Baudrillard, *The Consumer Society*.

Chapter 14

1. To be fair, many conventional economists, including Smith and Marx, have believed that labor has an intrinsic objective value, but that line of thinking was never very coherent and has had little influence on the profession for the last century.
2. See Coase, *The Firm, the Market, and the Law*.
3. For the philosophy, see the article by G Fassò on "Contrattualismo" in Centro di studi filosofici di Gallarate, *Enciclopedia filosofica*; and Manent, *La Cité de l'homme*. Weber, *Economy and Society* discusses the intellectual and practical novelty of socially unencumbered contracts.
4. I try to avoid castigating every foolish idea of conventional economics, but the notion that corporations can be described as having only one purpose, the good of equity shareholders, is too foolish and too widely believed to be left unmentioned. The idea was popularized in Friedman and Friedman, *Capitalism and Freedom*. It is a simple error of theory and observation, which does the profession a disservice.
5. For the history of labor organizations, see the articles by Laslett and Rimlinger in Mathias and Pollard, *The Cambridge Economic History of Europe*.
6. In the period between Plato, who argues (perhaps not very seriously) for something like sexual equality in labor, and Mary Wollstonecraft, who introduced a protomodern minimalist vision of sexual differentiation, the acceptance of a distinct economic position for women is so profound that it is never even discussed. Even Wollstonecraft did not think in anything like modern feminist economic terms, but rather argued, "Make women rational creatures and free citizens and they will quickly become good wives and mothers," (cited in Tims, *Mary Wollstonecraft*, 136). Only with Soviet economics did the expectation of equal work for women and men emerge from the shadows of utopian socialism into the mainstream of the modern worldview.
7. The vocabulary of caste is disputed, a linguistic controversy that reflects a profound dispute about the nature of society. See note 7 to chapter 7 for references.
8. "[Jesus] did not come to be served, but serve" (Matthew 20:28); "the chief of you [must bear himself] like a servant" (Luke 22:26). Spiritual authority and worldly power are granted only for the purpose of service. The relationship between the praise of service and a hierarchical social order did not bother premodern Christians, from Paul (see Philomen and Ephesians 6:5–9), to Leo XIII, *Rerum Novarum*—"Whoever has received from the divine bounty a large share of temporal blessings . . . has received them . . . that he may employ them, as the steward of God"s providence, for the benefit of others." Modern Christians often share the modern egalitarian distaste for all forms of social inferiority.
9. For postmodern labor, see Handy, *Beyond Certainty*. For evidence, none of which supports its existence, see Hvid and Hasle, *Human Development and Work-*

ing Life; Tomaney, "A New Paradigm of Work Organization and Technology?"; and Beardwell, Holden, et al., *Human Resources Management* (142–48).

10. The physiocrats were not proto-romantic enthusiasts for agriculture. They lived in a society in which most labor was agricultural and most nonfarm labor was nonproductive. So the statement that "land is the unique source of wealth" (Quesnay, Maxim III, translated in Meek, *The Economics of Physiocracy*, 232), which sounds polemical and erroneous to industrial ears, was made as little more than an observation of reality.

11. Peter Drucker contributed significantly to this new view. See his *The Concept of the Corporation* and *Management*.

12. See the descriptions of peasant life in Rösener, *Peasants in the Middle Ages*.

13. See the discussion in John Paul II, *Laborem exercens*, chapter 6.

14. See Gerhart and Rynes, *Compensation* for a sociological approach.

Chapter 15

1. "The life which God gives man is quite different from the life of all other living creatures, inasmuch as man, although formed from the dust of the earth, is a manifestation of God in the world, a sign of his presence, a trace of his glory" (John Paul II, *Evangelium Vitae*, section 34).

2. See Proctor, *Racial Hygiene* (178) and Burleigh, *Death and Deliverance*. Nazi propaganda emphasized the claim that the cost to society of supporting these lives was much too high. The essay by Jennifer Roback Morse in Bandow and Schindler, *Wealth, Poverty, and Human Destiny* defends the economic good of life in a more positive way.

3. See John Paul II, *Salvifici Doloris*.

4. The common usage is found in French, but not in German, Italian, or Spanish, not to mention Malayan or Chinese. The economic concept of a universal activity known as labor is very modern, and the words used have different etymologies.

5. See Melton, *The Individual, the Family, and Social Good* for the "socially toxic environment" of modern childhood. Dowrick and Grundberg, *Why Children?* provides supporting evidence.

6. Polsky, *The Rise of the Therapeutic State* provides some historical and cultural analysis.

7. On the moral philosophy of the artistic endeavor, see the articles "Art and Morality" by Michael Tanner and "Art and Truth" by Malcolm Budd in Craig, *Routledge Encyclopedia of Philosophy*. On the conventional economic view of art, see Klamer, *The Value of Culture* and see part 2 of volume 2 of Towse, *Cultural Economics*.

8. Aquinas, *Summa* Ia II.57.2, relying on a tradition that can be traced back to Aristotle and the Bible.

9. See Hocart, *Kings and Councillors* for an idiosyncratic introduction to this view. The social contract theory that dominates modern political philosophy takes a resolutely antitranscendental view of rule.
10. On premodern ideas about war, see Dawson, *The Origins of Western Warfare*.
11. Matthew 18:3. See von Balthasar, *Unless You Become Like This Child*; and, on play in general, the brilliant discussion in Gadamer, *Truth and Method*.
12. On Christian humility, see the relevant article in Catholic University of America, *The New Catholic Encyclopedia*; Kinsella, *Unprofitable Servants*; and Casey, *Truthful Living*.
13. See Melville, *Moby Dick* for the positive view and Verga, *The House by the Medlar Tree* for the negative.
14. See Mumford, *Technics and Civilization* "[T]he occupation itself was one of the lowest in the human scale. . . . [N]o one entered the mine in civilized states until relatively modern times except as a prisoner of war, a criminal, a slave." (67). "The mine . . . is the first completely inorganic environment to be created by man. . . . [T]he face of the mine is shapeless . . . [T]he miner . . . sees sheer matter. . . . Day has been abolished and the rhythm of nature broken" (69).
15. Smith makes this basic mistake in his emphasis on the division of labor in the famous description of a pin factory at the beginning of Smith, *Wealth of Nations*.
16. See the film *Modern Times* from 1936 or the stories in Swados, *On the Line*.
17. These statistics, compiled from the two volumes of Mitchell, *International Historical Statistics*, are flattered slightly by the tendency to build more "labor-intensive" factories in less prosperous countries.
18. Housework remains feminine. See Huber and Spitze, *Sex Stratification*; and Davidson, *A Woman's Work is Never Done* for historical and sociological analysis.
19. In their business senses, the first dates of use were 1902 for "executive," 1906 for "management," 1919 for "marketing," and 1936 for "service," according to the *Oxford English Dictionary*.
20. The financial industry certainly performs many useful functions. I have seen no studies of the proportion of labor that is useful, but my own estimate, based on many years of observation, is that no more than 20 percent of the time committed to the industry can be justified as improving efficiency.
21. The idea of instrumental neutrality can be seen as the direct descendant of the "sterile labor" of the physiocrats. See the discussions in Spiegel, *The Growth of Economic Thought*; and Mirowski, *More Heat than Light* (159–71). Also, Studenski, *The Income of Nations* shows (largely inadvertently) how an increasingly undifferentiated understanding of "national income" came to neutralize the earlier judgments of the different values of various types of labor. The key novelty in the notion of instrumental neutrality is that it is centered on the good rather than on production.

Chapter 16

1. The overall individual/social polarity, along with man/woman and body/soul, is identified in von Balthasar *Theo-Drama*.
2. See the classic discussion in part 3 of Weber, *Economy and Society*.
3. Veblen *The Theory of the Leisure Class*. See also Mason *The Economics of Conspicuous Consumption*; and Brennan and Pettit, *The Economy of Esteem*. In my presentation, I have developed the concept in accord with the concepts of human economics.
4. The preindustrial potlach is the most studied example. See Rosman and Rubel, *The Tapestry of Culture*; chapter 7 of Lewis, *Social Anthropology in Perspective*; and Douglas and Baron, *The World of Goods*.
5. Mass consumption has received too little scholarly attention, but see Miller, *Material Culture and Mass Consumption*; Williams, *Dream Worlds*; Strasser, *Satisfaction Guaranteed*; and chapter 1 of Lunt and Livingstone, *Mass Consumption and Personal Identity*.
6. The point is made strongly by some romantic economists, for example in Berry, *Home Economics*.
7. The literature on branding is enormous. See, for example, Mark and Pearson, *The Hero and the Outlaw*; and Hill and Lederer, *The Infinite Asset*.
8. For the intellectual history, see "Materialismo" by S. Caramella in Centro di studi filosofici di Gallarate, *Enciclopedia filosofica*; and Moser and Trout, *Contemporary Materialism*.
9. I exaggerate slightly. Growth is measured in terms of Gross Domestic Product (GDP), which includes the nebulous category of "services." Most of the conventional services are what I have been calling stuff—meals, travel, telecommunications—but some are payments for what I have been calling caring labor. In practice, the "service" and "goods" economy grow together (although "services" have been growing slightly faster for many years), so growth and increased production of consumption stuff can reasonably be treated as substitutes.
10. Many followers of Malthus thought absolute poverty was inevitable and argued that there was no harm in policies that would "decrease the surplus population," as Mr. Scrooge put it, using the classical economic vocabulary.
11. Philosophers have not given consumption the attention it deserves. Craig, *Routledge Encyclopedia of Philosophy* does not have an entry on the topic in its fourteen volumes. See Schervish, *Wealth in Western Thought*; and Crocker and Linden, *Ethics of Consumption*, especially the article by David Gill. The approach of the various philosophical schools to moderation is explained in the relevant articles of Centro di studi filosofici di Gallarate, *Enciclopedia filosofica*. Part 3 of de Geus, *The End of Over-Consumption* provides a more modern analysis of consumption moderation. Also, see Finley, *The Ancient Economy*. I was not much

aided by the anthropology of "material culture" in Lubar and Kingerly, *History from Things*; and Buchli, *The Material Culture Reader*.
12. The thinking in Lévi-Strauss, *Le cru et le cuit* lies behind this analysis, although he is a distinctly antitranscendental thinker.
13. This Catholic interpretation of contraception is defended in John Paul II, *The Theology of the Body*.
14. On the possibility that angels actually do consume, see Aquinas, *Summa* I.51.3.ad 5
15. See von Balthasar, *Leben aus dem Tod*, which blames this incomplete Christianization of historic Christian thinking on the reliance of theologians on stoic and platonic antimaterialism.
16. St. Benedict explains that the lack of personal property reminds the monks of their obedience to God through the abbot—"[M]onks may not have the free disposal even of their own bodies and wills. For their needs, they are to look to the father of the monastery.... Whoever needs more should feel humble because of his weakness, not self-important because of the kindness shown him," Benedict, *The Rule of St. Benedict*, chapters 33–34. See also Aquinas, *Summa* III 186.3.

Chapter 17

1. The division of necessities, comforts, and luxuries dates back to the eighteenth century. See Blaug, *Economic Theory in Retrospect* (76) and Crowley, "The Sensibility of Comfort."
2. For example, "How can it be that even today there are still people dying of hunger? Condemned to illiteracy?" John Paul II, *Novo Millennio Ineunte* section 50.
3. Plato, *Republic* 372.
4. See Sen and Drèze, *The Political Economy of Hunger*.
5. Cited in Crowley, "The Sensibility of Comfort."
6. On luxuries in an economy of mass consumption, see chapters 5 and 6 of Williams, *Dream Worlds*.
7. On asceticism and luxury, see the entry "Ascesi" by A. Marchetti in Centro di studi filosofici di Gallarate, *Enciclopedia filosofica*. Hardman, *The Ideals of Ascetism*, a reasonably modern description of the ascetic life, combines the two criticisms, "Luxury in every form is economically bad, it is provocative to the poor who see it flaunted before them, and it is morally degrading to those who indulge in it" (212).
8. See Snooks, *Economics Without Time* and Snooks, "Great Waves of Economic Change" for some analysis of the idea of historical economic choice.
9. Manuel and Manuel, *Utopian Thought in the Western World* say that "the key economic question" in utopian thinking is the relation between labor and "the amount and duration of indulgence in the pleasures of consumption" (129–30).

Chapter 18

1. United Nations Development Program, Human Development 1998 presents some relevant statistics (46–50). From 1960 to 1995, life expectancy in "developing countries" increased from forty-six to sixty-two years, and infant mortality fell by almost two-thirds. Meat consumption has almost tripled since 1970, electricity usage and car production have almost doubled, paper consumption more than doubled, and telephone penetration multiplied by a factor of five. In India, which was not considered a development success, 41 percent of the families below the poverty line had bicycles, and two-thirds of all families had sewing machines. See also Steckel and Floud, Health and Welfare during Industrialization; Simon, The State of Humanity; Johnson, "Population, Food, and Knowledge"; World Health Organisation, The World Health Report 2002; and Melchior, "Global Inequality: Perceptions, Facts and Unresolved Issues." Absolute poverty is increasingly limited to sub-Saharan Africa and regions that have suffered some sort of political or military disaster.

Index

Aquinas, Thomas, 50, 223
Arendt, Hannah, 98

Bentham, Jeremy, 24, 26, 55, 114, 247
Bible, 186, 276
    Genesis 1:26–27, 59; 3:6, 99; 3:17–19, 99; 9:20–23, 186
    Mark 10:17–31, 4; 10:23, 253
    1 Timothy 6:10, 250

caring economy, 10–12
Carlyle, Thomas, 29, 35, 42
Catholicism, 36, 43–45, 55–56, 66, 73, 74, 84, 99, 122, 252
Catholic social teaching (CST), 43–46
Christianity, 21, 67, 173, 216
communism, 40–41, 45, 176
consumption, 6, 9, 21–23, 33, 37, 44, 51, 57, 60–61, 69–73, 78, 82, 84, 87–97, 99–104, 106, 108–9, 113, 115, 117–19, 121–24, 126, 128–31, 133–34, 136–39, 142, 144–51, 153–54, 156, 158, 162, 166, 168–69, 171–72, 175–77, 179, 182–89, 191, 194, 196–97, 199, 201, 203, 206, 211–12, 224–28, 231–32, 235, 237–71, 277, 279, 281
contemporary economies, 2–3, 172
conventional economics/economists, 3, 5–6, 9, 11, 12, 14–15, 17–19, 21, 23, 27, 30, 35, 40, 42–45, 54–56, 57–58, 61–62, 77–78, 80, 83–84, 88–89, 90–92, 94, 97, 99–100, 102, 104, 106–7, 113–15, 120, 129, 132, 136–37, 148, 150–52, 155, 157, 162, 164, 170, 173, 184, 189, 193, 195, 214, 229, 239, 247–49, 280, 282

Darwinism, 22, 38, 55
Descartes, René, 77–78
Discourse on Method, 77

Enlightenment, 29–30, 49, 51, 278–79
Epicurus, 249
external goods, 129–30, 134, 136, 148, 149, 150, 167, 170

feminism, 38, 74
Franklin, Benjamin, 262

Gross Domestic Product (GDP), 26, 81, 120–21

Hobbes, Thomas, 55, 163
Homer, 222, 265
human economics, 31, 33, 55, 77–78, 84, 87–88, 96, 191, 238, 253

industrial economies, 3–7, 9, 11–14, 17, 19, 22, 25, 27, 29–30, 33, 35, 39–46, 52, 57, 61–62, 67, 71, 78–79, 81–83, 96–97, 101, 104–7, 111, 119, 122, 125, 129–30, 133–35, 137–38, 141, 144, 151–53, 158, 163, 166, 174, 177, 183, 185–87, 194, 198, 204, 206, 217, 221, 224, 226, 228–

37, 240–46, 251, 260–65, 268–69, 271, 273, 275–82
industrial societies, 9, 24, 74, 82–83, 107, 109–11, 119–20, 132, 138, 143, 152, 162, 168, 174, 184, 186–87, 194–95, 207, 211, 213, 220, 230–31, 235, 237, 241, 270, 275–77
internal goods, 129, 136, 141, 143, 145, 147–48, 155–56, 167, 181

labor, 3, 7–8, 10, 12–13, 22, 26, 28, 38, 40, 44, 51, 54, 57, 60–61, 65, 69–74, 77–78, 81–82, 84, 87–89, 91, 94–106, 108, 111, 113, 115, 118–20, 122–23, 128–32, 134–40, 144–54, 156, 158, 162–63, 166, 168–70, 173–85, 188–241, 244–46, 251–52, 257–59, 261, 264, 266, 270–71, 275–77, 279, 281

Malthus, Thomas, 30, 32
Marx, Karl, 16, 40–41, 82, 88, 97, 152, 160, 175–76, 196, 201, 247
Marxism, 38, 40–41, 44–46, 49, 62, 98, 122, 141, 176, 204, 226
Maslow, Abraham, 37
Mill, John Stuart, 55, 74, 115

North, Douglass, 37

Plato, 50, 58, 126, 222, 259
Pope John Paul II, 43–46
  Laborem exercens, 43
preindustrial economies, 3–4, 8, 12, 51, 82, 106, 129, 132, 134–35, 139, 174, 176, 184, 204, 206, 217, 220–21, 225–28, 232, 242, 244, 251, 259, 261, 265, 269
preindustrial societies, 4, 11, 16–17, 74, 142, 152, 172, 199, 207, 213, 220

Renaissance, 29, 51, 140, 265

satiety, 5–7, 83, 117–22, 126–27, 143, 150, 171, 182, 184, 187–88, 235–36, 243, 248, 262–64, 266, 269, 271, 281
Simon, Herbert, 37–38
Smith, Adam, 98, 152, 183
socioeconomic organizations, 107–8
stuff economy, 5–8, 10–11

utilitarianism, 24–26, 38, 43, 55, 114, 125–26

Veblen, Thorstein, 37, 242, 244

Weber, Max, 152

About the Author

Edward Hadas, who holds a B.A. in philosophy from Oxford and an M.B.A. from the State University of New York, writes about economics and finance for Breakingviews.com, an Internet financial commentary service based in London. He also teaches and writes about Christian citizenship and social and political philosophy at the Maryvale Institute in Birmingham, UK.